THE UNITED STATES
IN A DISARMED WORLD

Other Hopkins books from The Washington Center of Foreign Policy Research, School of Advanced International Studies

Nations in Alliance: The Limits of Interdependence
George Liska

The Exercise of Sovereignty: Papers on Foreign Policy
Charles Burton Marshall

International Peace Observation: A History and Forecast
David W. Wainhouse and others

Discord and Collaboration: Essays on International Politics
Arnold Wolfers

Alliance Policy in the Cold War
Arnold Wolfers, ed.

Changing East-West Relations and the Unity of the West
Arnold Wolfers, ed.

THE UNITED STATES IN A DISARMED WORLD

A Study of the U.S. Outline for General and Complete Disarmament

Arnold Wolfers
Robert E. Osgood
Paul Y. Hammond
Laurence W. Martin
Robert W. Tucker
Charles Burton Marshall
Livingston T. Merchant

Prepared at The Washington Center
of Foreign Policy Research,
School of Advanced International
Studies, The Johns Hopkins University

The Johns Hopkins Press: Baltimore 1966

PREFACE

One of the striking features of international relations in the twentieth century is the extensive proposals and negotiations of disarmament agreements among the major states. The basic reason for this emphasis is clear: it reflects the new impact of competition in armaments upon international politics. This impact has been growing ever since large-scale arms production and a high rate of technological innovation became prerequisites of peacetime military preparedness in the latter part of the nineteenth century. From the outset, modern arms competition was regarded as an expensive diversion of national resources from the enrichment of the civilian economy and, in some cases, a serious drain on national treasuries. It was also regarded, especially after World War I, as an aggravation of international tensions and a danger to peace. The nuclear age has greatly accentuated the latter concern and has added a new reason for disarmament: the elimination of weapons so destructive that in a major war even the victor and hundreds of thousands of non-belligerents would be destroyed.

It is in the light of this new prospect of catastrophic war that so-called general and complete disarmament (GCD), in contrast to selective and partial arms reduction, limitation, or control, has attracted international attention far greater than before World War II. In the interwar period only the Soviet Union supported GCD, while the other major states were busy attending conferences on arms reductions and limitations. In 1959, after the original failure of the Baruch plan for atomic disarmament and successive failures of comprehensive arms reductions and more limited arms control proposals, the Soviet Union and the United States endorsed the concept of GCD and subsequently adumbrated general proposals for achieving it through graduated and balanced reductions. The United States proposal was suggested in the "Outline of Basic Provisions of a Treaty on General and Complete Disarmament in a Peaceful World" (hereafter referred to as the *Outline*), which it submitted to the Geneva Disarmament Conference in April, 1962. The *Outline*, however, differs fundamentally from the Soviet concept of GCD in that it emphasizes the essential principle of correlating the three proposed stages of disarmament with ever more stringent peace-keeping measures until, at the conclusion of the final stage, an international military force would replace all national military establishments beyond those needed for internal security. The Soviet proposal, on the other hand, takes the view that the abolition of arms would by itself establish a peaceful international order.

The utility and mutual acceptability of such a radical change in international affairs as GCD would entail are, of course, highly doubtful, if not absolutely out of the question, so far as most students of international politics—the present authors included—would judge from the historical record and their understanding of the nature of power among states. Whatever value the *Outline* may have as a general statement of United States views about the hypothetical conditions of GCD, it has failed to attract intensive scholarly attention as a negotiable proposition. On the other hand, students of international politics should find it illuminating to explore the practical implications of the concept of GCD, since it enables one to examine from a novel perspective one of the most basic aspects of international politics: the relationship of force and order in a system of independent states. It is as though one were to conduct a controlled experiment in one's imagination, reducing and finally eliminating the external military forces of states in order to determine their role by observing the effects of disarmament upon other elements of the international system.

For this purpose the *Outline* is very useful, since it is the most comprehensive and detailed effort ever undertaken by any government to indicate the nature of an acceptable agreement on GCD. Therefore, in the belief that a wider audience will be

interested in a study of this document, The Washington Center
of Foreign Policy Research of The Johns Hopkins University
School of Advanced International Studies is publishing the
present examination of the peace-keeping proposals of the
Outline, which it completed for the United States Arms Control
and Disarmament Agency in July, 1964. It is the work of seven
members of the Center, who met periodically in the course of a
year as a panel under the direction of Arnold Wolfers, then
Director of the Center, and wrote separate essays expressing their
individual views on different but related issues posed by the
Outline.

The first three essays deal with policy means and ends in the
environment of a disarming and disarmed world. They explore
the interests of the United States that require protection and
inquire into the resources for deterrence and defense that the
United States would command, apart from whatever peace-
keeping instrumentalities might be placed at its disposal. The
following four essays evaluate the proposed peace-keeping
measures both in terms of their practicability and in terms of
their effectiveness as supplements to or substitutes for the
armaments that would be eliminated in the process of disarmament. All of the essays deal in varying degrees with highly
technical problems—questions of international law, military
organization, the balance of power process, and the like—but the
aim of the study is not a technical one. Instead, the intention
throughout is to probe the assumptions that underlie propositions
about the relations between peacekeeping and disarmament and
to look into the future on the basis of historical experience and
theoretical reflection.

The views and judgments expressed in this volume are solely
those of the authors and do not necessarily reflect the views of
the United States Arms Control and Disarmament Agency or of
any other department or agency of the United States Government.

Robert E. Osgood, Director
The Washington Center of Foreign Policy Research
School of Advanced International Studies

November, 1965

CONTENTS

THE CONTRIBUTORS

ARNOLD WOLFERS   Special Adviser and Research Associate of the Center; Sterling Professor Emeritus of International Relations, Yale University; Consultant to the Department of State and the Department of the Army; Consultant to the Institute for Defense Analyses; Director of the Center, 1957–1965; member of faculty of the National War College, 1947. Author of *Britain and France between Two Wars*, 1940; *Discord and Collaboration: Essays on International Politics*, 1962. Editor and co-author of *The Anglo-American Tradition in Foreign Affairs*, 1956; *Alliance Policy in the Cold War*, 1959; *Changing East-West Relations and the Unity of the West*, 1964.

ROBERT E. OSGOOD   Director of the Center; Professor of American Foreign Policy, The Johns Hopkins University School of Advanced International Studies; Associate Director of the Center, 1964–1965; Consultant to the Department of Defense, 1962–1963; Research Associate of the Center, 1961–1964; Professor of Political Science, University of Chicago, 1956–1961. Author of *Limited War: The Challenge to American Strategy*, 1957; *NATO: The Entangling Alliance*, 1962; *Ideals and Self-Interest in America's Foreign Relations*, 1963.

PAUL Y. HAMMOND   Member of the Social Science Department, The RAND Corporation; Consultant to the Joint Committee on Atomic Energy, U.S. Congress; Research Associate of the Center, 1962–1964; Consultant to the Institute for Defense Analyses, 1961; Assistant Professor of Political Science, Yale University, 1957–1962; resident faculty member, Naval War College, July–December, 1955. Author of *Organizing for Defense: The American Military Establishment in the Twentieth Century*, 1961; "NCS-68: Prologue to Rearmament," Chapter II of *Strategy, Politics, and Defense Budgets*, 1962.

LAURENCE W. MARTIN   Wilson Professor in International Politics, University College of Wales; Research Associate of the Center, 1961–1964; Associate Professor of Political Science, The Johns Hopkins University School of Advanced International Studies, 1961–1964; Assistant Professor of Political Science, Massachusetts Institute of Technology, 1956–1961. Author of *Peace without Victory*, 1958. Co-author of *The Anglo-American Tradition in Foreign Affairs*, 1956. Editor of *Neutralism and Nonalignment: The New States in World Affairs*, 1962.

ROBERT W. TUCKER   Research Associate of the Center; Professor of Political Science, The Johns Hopkins University; Consultant to the Executive Office of the President, 1959; Consultant to the Department of State, 1958–1959. Author of *The Law of War and Neutrality at Sea*, 1956; *The Just War: A Study in Contemporary American Doctrine*, 1960.

CHARLES BURTON MARSHALL   Research Associate of the Center; Visiting Professor of International Politics, The Johns Hopkins University School of Advanced International Studies; Political Adviser to the Prime Minister of Pakistan, 1955; member of Policy Planning Staff, Department of State, 1950–1953; Consultant to Committee on Foreign Affairs, House of Representatives, 1947–1950; Harvard University Fellow, 1935–1936. Author of *The Limits of Foreign Policy*, 1954; *The Exercise of Sovereignty: Papers on Foreign Policy*, 1965.

LIVINGSTON T. MERCHANT   United States Executive Director, International Bank for Reconstruction and Development; Consultant to the Arms Control and Disarmament Agency; Consultant to the Secretary of State; Trustee, Princeton University; Research Associate of the Center, 1962–1964; Under Secretary of State for Political Affairs, 1959–1961; Ambassador to Canada, 1956–1958, 1961–1962; Assistant Secretary of State for European Affairs, 1953–1956; Deputy Assistant Secretary of State for Far Eastern Affairs, 1949–1951.

I
POLICY ENDS AND MEANS

1.

DISARMAMENT, PEACEKEEPING, AND THE NATIONAL INTEREST

Arnold Wolfers

THERE IS NO serious quarrel about the principle that national governments shall be guided in their policies by the national interest. What is controversial and frequently disputed is what constitutes the national interest or the national interests of a given nation at a given time.[1] Measures and agreements directed towards arms reduction or towards the establishment of peacekeeping devices as acts of national policy are ruled by this same principle and will continue to be so unless the process of disarmament and peacekeeping should ever bring the existing nation-states to merge with one another and to transfer the responsibility for peace, order, and the welfare of their people to a supranational authority.

[1] The term "national interest" is used here in a neutral sense to cover all those matters a nation feels constrained to foster and protect, not in the narrower sense in which it implies national selfishness, or is limited to the concept of "interest defined in terms of power," as Hans Morgenthau puts it (*Politics among Nations* [3d ed.; New York: Knopf, 1960], p. 5). See also the criticism of his views implicit in Thomas Cook and Malcolm Moos, *Power through Purpose* (Baltimore: Johns Hopkins, 1962), pp. 148–49. Using the term in the wider and neutral sense, Charles Burton Marshall states: "I am sure that everything expressible as an interest of the United States is expressible also as a responsibility . . . and though it may sound very righteous to say we should overlook our national interests, it sounds quite different to say we should overlook our responsibilities" ("Foreign Policy: Rhetoric and Reality," *World View*, September, 1959, p. 5).

3

It is a special feature of the official American approach to the disarmament problem that it makes progress in the direction of complete and general disarmament conditional on simultaneous progress in the field of peacekeeping. Implicit in the insistence that the two types of policy be linked together is the assumption that arms reductions taken by themselves risk harming those interests that depend for their protection or satisfaction on the existing military power of the country. As a first approximation to the truth, this assumption is valid. It is paradoxical, after all, that a government should decide to cut back armaments when for reason of costs, if for no other, it will have sought to arm the nation only to a level deemed necessary for the adequate protection of the national interest. But governments may gain leeway for arms reductions—even for drastic reductions or the total elimination of all national armaments—if other changes, external or internal, take place simultaneously and reduce the need for national armaments. One such set of changes, though not necessarily the most potent, can consist of peace-keeping measures deliberately undertaken either to diminish the threats against which armaments are directed or to shift the burden of protection from national to international armed forces, as proposed by the United States *Outline* in the form of an International Peace Force.

In order to provide a perspective by which to judge the leeway that governments enjoy with respect to disarmament in the absence of such peace-keeping measures and to define the limits beyond which the need for effective peace-keeping devices becomes imperative in the process of arms reductions, this essay will explore the relationship between disarmament and the interests of a nation. Some attention will also be devoted to a second assumption implicit in the requirement of parallel advances in disarmament and peacekeeping. The assumption is that the kind of peace-keeping measures described in the United States *Outline* will necessarily be beneficial by offsetting otherwise harmful effects of arms reductions. Such beneficial effects cannot be taken for granted, at least in the case of an international peace force. In fact, it will be argued that a condition in which the establishment of a preponderant force under the control of an organization like the United Nations might increase the requirements of some nations for national armed forces is conceivable.

A direct relationship exists between the armaments of a nation and those national interests deemed vital. By definition, interests in this category are valued so highly by the nation in question that it will rely on its national military power as a last resort to deter, stop, or defeat those who threaten them. Since the extent and character of the threats to such vital interests and the dependence on national armaments with which to meet such threats determine the level to which a country will seek to raise its national armor or at which it will seek to maintain it, the problem arises of how to account for voluntary arms reductions, unilateral or bilateral.

The case of unilateral disarmament requires special treatment. If it occurs—and it is by no means rare—it would seem to run counter to the proposition that nations enjoy at best the military protection that meets their minimum requirements. By definition, unilateral disarmament occurs without any assurance of a corresponding reduction of the military power of the adversary, and such a reduction may in fact be neither expected nor considered necessary. Yet quite aside from the particular philosophy and arguments of the "unilateralists"—the exponents of unilateral nuclear disarmament—it is possible to conceive of many situations in which unilateral arms reductions may appeal to governments and turn out to be wise policy. While a diminution in relative military power compared with that of existing adversaries is an almost inevitable consequence of unilateral arms reduction, changes other than those in the actual military power of the opponent—either in the environment or in the expectations of responsible statesmen—may justify unilateral action by making the existing level of armament excessive.

Changes may occur in estimates of the military strength of the adversary or adversaries. Because estimates are bound to be uncertain and to fluctuate, a rational military policy will cut back or raise the level of armaments, as the case may be, in order to preserve the desired relationship to the military strength of the opponent as estimated at a given time.

Similar fluctuations may occur in the estimate of an adversary's intentions. It takes more to deter an opponent whose assumed intention it is to extend his territorial control—if necessary, by resort to military force—than it does to check an opponent whose armaments are believed to be intended solely to preserve the *status quo* or to provide him with an adequate sense of security. The intentions of other governments and nations are at best, however, a matter of informed guesses, and it is a risky enterprise to reduce armaments in response to assumed changes in intentions. Also, the ticklish question may arise of whether a given "relaxation of tension," if it occurs, reflects the kind of change in adversary intentions that will diminish the threat to national interests. Some risk-taking in such instances may be justified if the refusal to take the risk would threaten even greater harm, as it might do if the existing level of armaments should prove provocative.

Changes may occur in the pattern of a nation's interests themselves, thereby reducing the requirements for armed protection: a nation may abandon some interests altogether or cease to regard others as vital. To give an example, a country may have armed in part to protect a vulnerable ally; if this ally turns neutral or switches to the opposing camp, military strength earmarked for its protection is no longer needed. However, if such a switch by an ally were to make its military resources available to the adversary, the change would raise rather than reduce the need for armaments.

A change in ranking of interests from a vital to a less vital level, occurs rather frequently. The Soviet Union might decide to disband some of its forces if it lost serious interest in other people's "wars of liberation," wars which it now says it is willing to back with its military power. Another case, the possibility of a great power's losing interest in remote and vulnerable strategic positions after suffering a radical diminution of its power, will be discussed later.

Then again, changes may take place in a government's expectations of the adversary's reaction to its armament policy. If it was discovered that present armaments were provoking apprehensions and, as a consequence, leading to an unprofitable stepping up of the arms race, such a government might decide to revise downward its earlier estimate of the optimum of national preparedness. In such an event, what might first take the form of a unilateral cutback of forces might turn itself into reciprocal arms reduction, tacitly or formally agreed upon.

Finally, unilateral disarmament measures—though in this case in the form not of across-the-board cuts but of cuts limited to certain arms or forces—may justify themselves in the wake of technological change. As an illustration, if manned bombers should lose their ability to penetrate the territory of an opponent, their elimination would have no adverse effect on the existing military power relationship. The same would be true if some day nuclear missiles designed to be used exclusively against counterforce targets faced conditions in which such targets had for all practical purposes become invulnerable. One might question whether it is proper to speak here of disarmament measures because weapons that have lost their utility do not really constitute "armaments" in any meaningful sense of the term. Yet it could be argued that even under these conditions unilateral "disarmament" measures would be harmful to the national interest on the ground that a nation can never have too many arms; some day they may come in handy, even if with functions not yet foreseeable. As a general rule, the argument in favor of maximum armaments is not convincing. Any build-up of "military power in reserve" may provoke increased counterarmaments on the part of the opponent and thus in the end step up the risks and costs of the arms race. Yet an exceptional case is worth mentioning. A quest for the maximum effective armaments a nation can afford irrespective of needs may be profitable when there is a chance of defeating an adversary by exhausting him economically.

Unilateral disarmament measures that can only be justified by one or more of the changes discussed above are not what the "unilateralists" have in mind when they call for the abandonment of nuclear weapons, if not of all armaments, without regard for

whether or not the adversary follows suit. They rest their case
alternatively, if not simultaneously, on two separate arguments.

Some argue that nuclear armaments—or all extensive armaments in a nuclear age, with its danger of escalation—have become incompatible with the national interest. Armed power, it is
said, represents a threat to national survival and thus to the
interest that outranks all others.[2] Whether it does outrank them
is a matter of ethical judgment and a subject of heated controversy which cannot be resolved here. It is worth mentioning,
however, that not everyone who believes that none of the interests traditionally considered vital, such as political independence
or territorial integrity, could ever justify a nuclear holocaust
counts himself in the unilateralist school of thought. There are
those who hold that the possession of nuclear arms, and of
adequate armaments generally, remains indispensable as a means
of deterring attack on vital interests and thereby of preventing
the outbreak of violence. The unilateralists can respond that
deterrence based on the threat of nuclear retaliation is either a
bluff, and thus of very doubtful reliability, or a decision to accept
national self-destruction if deterrence fails and vital interests
cannot be protected short of war. Actually, no way has been
found to escape from this dilemma of nuclear deterrence, but the
"escape" suggested by the unilateralists leads into another and no
less serious dilemma. While unilateral nuclear disarmament

[2] See Erich Fromm's article, "Unilateral Disarmament" (*Daedalus*, Fall,
1960, p. 1016), in which he points out that one of the premises underlying
proposals for unilateral arms reductions is that "without achieving complete
disarmament, the armament race will continue and lead to the destruction
of our civilization as well as that of the Russians or, even without the outbreak of war, will slowly undermine and eventually destroy the values in
defense of which we are risking our physical existence." Charles E. Osgood
has termed the threat to security from arms one of the "paradoxes of the
nuclear age." "The more nations spend for what they call 'defense,' the
less real security they have. Who will deny that over the past ten years
we have been steadily increasing our expenditures for weapons? And who
will deny that now we are really less safe, less secure, less defended than
ever before in our national history?" (*An Alternative to War or Surrender*
[Urbana: University of Illinois, 1962], p. 20). See also C. Wright Mills for
an unequivocal statement of the incompatibility of war with the national
interest (*The Causes of World War Three* [New York: Simon and Schuster,
1958], p. 3).

would remove the danger of future nuclear war, it would do so by means of a policy that would place the nation and its interests at the mercy of any adversary who possessed nuclear weapons. It calls ultimately for surrender at no risk or cost to the enemy.

Some unilateralists would not agree that such a dilemma exists. They assert that in depriving itself unilaterally of military power, a nation thereby removes the very threats to its vital interests against which it has sought to protect itself by means of armaments.[3]

There are two variations on this theme of what might be called the self-generating compatibility of disarmament with the national interest. According to the first, which has all the earmarks of Gandhi's policy of passive resistance, no nation is psychologically capable of resorting to force against a country that has given up its means of military resistance.[4] There is no need to discuss this version because it patently lies outside the present range of practical international politics. The second variation deserves careful scrutiny. It rests on the theory of the security dilemma, which has received much scholarly recognition and according to which fear of what other nations may do provokes steps in behalf of security which in turn create fear in others.

This theory is sound in pointing out that armament policies pursued in a quest for security may lead to a vicious circle in which insecurity breeds more insecurity and the expected protection of interests through armaments becomes the cause of

[3] "The most likely result of unilateral disarmament—whether it be undertaken by the United States or the Soviet Union—is that it would prevent war. The main reason which could impel either the Soviet Union or the United States to atomic war is the constant fear of being attacked and pulverized by the opponent" (Fromm, "Unilateral Disarmament," p. 1020). C. Wright Mills takes the same position when he says, "The immediate cause of World War III is the military preparation of it" (Mills, *World War Three*, pp. 82, 89).

[4] "Finally, it would seem at any rate up to the present time that in a dispute between a nuclear Power and a non-nuclear Power, even if it came to war, the whole weight of world opinion would make it very difficult for the nuclear power to use its nuclear weapons . . ." (Stephen King-Hall, *Power Politics in the Nuclear Age* [London: Gollancz, 1962], p. 108).

more threats to these interests.[5] It can be illustrated by the case of air or naval bases on foreign territory. Under certain circumstances bases can become a source of international friction or of intensified conflict. Therefore, if the security gained from a particular base is less than the additional insecurity arising from the friction it produces, the country in question could enhance the protection of its national security by abandoning the base, which amounts to carrying out a disarmament measure. More generally, whenever the possession of assets such as a strip of territory or access to the territory are valued not for their sake but because of the service they are expected to render as instruments of national security, conflicts arising over their possession may turn them into a liability.

One cannot conclude from such cases that most territorial disputes, the cause of so many international conflicts and wars, would disappear if only nations were to disarm and thereby ceased to engender fear in one another.

Some boundary disputes are obviously related to national security, as when the issue is one of providing a nation a more easily defendable frontier. Well-known examples are the former French quest for a boundary on the Rhine and the recent concern of India about a strategic boundary on the crest of the Himalaya Mountains. But most territorial conflicts are of a different nature. The NATO powers may have some reason to desire the liberation of East Germany because it would provide them with more space for military deployment and defensive depth, but neither Germany's allies nor Germany herself would be less concerned about Germany's partition, the isolation of West Berlin, and Communist domination of the eastern zone of Germany if they had no need or desire for more central European territory to make their military position more secure. Whenever a territorial conflict arises out of a quest for self-determination or

---

[5] On the "security dilemma," see John Herz, "Idealist Internationalism" (*World Politics*, II, No. 1 [January, 1950], p. 157), and his study on *Political Realism and Political Idealism* (Chicago: University of Chicago, 1951), pp. 1–16; see also Herbert Butterfield, *History and Human Relations* (New York: Macmillan, 1952), pp. 19–20, who speaks of the Hobbesian fear as causing the vicious circle.

is pursued for the redress of grievances or reflects an ambition for grandeur and prestige, disarmament is likely to do nothing to end or moderate the conflict. It is even likely that disarmament measures that changed the existing distribution of military power would bring new territorial conflicts to the surface, rather than eliminate old ones. Conflicts may remain dormant as long as nations with an incentive to push for territorial change lack the military power to make their claims good. Therefore, any military advantage they gained over nations interested in preserving the territorial *status quo* would tend to activate new demands and thereby cause or intensify conflict.

What the theory of the security dilemma overlooks is the very factor that accounts for most serious threats to national interests and offers the chief explanation for the value that nations attach to means of deterrence and defense. The fear that another nation might be tempted, or might actually decide, to violate the interest of another need not rest on unwarranted suspicions, as the vicious circle thesis implies. Instead, nations are frequently so eager to change the established distribution of values—usually referred to as the *status quo*—that they become willing, given a chance of success at a tolerable cost, to resort to the threat or use of military force rather than to resign themselves to the existing state of affairs. If others who would suffer from a change of the *status quo* prefer resistance to surrender—and equip themselves with the military means by which to make resistance effective—the arms competition is not the cause but the result of the conflict. In order that arms reductions may become compatible with the national interest under such conditions, the underlying conflict itself first has to be resolved or attenuated. If it is, arms reductions are likely to follow as the logical reaction of the parties to the changed environment, even in the absence of formal disarmament agreements.

If we turn now to bilateral or multilateral disarmament, whether tacitly or formally agreed upon, where parties whose armaments are directed against one another cut back or eliminate their military forces and weapons, the question of compatibility appears in a different light. Armaments serve to protect interests from threats emanating from the military forces of an adversary, and their value is measured by their strength relative to that of the opposing forces. Thus, while the puzzling thing about unilateral disarmament is that it should ever prove compatible with the national interest, what may appear to be puzzling in the case of bilateral disarmament is, rather, that it should ever be found to be incompatible with that interest.

Simultaneous bilateral disarmament, even to the point of total disarmament, should not harm either party, provided that the distribution of military power existing prior to disarmament remains unchanged. When this condition is fulfilled, one can say that the measures taken by both sides are proportionate. But it is one thing to state the principle of proportionality theoretically and quite another to put it into practice. There is no easy way, and in many instances no way at all, by which the parties can assure themselves against unbalancing consequences of bilateral cutbacks in armaments. Even the best intentions on the part of all participants and the most careful calculations may not produce the desired result or make it enduring. The fact is too well known from the experience of all disarmament negotiations to need elaboration here.

Two aspects of the proportionality issue which may be overlooked deserve to be mentioned, however. First, efforts to leave the relative power position of the two sides unchanged will, in many cases, be found to be incompatible with total disarmament. Whenever one party enjoys superiority in armaments, arms reductions down to the zero level of complete disarmament must inevitably eliminate such superiority. They turn out, therefore, to be beneficial to the formerly weaker side. As a result, nations occupying a disadvantageous position in an arms race have a special incentive to favor total disarmament over partial reductions of armaments; the latter—in principle at least—can be made to conform with proportionality. One need only imagine how favorably changed the world would appear to scores of states that are at present militarily impotent if all the great powers decided to disband their armed forces completely!

Second, nations do not rely exclusively on military power to protect or promote their interests against others or even to coerce others. To a varying degree, they also use or can fall back on other instruments of policy. While the limits within which non-military means of pressure or coercion can effectively substitute for military force may be narrow, it is true, nonetheless, that drastic reductions of armaments could play into the hands of nations better equipped with nonmilitary instruments of policy or more skilled in putting them to use. If there is inequality here, then even proportionate reductions in armaments would not leave the relative power position of the two opponents unchanged. The side that was at a disadvantage on the nonmilitary level of preparedness and skill could provide the former degree of protection to its interests only by either retaining enough military power to meet the nonmilitary challenges of its adversary or by enhancing its own ability in the field of nonmilitary coercion.

Another much-discussed danger to the national interest arises from the possibility that the adversary may cheat by failing to carry out his disarmament commitment or, having disarmed, by rearming secretly. Whether this danger can be eliminated or reduced to a tolerable minimum depends, obviously, on whether agreed arms reductions by the parties can be effectively verified and enforced. Nations that fear being at a disadvantage here, believing themselves to be either more faithful to their pledges or unable to catch up in a rearmament race if it were initiated by the opponent, have reason to attach particular importance to reliable machinery for verification and enforcement; the protection of their interests in a more or less remote future is at stake.

What has been said so far shows that unilateral disarmament within narrow limits and bilateral disarmament within much broader limits may leave the national interest protected. It follows logically that within these limits peace-keeping measures need not be made a prerequisite of partial disarmament. But it does not follow that improved peace-keeping devices would not be beneficial even in such instances. They can serve to raise national security above what is at best the painfully precarious level it can attain under the conditions of an armed world. They become indispensable if disarmament goes beyond the limits within which it is compatible with the national interest, which it risks doing for many reasons, no matter how carefully nations may seek to avoid such an outcome. Nations may err in estimating the strength or the intentions of their opponents; they may miscalculate the requirements of proportionality. They may be taken by surprise by technological advances favoring their opponent or discover themselves unable to cope in time with the unbalancing effects of such advances.

I shall not attempt a general analysis of the peace-keeping measures that are discussed in the essays of this study in order to discover what the chances are that such measures might compensate for the risks or actual losses of protection connected with the disarmament process. But something needs to be said here about the way in which peacekeeping and threats to national interests are related because the leeway for nonharmful arms reductions will vary as peace-keeping measures increase or reduce such threats.

Peace-keeping measures can operate simultaneously or alternatively along two different lines. The first consists in reducing the need for national armaments by substituting other forms of military power, presumably in the form of internationally controlled military forces. In the American *Outline* this approach is given the form of proposals for an international peace force which would serve to transfer some or all of the responsibility for legitimate deterrence and defense from national to international armed forces.

In order that an international force may be able to provide a nation with the same protection that it derived from national armaments, it has to meet several conditions. One condition is that the nation in question must be able to rely on the availability and effectiveness of the international force when its vital interests are threatened or violated. What is involved here is not only the problem of making the international force effective as a fighting instrument; an even thornier problem is how to assure nations that the authority controlling the force will order it into action in favor of their side, or at least not in favor of the opposing side. By giving every nation a veto, action in behalf of the adversary can be prevented unless it takes place in violation of the rules, but the force may be paralyzed by veto rights for all nations. Whether a nation can safely regard the international force as a substitute for national armaments or whether its existence will instead cause a nation to retain larger forces to protect itself against international forces operating on the side of an adversary depends largely on those who control it. The struggle for control of these forces might become a serious source of dispute, particularly if they should become substantial or militarily preponderant. Competing quests for control might in such a case aggravate rather than mitigate the arms race.

The second type of peace-keeping measure is directed at the reduction and, if possible, the elimination of the danger that conflicts among nations will erupt into violence. It is addressed, therefore, to threats to interests rather than to the protection of interests when they have come under threat. It calls, for instance, for guarantees that disputes will be settled peacefully and within the framework of agreed rules of conduct, or that change when justified will take place without resort to military force. It seeks thereby to reduce or eliminate the incentives for a resort to violence. Obviously, if it were possible to assure the just and peaceful settlement of all international disputes, any need for armaments, national or international, would be removed once this ultimate goal had been reached. After all, a peaceful settlement is one reached without the resort to force, and a just settlement, if regarded as just by both sides, would provoke no demands for change that could lead to violence.

However, such a high state of peacefulness is Utopian; it does not exist even in the most orderly nations, for if it did, this would spell the end of police and internal security forces. When measures of this type are suggested in connection with disarmament, what is meant is that countries could reduce the risks arising from disarmament to the extent to which they succeeded in increasing the chances of peaceful settlement and peaceful change. One can imagine, for instance, that an economically weak country would be more inclined to forego costly national armaments if, in disputes in which its interests were threatened, it could count on the friendly intervention of an international peace-keeping organization. Under another set of conditions, one could conceive of two major adversaries becoming more willing to scale down their armaments and accept the risks involved if they had gained confidence in peace-keeping agreements among themselves that made the resort to coercive means by the other side appear unlikely.

Turning now to the United States, it is worth noting that the relationship of its national interest to disarmament measures is in some ways unique. No other country is subjected to quite the same contradictory and powerful pulls when it comes to deciding whether to reduce, if not to disband, its armed forces.

American policymakers have been exposed to two experiences. In the first place, they have witnessed with satisfaction how well the vital interests of their country have fared under the greater armament efforts of the Cold War era. Having had no intention of threatening or using armed forces to change the *status quo* or to acquire new possessions, they can count it as a major success that the Soviet Union and, subsequently, Red China with few exceptions have been deterred—and, in the case of North Korea, prevented—from expanding their controls to new territories and peoples by means of military power. While there is no way of knowing what would have happened had the United States been militarily less well equipped, especially with strategic nuclear forces, there is good reason to believe that much of the success in preserving the security of the United States and of a score of non-Communist countries can be credited to American military might. Even if it could be proved that the Soviets never did have the intention of resorting to military power for action beyond the borders of the "Bloc," it could still be plausibly argued that their intentions would have been different if Western defenses had not made the price of such military action prohibitive.

The Soviet Union and Red China have less reason to be satisfied with the advancement of their interests resulting from their impressive armament efforts. If it is correct to assume that their leaders wished to expand Communist control over far more extensive areas than had been subjected to Communist rule by the end of World War II and the early "fall" of Czechoslovakia and continental China, the fact is that after this time their armaments did not help them to satisfy further territorial ambitions. America's friends and allies have reason to credit the armaments of the United States for much of the security they have enjoyed since the close of World War II. But not all of them are prepared to do so, either because they take a less grave view of the threats to which they have been exposed, or because some of them look to American armaments with misgivings as being provocative if not actually a sign of American militaristic proclivities.

Under these circumstances, one would expect a particularly strong reluctance on the part of the United States to let go of any part of its armed strength; at least one would not be surprised to find the United States especially insistent upon iron-clad guarantees that any disarmament measures it carries out or to which it agrees will leave those of its interests that have been protected militarily as safe as they were before. The fact is that in its proposals for disarmament the United States has been insistent on accompanying provisions for strict inspection and enforcement and for peace-keeping arrangements designed to maintain protection of American interests.

However, the United States has also undergone a second and exceedingly harrassing experience which has led to a vivid realization of the dangers inherent in the reliance on military means under conditions of nuclear armaments. No other country, except perhaps the Soviet Union, has been able to acquire such an intimate knowledge of the forces compelling nuclear countries engaging in nuclear deterrence to go on occasion to the very brink of thermonuclear war, or obtained so clear a view of the dangers of such a war to national survival. Such knowledge has made the United States very disarmament-minded.

As was stated above, the way for a nation to get the best of two worlds is to retain adequate military protection of its vital interests where such protection continues to be needed, while at the same time it pushes disarmament to the limit of its compatibility with this protection. The United States, like every other

country, has an interest in either initiating arms reductions—or in
reciprocating in kind if the adversary reduces his armaments—
whenever it can prudently afford, in the light of new evaluations
of the military strength or the intentions of its opponents, to
revise downward its estimate of American force requirements.
All it would be doing would be dispensing with the costly and
provocative luxury of militarily superfluous armaments.

Bilateral disarmament agreements, by which arms reductions
or the abandonment of armed forces are synchronized with those
of the Soviet Union and of other substantially armed countries,
would be in the United States national interest provided that it
could be made certain, in accordance with the statement of
agreed principles, that no one state or group of states will be
allowed to obtain military advantages from the disarmament
process.[6] This is the principle of proportionality, referred to
earlier. It applies to disarmament by tacit as well as by formal
agreement. However, by implication, the United States government made it clear that it shared the doubts about the universal
practicability of proportionate moves; otherwise, why would it
insist that peace-keeping measures, some of them drastic in
nature, accompany every stage of arms reduction, thereby to
assure the continued and undiminished protection of American
interests? Skepticism about the applicability of the principle of
proportionate reduction, though justified in principle, may be
carried too far. In the case of partial disarmament, it is not impossible that arms reductions might be devised and executed that
would not give a military advantage to either of the two opposing camps.

Any meaningful analysis of what the present and foreseeable
minimum requirements of United States military power are, as
measured in terms of the protection of United States national
interests, would require a study far exceeding the limits of this
discussion. In order to do justice to the subject, a score of

    [6] "All measures of general and complete disarmament should be balanced
so that at no stage of the implementation of the treaty could any state or
group of states gain military advantage and that security is ensured for all"
(United Nations, *Joint Statement of Agreed Principles for Disarmament
Negotiations* [A/4879, September 20, 1961]).

variables and their interactions, some of them of a highly technical nature, would have to be taken into account and evaluated in terms of their scope and impact. What I propose to do is to limit the discussion to two particularly important factors, both directly relevant to the subject of interests that is under discussion here. They bear first on the scope of those United States interests that are deemed vital and, for this reason, fall under the direct protection of United States military means, and second, on the threats to these vital interests, on which the requirement for military protection is dependent.

What the vital interests of the United States are or should be cannot be derived by mere logical deduction even from the most accurate estimates of the condition in which the country finds itself. Rather, their determination is the result of basic decisions on national strategy and is therefore frequently a subject of heated political controversy between men and groups holding different value judgments. One can only hope that once the decision has been reached, as it has been in the United States for the time being, the choice will prove to have been in the best interest of the country.

That the protection against military attack of the American homeland, or more properly of the North American continent, should figure among these vital interests, presumably topping the list, has only rarely been questioned. As a consequence, any military support needed to deter or ward off such an attack is indispensable. Some opposition to this proposition has been voiced recently by radical pacifists, who insist that in an age of thermonuclear weapons the resort to military force, meaning war, can no longer be justified even in defense of the national territory; war has become impossible, they say, because it would spell national suicide. Not all who concur with this view conclude that nuclear armaments—not to speak of armaments generally— should be discarded, even by unilateral action, nor do they believe that such a view should be openly expressed. They want an American offer never to retaliate with nuclear weapons to be made contingent on a similar Soviet commitment, or they wish to leave the Soviets in doubt about the way the United States would react once the chips were down, such doubts presumably assuring the continuing deterrent effect of America's strategic forces.

What was controversial after World War II, until a broad consensus was reached, and what might become controversial again was the decision by the American government to consider interests other than that of the defense of North America vital in the sense here defined. It is still controversial how the circle circumscribing these other interests should be drawn. Is the freedom of Quemoy and Matsu from Communist control vital to the United States? Is the liberation of the East European satellite countries vital? Is the nonrecognition of the East German Communist regime vital? What armaments the United States must possess in order to be able to safeguard all of its vital interests, and therefore what forces it could under certain circumstances agree to discard, will depend on the answers to these questions.

At the close of World War II, the United States had three broad options regarding what it should treat as its vital interests. The first option goes under the name of an isolationist or Fortress America policy. The second could be called an offensive policy directed at changing the *status quo* by force in favor of the non-Communist world. The third will be discussed under different names, as a policy of containment, of collective defense, or of a balance of world power.

Had the first option been adopted—or should it be adopted in the future—the United States would, under the most extreme interpretation, regard no interest as vital except the safety of North America. Only an attack on this continent would call for a resort to military force, and in the absence of such an attack this territory alone would be protected through military deterrence. According to less extreme versions, the rest of the Western Hemisphere and possibly even Great Britain would be added to the vital sphere. (The far-reaching military consequences of any such extension have, to my knowledge, never been spelled out. They might make this option almost as exacting and costly as the third option, which will be discussed below.) Leaving aside such extensive interpretations, the demands on American armed forces resulting from the first option would be much more moderate than they are today and would, other things remaining equal, greatly extend the leeway for arms reduction, even of a unilateral kind. This helps to explain why the United States felt justified in disarming its wartime military forces in a rapid and radical way at the close of both World Wars, when vital American interests beyond the borders of North America had not yet been recognized and when, in addition, no hostile power was in sight that had the means of either striking from the air or the sea at targets on the North American continent. Substantial landings on North American territory did not then, and do not today, represent a serious military danger.

The invulnerability to attack that the United States enjoyed, first in the days when a friendly British navy controlled the seas (in that era the only avenue to American territory) and again immediately after World War II, when control of the air as well as of the sea routes was assured, is not likely to return other than by arms control agreements in an age of long-range and medium-range missiles capable of operating from land, sea, and air, and possibly from outer space. It makes sense, therefore, to speculate about a way, through arms control, of depriving America's opponents of their ability to take advantage of her vulnerability. Disarmament measures could do so if the Soviet Union—which alone among adversaries has the capacity today to strike at targets within the United States—could be induced to give up all of its long-range and medium-range rockets and manned bombers. The United States is in an unusual position: its most vital interest, the security of its homeland, is presently under only one single threat, namely, Soviet medium- and long-range capabilities for nuclear attack. This being so, American vital interests, by the assumptions of a Fortress America strategy in its extreme interpretation, would become safe even in the absence of most of the military power that the United States presently commands if the Soviets were to join in a prohibition of all carriers of nuclear weapons capable of reaching North America and could be made to live up to such a prohibition.

If it were not for other reasons that militate against the first option and thereby preclude the remedy just suggested, the United States would stand to benefit enormously from a controlled prohibition of long- and medium-range nuclear striking power. If executed in good faith, such a prohibition would return the United States to the same privileged position of immunity against external attack that it once enjoyed. Whether the Soviets could be induced to agree to such a prohibition, if it were to be carried out in isolation from other measures of disarmament, is another matter. Moreover, at least two asymmetries would render agreement exceedingly difficult for both parties unless the disadvantages arising from these asymmetries could be made to cancel each other out. Both arise from differences in the geographical position of the two superpowers.

The first asymmetry favors the United States. Soviet territory can be subjected to military punishment not only by means of strategic forces but also by almost any other type of force operating from land, sea, or air. The second asymmetry, which gives the Soviet Union a military advantage, is that the Soviets can attack many of America's allies over land, while the United States has to cross wide spaces and oceans to reach any of the allies or satellites of the Soviet Union or to assist in the defense of its own allies. Only the prohibition of strategic forces, which would put an end to American nuclear superiority, synchronized with reductions of conventional forces in a way that would wipe out Soviet superiority on land, might conceivably leave the military balance of power intact.

A second option, which to my knowledge has never been seriously considered by any American administration, lies at the opposite pole as far as the range of United States vital interests is concerned. Resting on the assumption that the continued existence of Communist power anywhere in the world is intolerable to the United States because it would eventually spell the destruction of freedom everywhere, this option makes it a vital American interest to eliminate all existing Communist regimes and to prevent new ones from arising. It requires that this be done by military force if necessary. It is worth stressing that the third option, which will be discussed below, does not preclude the use of noncoercive means to "roll back" the Iron and Bamboo Curtains; it merely excludes, in contrast to the second option, the initiation of military violence or other coercion to bring about such a result.

If the United States were ever to adopt the second option, the need would be not for disarmament measures but, on the contrary, for new and strenuous efforts to beat the Soviets in the arms race. Any attempt to force a rollback would obviously be folly unless the United States had first achieved unquestionable nuclear supremacy, which would mean a strategic counter force capability sufficient to destroy almost all Soviet nuclear retaliatory power in a first strike, thereby preventing intolerable damage to the United States and allied countries. Today, even the most optimistic estimates of United States superiority in nuclear striking power fall far short of assuming such supremacy, and the chances of attaining it in the future will decline as Soviet targets become less vulnerable. Only a technological breakthrough in favor of the United States might conceivably change this forecast. An unrestrained and spiralling arms race, rather than disarmament, would be the most likely result of a United States policy of the second option.

The third option has been the American choice ever since the Cold War began and has been the basis of American armament and disarmament policy under all postwar administrations. The term "containment" describes fairly well the negative aim of the strategy of the third option, although like any other term it is an oversimplification that does not take into account the many deviations introduced into long-range policy by the pressures of expediency. According to this strategy, the United States regards itself as vitally interested in preventing, if necessary by the threat or use of military force, any expansion of the Soviet Union or Red China beyond the lines they reached with the communization of Czechoslovakia and of continental China. Korea and West Berlin are illustrations of this policy, while North Vietnam, Tibet, and possibly Cuba can be interpreted as deviations because the "line" was not held in these latter instances. There is nothing

in the term containment to explain why the highly accidental
borders of the Soviet bloc that had come to exist by 1949 should
be considered the line beyond which Soviet or Red Chinese expansion would represent an intolerable threat to United States
security. By turning to other symbols for option three one may
gain some clarification on this point.

While containment stresses the negative goal of the third option,
the term "collective defense" emphasizes the common interest
of non-Communist countries in retaining their freedom from
Communist control. The United States defense perimeter now
extends beyond the shores of North America and the Western
Hemisphere to the distant borders of countries adjoining what,
for the sake of brevity, may still be called the Sino-Soviet bloc.
A large network of alliances, usually referred to as collective
defense agreements, were entered upon and testify to the wide
extension of the vital area. Obviously, the United States did not
assume the immense burden of protecting such an array of countries, many of them weak and highly vulnerable, and all of them
very distant from the American arsenal, for reasons of sheer
friendship, although a sense of close affinity was an important
contributing factor in the alignment with the European members
of NATO. Collective defense rests on the conviction that United
States security is at stake, if indirectly, in any Soviet or Red
Chinese attack across the Iron and Bamboo Curtains and that the
United States needs the assistance of overseas allies to deter or
ward off such indirect threats to its own security. There is at
present in the United States very little dissent from these propositions and little quarrel, therefore, with this option.

The concept of collective defense does not explain why the
United States should feel compelled on occasion to assist a country—as it was prepared to do when India was invaded by Red
China—that had rejected the idea of collective defense in the past.
Under some circumstances the United States may even feel compelled to defend a country that does not wish such assistance or
actually resents it. Apparently, what the United States is seeking
to accomplish under option three, though the government may
not be consciously guided by this aim, is to preserve a reasonably

reliable balance of power between "the East" and "the West," with these terms standing for the two parties to the Cold War.

A world balance of power can best be defined as a distribution of power that promises to assure to two opponents the capacity to deter each other from resorting to war. A condition of mutual deterrence or of balance constitutes a highly rational goal for the United States, no matter how difficult it is to decide when it has been reached. In fact, the United States would appear to have little choice but to make such a balance not merely its minimum goal but also the maximum goal of its military effort, though of its military effort only. This does not suggest that the present *status quo* is desirable (it obviously is not) but that the United States has no intention of changing it at the price of war. The United States thereby resigns itself for the time being to many highly distasteful features of the *status quo* such as the partition of Germany, Vietnam, and Korea, the exposed position of West Berlin, the subjection of the East European countries to Moscow's overlordship, and the Communist dictatorship over the peoples of the Soviet Union and continental China itself. But, if successful, the United States policy also prevents its adversaries from employing military force to change the *status quo* in their favor.

If option three is interpreted, then, as a policy of containment, collective defense, or the balance of power, it follows that the United States must measure its requirements for coercive power —and thus the limits it will impose on the reduction of this power in the absence of peace-keeping substitutes—by what it takes to achieve this goal in the light of Soviet and Communist offensive capabilities and intentions. One cannot conclude that a balance is achieved merely because both sides have the same amount of military power. It takes more to deter some than it takes to deter others, depending on their intentions as well as on their willingness to take risks and use force.

So far, the discussion has proceeded on the assumption that serious threats to American vital interests, both direct and indirect, actually exist and that these threats are of a kind that can be countered effectively only by adequate military means of deterrence and defense. If it were not for this assumption, there would be no rational justification for the immense military effort that the United States, together with its allies, has undertaken in the period since the defeat of its wartime enemies. Obviously, the danger of expansionist offensive moves on the part of the Soviet Union and Red China overshadows today all other dangers motivating Western military preparedness. The question might be raised, and in some quarters has been raised, as to whether the United States is correct in assuming a continuing danger of Soviet military attack on free countries. One could point out that the Soviets have not so far moved or attempted to move any of their military forces beyond the territory they came to control at the close of the war. But we do not know whether they would have done so if they had not been deterred by the risks involved and thus by the military power of their opponents. In the case of Red China, military expansionism has been openly manifested both in Korea and in the Taiwan Straits. Because the threat from potential initiators of war and violence depends on their intentions as well as on their coercive powers, all one can say is that neither the expressed intentions of the Communist leaders nor the build-up of military power in their camp have been sufficiently reassuring to permit the United States and its allies to let down their military guard or to downgrade the value of their deterrent efforts. But if at some future time the United States became convinced that the Soviet Union had at least resigned itself to the *status quo* in the same sense that the United States has already done, it could reduce its military power drastically, even by unilateral measures.

Let us assume, for the sake of identifying other threats (which might still put a limit on arms reductions compatible with the United States national interest), that both the Soviet Union and Red China had ceased to constitute a military threat, either because their intentions had changed or because drastic disarmament had permanently deprived them of the means to make good on their continued aggressive intentions. In such a situation, hard as it is to imagine today, certain American national interests under option three might still require military protection because of at least three types of threats remaining.

1. The Soviet Union and Red China would continue to be the source of threats of indirect aggression or subversion. No matter how radically armaments might be reduced by all parties, it would be unrealistic to expect that enforcement measures could prevent the military training of guerrilla leaders and revolutionaries, or the export of small arms and advisers to revolutionary and insurrectionist movements outside the borders of the Sino-Soviet bloc. But independent of indigenous revolts arising in the third countries themselves, Sino-Soviet offensive action below the level of conventional forces could hardly call for a degree of Western preparedness that would interfere seriously with partial disarmament. Only in the case of general and complete disarmament would an international force become indispensable to meet threats of this type.

Apprehension is widespread about the alleged superiority of the Communist countries in the field of economic coercion and ideological warfare. Such instruments of coercion and the threats to American interests emanating from them would rise in significance as military and paramilitary means of coercion were reduced or eliminated by disarmament, but there are reasons why Soviet and Red Chinese ability to employ economic and ideological coercion would not seriously disadvantage the United States. Any assumption of a sweeping Sino-Soviet superiority on the nonmilitary and paramilitary levels of confrontation deserves to be questioned. Aside from the exceptional case of West Berlin, which is vulnerable to economic strangulation, it is hard to imagine where the Soviet Union or Red China could exert dangerous coercion by purely economic measures such as a blockade or an embargo. Surely the West, with its superior economic capabilities, should be able to absorb or counteract Communist attempts at expansion by economic means. One cannot speak as confidently about Western abilities to balance the Communist potentialities for ideological warfare, although communization of other countries has so far depended on either Sino-Soviet military backing or the victory of indigenous Communist forces, as in China and more recently in Cuba. Moreover, it would be a mistake to underestimate the deterrent effect that American and allied threats of ideological countermeasures might have after the

Soviet Union and Red China had disarmed. These two nations might prove to be highly vulnerable to nonmilitary pressures from the surrounding non-Communist world, especially the "subversive" attraction of freedom and prosperity for Communist-controlled peoples. Using only a small part of the funds going into armaments today, the West could not only contain an effectively disarmed Sino-Soviet bloc but could also stage very potent ideological offensives directed at the liberation of nations from Communist dictatorship and from control of Moscow or Peiping. It should also be remembered that the harm that might be suffered by American interests because of Sino-Soviet nonmilitary blandishments or punishments of third countries cannot as a rule be prevented by military power, and thus no limitation of arms reduction would be necessary for this reason.

2. A second category of threats which may limit United States ability to participate in even the most carefully calculated and enforced proportionate disarmament has its source in countries lying outside the borders of the Sino-Soviet bloc. It might seem fantastic to include here any of the countries presently allied with the United States. But although it seems almost inconceivable that the United States would use or threaten to use its military power against any of its present friends, drastic disarmament would wipe out American military superiority over its allies and thereby eliminate much of the influence it is presently able to exert in Europe or the Far East. Allied nations who need American military protection and assistance are now under varying degrees of pressure not to antagonize the United States. One may ask oneself what would become, for instance, of American influence on the future of Germany if the American military presence in Europe and American nuclear power were to become things of the past. However, the loss of influence and leadership within the present alliances might not be a prohibitive price to pay for general and complete disarmament if the simultaneous elimination of Soviet and Red Chinese military power made the alliance worthless anyway.

3. More serious existing and potential threats come from what is frequently referred to today as the "Third World" or what is

pictured as the "South" in a "North-South struggle" between economically underdeveloped, colored peoples of the Southern Hemisphere and industrialized, white, non-Communist nations of the Northern Hemisphere. It may sound ridiculous to suggest that the countries of the Southern Hemisphere, who are so lacking in military potential and so heavily dependent on outside economic aid, could ever turn themselves into a serious threat to American interests, especially into a threat that could be met only by a United States endowed with military power. After all, the military effort that has been directed by the United States in the past at such countries as Lebanon, the Congo, or Vietnam, chiefly in the form of military assistance or the deployment of forces, was not directed at these weak countries themselves but at their Soviet and Chinese backers, who, under conditions of drastic disarmament, would cease to give them the kind of support that could create serious dangers to the United States. It might also be argued that the rather astounding leverage that the underdeveloped states have had on the great powers has been a side effect of the East-West struggle. But the East-West confrontation would not necessarily end merely because the Soviet Union and Red China no longer had the intention or the means of military offensive action. On the contrary, the nonmilitary competition for the Third World might be intensified.

American interests that might be at stake in a struggle with the countries of the South are not territorial integrity or national independence. What might come under attack in situations of social or racial upheaval would be such assets as United States industrial installations, harbor facilities, indispensable raw materials, or canal rights abroad, as well as the other prerequisites of orderly world trade on which so much of the prosperity of the industrially advanced nations depends. Revolutionary disturbances could also threaten what there is in those countries of democratic institutions, civil liberties, and the freedom of private enterprise; the United States regards all these things as essential parts of the economic and political world order to which it is attached, and considers itself especially responsible for their protection.

So far the United States has not had to resort to the threat or use of force for the sake of protecting these interests, in part because the Cold War has forced it to concentrate on conflicts in which the East-West balance of power is directly at stake, in part because the South has directed its main effort against the colonial holdings of European countries, which the United States did not regard as vital. However, recent outbursts against "neocolonialism," directed chiefly against American positions, have given an inkling of what might happen if American influence, through drastic disarmament measures, ever dropped to a level as low as that of the Dutch and British at the close of World War II. Even in the absence of significant Communist backing from abroad, a militarily impotent United States might under such circumstances find its own means of protecting its interests inadequate.

It could be objected that the United States, however much disarmed, would still continue to be a leading power because of its prominence in the economic field. But it would be a dangerous illusion to assume that economic strength alone would suffice to deter, stop, or defeat revolutionary movements. The denial of markets, embargos, and other punitive economic measures, while harmful to enemy populations, has not proved a strong weapon against fanatic leaders and elites, and some of these measures, especially a blockade without the support of superior naval or military power in the area, can be made effective only in exceptional cases (e.g., West Berlin).

One way in which the situation could be remedied might be a downgrading in the value attached by the United States to those interests that are vulnerable to attack or violation by the South. It is a well-known phenomenon that the loss of great-power status tends to induce a retrenchment in the scope of the national interests deemed vital or even significant. Thus Sweden in an earlier era and Germany, Japan, and Italy in more recent times have transformed themselves by cutting back their ambitions, for the time being at least, and turning themselves from imperial into local powers. Britain and France, on the other hand, are showing today how hard it is for the once great to shed themselves of their responsibilities: while neither of these countries appears prepared to fight for all of the positions it once treated as vital in Asia, both have returned, with military power, to the African areas on which they turned their backs in the process of decolonization.

Another way in which the United States might seek protection for its interests might be an appeal for intervention by an international force of the kind proposed in the United States *Outline*. Rather than expecting such a force to operate against one of the present great powers, one could imagine it to be adequate to hold down even substantial violence in underdeveloped countries, at least if a rash of uprisings and violations of the peace did not occur at once. But would such a force constitute a reliable substitute for the protection United States interests presently enjoy vis-à-vis the South? The military quality alone of such a force, even assuming it to be of a very high order, would not suffice to make it a reliable instrument of United States defensive policies. The answer to the question would depend on what assurance the United States would have that the force would actually take on its opponents when it deemed action necessary, rather than standing by, paralyzed, or, worse still, siding with the party hostile to American interests. One thing seems certain: if such a force were controlled by the United Nations as presently constituted (an arrangement that it is hard to imagine the United States ever accepting, however), there would be little chance that it would be ordered into action against "liberation movements" or against groups acting against a Western nation in the name of "anti-neocolonialism."

The idea that an international police force might take action against the United States itself may seem preposterous, and I shall not attempt to draw up a detailed scenario to depict the way in which this might happen. Yet, if ever a central authority were endowed with a global monopoly of military power, one can foresee what might occur once this authority became engaged in a process of international legislation which it could not long avoid if it wished to retain its power. Given the present attitude of the Communist countries and of the bulk of the members of the Third World, such legislation might so affect American interests and convictions that it would be utterly unacceptable to the American people. It might, for instance, call for the abolition of all obstacles to free migration, or impose taxes on the rich nations for the benefit of the poor, or be directed at any of a long list of alleged iniquities ascribed to the "capitalist" nations. If the United States were to refuse to subject itself to such new laws, it is surely conceivable that the central authority would apply sanctions against a disobedient United States deprived of everything but an internal security force and incapable, therefore, of putting up more than token resistance. While such rather far-fetched speculations may not be a conclusive argument either against a powerful international peace force or against general and complete disarmament, they do suggest that American vital interests could become exposed to new threats emanating from such a force, instead of being protected by it. Even the right to veto its intervention would not be a guarantee against such threats. One need not be cynical, after all, to suggest that majorities enjoying strong and possibly fanatical popular backing have, as a rule, little difficulty in getting the law interpreted according to their wishes and in obtaining permission to satisfy what they regard as their legitimate demands. It would be ironical if an international force, intended as a means of safeguarding the American national interest, should constitute a new threat to this interest and thus bar American acceptance of sweeping disarmament measures.

2.

MILITARY POWER
IN A DISARMING
AND DISARMED WORLD

Robert E. Osgood

THE SOVIET PLAN for general and complete disarmament is based, avowedly, on the proposition that the establishment of a just and peaceful international order will follow simply from the elimination of all armed forces except those needed for internal security because armaments themselves pose the chief threat to international peace and security. According to a contrasting assumption reflected in the American approach, a just and peaceful international order in a world without national arms would require an international military force and more effective procedures for the peaceful settlement of national disputes. Otherwise, according to this assumption, international relations would lapse into the chaos that Hobbes posited as the natural state of human relations without government, and the beneficiaries, if any, would be the most lawless and aggressive states.

Thus the premise underlying the American approach contradicts the Soviet proposition that serious international conflicts leading to aggression and war could be eliminated or mitigated merely by disarming states. The American premise is sound, as other parts of this study demonstrate. It raises the question, however, of how serious the danger of aggression and war would be in a situation of general and complete disarmament. This question, in turn, leads to a larger question: what would be the effects upon international relations of the capacity of states to coerce one another in a completely disarmed world without an effective international military force to enforce a just international order? This is the principal question to which this chapter is addressed. Because the process of reaching general and complete disarmament might raise problems almost as serious as those of full disarmament, and because these problems might forestall the achievement of full disarmament, I shall first briefly examine the possible effects of armaments upon the international environment during the three stages of disarmament projected in the Soviet and American plans.

The Disarming Process

As an obviously valid requirement, which has been recognized in all proposals for an agreed voluntary reduction of arms, the American suggestion specifies that in each of the three stages of disarming there should be a "balanced" reduction, "so that at no stage could any state or group of states obtain military advantage." Yet the history of disarmament efforts shows that even in an age of simpler, less diversified weapons systems, as between the two world wars, states have encountered extraordinary difficulties in reaching agreements upon the precise reductions and limitations that should be embodied in a treaty in order to maintain a mutually satisfactory military balance.

These difficulties do not spring only from the dissatisfaction of prospective signatories with the political *status quo* and, therefore, with the military ratios that sustain it. Even when statesmen are otherwise content with a particular distribution of military potential, they are rightly reluctant to commit their governments to a treaty fixing that distribution, since altered circumstances may require some unilateral change of armed forces which is prohibited. Their reluctance is reinforced by the practical difficulty of knowing precisely what configuration of military power would provide a sufficient protection of vital national interests. With the profusion of military technology untested in battle, the

ultimate test of sufficiency, successful combat, has become increasingly difficult to determine. The requirements for successful
combat have become increasingly changeable because of the
rapid rate of innovation and obsolescence of weapons. The difficulty that any one state meets in determining the constituents of
military sufficiency is vastly compounded by the problem that
a number of states must encounter in measuring and restricting
their armed forces in comparable terms: different political,
geographical, economic, material, and other conditions affecting
the military security of states lend different military significance
to particular kinds and quantities of arms and armed forces. In
the nuclear age the test of military sufficiency—for the nuclear
powers, at least—tends to be less the capacity to win a war, from
which neither side would be likely to profit, than the ability to
convince the adversary that his transgressions will incur an unacceptable risk of a devastating war that no one can win. But
this test, in all its imponderable political and psychological ramifications, is even less calculable and measurable, and its material
requirements are no less subject to unpredictable change.

One must assume, therefore, that only some extremely compelling incentives could lead national governments to agree to a
disarmament treaty that committed them to proceed through
precisely formulated stages of prescribed arms reductions. Presumably, the overriding incentive for most states would be the
determination to achieve general and complete disarmament so
as to eliminate the danger of sudden, catastrophic war. Whatever the risk of disarming might be, the signatories would thus
have decided that the risks of remaining armed were greater.
For this reason they might be less concerned and exacting about
the precise distribution of military power during the disarming
process than if a balanced reduction of arms were the final
instead of the transitional stage. In any case, once governments—
especially accountable governments—had succeeded in com-
mitting their people to embark upon such a radical venture as
general and complete disarmament, there would undoubtedly be
tremendous pressure upon them not to disrupt the venture merely
because they feared that the military ratios were turning out to
be disadvantageous.

On the other hand, one cannot prudently assume that all major signatories would be completely satisfied with the political *status quo* at the time of the disarmament agreement or that serious conflicts of interest would dissolve during the disarming stages. Furthermore, although the reduction of arms and the universal commitment of nations to full disarmament would probably eliminate some international conflicts and mitigate others, the changing military balance could also be expected to stimulate some new suspicions, insecurities, antagonisms, and ambitions among states. Old adversaries might find new threats and temptations in the drastically altered configurations of power. Even traditional friends, previously bound by their fears of a common military threat, might find old grievances rekindled or new quarrels generated as the common threat diminished.

Some unavoidable changes in the components and configurations of military power would be especially disturbing from the standpoint of the United States in the absence of an international military force that could protect America's far-flung security interests. At some point in the disarming process, probably by the end of Stage II, the United States's capacity to support its overseas interests with force—either from overseas or on the spot— would be substantially reduced in relation to the capacity of adversaries to threaten these interests. Probably this effect would be most acute in the nonaligned areas close to the Sino-Soviet periphery, where the capacity of Communist China and its satellites to undertake indirect aggression and wage internal war would be especially dangerous. In Stage III the United States's capacity to project its restraining power abroad would be even more significantly reduced by the elimination of nuclear weapons and, as a result, the enhanced significance of disparities in local nonnuclear power.

Might not the threat of rearmament supplant the deterrent effect of existing forces as an instrument of containment? Considering the domestic and foreign pressures against disrupting the disarming process, this is doubtful. The United States would be especially disinclined to incur the onus of rearmament in order to contain overseas guerrilla warfare and other forms of indirect aggression. Yet whereas the United States would have political difficulty in countering even direct military threats against its overseas interests at the price of openly violating the disarmament agreement, the Soviet Union could maintain the option and, to a much greater extent, the physical capacity of sudden rearmament, both in order to deter American military action or rearmament and to achieve military superiority for some major offensive objective. The Soviet advantage would arise from the ability of the aggressor to pose ambiguous threats that can be countered only with unambiguous responses and from the superior capacity of an authoritarian government to mobilize national resources and resort to coercion for policy ends, including those at variance with international agreements, without the necessity of eliciting popular approval of such policies. An authoritarian government could readily rearm and maintain comprehensive preparations for rearmament by subterfuges and clandestine violations which are simply not available to responsible democratic countries—except, perhaps, at the price of their political integrity. Thus during partial as well as total disarmament the Soviet capacity to rearm, in the absence of an effective international military force to enforce order, might supplant some of the principal functions of Soviet nuclear forces in the armed world, but the United States would be at a disadvantage in trying to counter these functions with its own rearmament capacity or its capacity to assist local resistance overseas.

The Elements of Military Power in a Disarmed World

Both the Soviet and American plans for full disarmament are based on the assumption that, once the final stage of disarmament has been completed, peace and national security will no longer depend on the maintenance by sovereign states of a balance of countervailing military power. According to the Soviet plan, peace and security will depend simply on the absence of external armed forces. According to the American plan, they must depend on an international military force. The Soviet assumption that getting rid of arms gets rid of the problem of enforcing order with the power of armed coercion is obviously wrong, for we know that even the public order of a well-established state requires the ultimate sanction of force. It does not necessarily follow, however, that a tolerable international order cannot be achieved in a disarmed, as in the armed, world by a balance of countervailing coercive power among states rather than by a preponderance of coercive power under an international authority. Before one can decide that question, one must try to imagine, realistically and systematically, what the role of military power would be in a fully disarmed world.

This inquiry must start by recognizing that, contrary to the phrase "general and complete disarmament," the capacity of states to employ armed coercion and the threat of armed coercion against other states cannot be abolished entirely. Quite apart from the fanciful prospect of states resorting to clubs and knives, they would retain the following instruments of external military power: internal security forces that were not needed at the time to preserve domestic order; cadres of disguised paramilitary forces that could incite and assist local insurrections, subversion, and sabotage; a civilian technology readily convertible to military uses (especially for transportation and communication); rearmament and the capacity to rearm (that is, military potential). Whether or not a tolerable international order could be achieved under what is called complete disarmament without effective international substitutes for national peace-keeping forces would depend largely on whether the disarmed states, pursuing their interests with these remaining instruments of coercion, would create a sufficiently constraining balance of power to protect their mutual independence and security. I shall examine this question in terms of (1) the role of military power under effective general and complete disarmament; (2) the stability, or continuity, of general and complete disarmament; and (3) the consequences of rearmament in violation of the disarmament agreement

Military Power under Effective General and Complete Disarmament

Since states would still have the means of coercing and threatening to coerce each other with violence under general and complete disarmament, and since they would continue to have serious conflicts of interests not susceptible to peaceful resolution, general and complete disarmament would not eliminate the problems of military security and countervailing power that exist in the armed world. States would have to grapple with these problems, however, in a radically different military environment—an environment in which the size, striking power, and reach of armed forces would be drastically reduced, the configurations of relative military power would be greatly changed, and the ability of states to employ or even adjust their military power to meet changing circumstances without violating the disarmament treaty would be severely limited.

How would this strange military environment affect American security and other American interests, and how would it affect the general quality of international order? That would depend very much upon (1) the distribution of military power and the relative capacity of states to use it, and (2) the frequency and dimensions of warfare.

General or complete disarmament would enhance the protection of states from direct attack and invasion almost in proportion to their remoteness from adversaries. It would eliminate powerful long-range weapons, greatly reduce the number of troops that could be sent to foreign soil, and severely limit the means of getting them there. Therefore, general and complete disarmament would greatly reduce the capacity of states to project their military power openly and directly beyond their borders, either to inflict sudden devastation in an offensive strike or to protect noncontiguous states from attack by local defense or retaliation.

On the other hand, states which were contiguous or nearly so would have comparatively easy military access to each other with their internal security forces. The difficulty of intervention by other states to defend those under attack would help offensive states to use this access with impunity. If the size and armament of internal security forces roughly reflected the extent of territory and population of states, large and populous states with internal stability would have numerous forces with which they could achieve a significant local military superiority vis-à-vis smaller states within their reach simply by concentrating for external use the forces that were not at the moment essential to domestic order. In other respects, however, the power of small states in relation to large ones might be increased. For example, the enhanced importance of the local balance of internal security forces might enable small states that are now militarily weak to attack and harass with relative impunity the foreign property and facilities, the far-flung ports, canals, and lines of commercial transportation and communication upon which the major maritime and trading states depend. They might do this on their own initiative or as proxies for major powers.

Without trying to anticipate all the changes of relative military power that might result from the restriction of armed forces to the purposes of internal security, one can be sure, at least, that general and complete disarmament would produce some significant changes in the distribution of military power available for external use among hostile and potentially hostile states, and that other states could not readily counterbalance these changes by extending military assistance. For the composition, armaments, and size of forces available for external use would have been fixed by the disarmament treaty on the basis of criteria bearing only a coincidental relationship to the requirements of military security and the protection of foreign interests. Yet the disadvantaged states would be legally prohibited from making compensating adjustments by increasing their armed forces or altering military deployments outside their territories. Therefore, barring a transformation of national psychology and the international system, one must conclude that the resulting legally unalterable imbalances of power among states with conflicting interests would create more insecurity and tension among states than the laissez-faire power politics of the armed world.

Yet one should take into account the possibility that states might be deterred from using or threatening to use internal security forces in the ostensibly disarmed world by their consciousness of the penalties of violating the spirit of the disarmament treaty and touching off a rampant rearmament race. At the least, one might expect that states contemplating external military action with their internal security forces would estimate the danger of precipitating rearmament by their immediate adversaries. Thus the imbalances of power resulting from disparities in the offensive and defensive capabilities of internal security forces might be offset in some cases by countervailing disparities in military potential.

Military potential would include the capacity to employ civilian technology with inherent or readily convertible military utility, as well as the capacity to produce new arms and to mobilize additional military manpower. Depending upon how well they planned their administrative, financial, scientific, and industrial structures for mobilizing their military potential, the major industrial states should be able to develop devastating striking power within a period of a few months, although it might take them longer to train, to organize, and to deploy great numbers of armed forces. In a very short time they could convert much of their civilian technology—especially their transportation vehicles and communications facilities—to military uses. Consequently, an armed conflict of any duration that impinged seriously upon the interests of a major industrial state would raise a serious threat of rearmament, which any state contemplating military action with internal security forces would have to weigh beforehand. In the disarmed world, therefore, threats and counterthreats of rearmament, whether implicit or explicit, might be as important for deterrence as nuclear forces are in the armed world.

The capacity of states to rearm, however, would probably, as in the case of nuclear forces today, have only a limited deterrent effect against the whole range of possible military actions by adversaries: expansionist or revisionist states would have the advantage of being able to pose threats that might not seem worth resisting at the price of openly violating the disarmament agreement and possibly touching off a rearmament race. Rearmament capacity would be especially limited as a deterrent to incursions upon other states which were geographically vulnerable and which possessed little war potential of their own. In such cases there would be a premium upon a quick, limited attack that could achieve its objective before the rearmament of supporting states could have any effect. Deterrent threats of rearmament by one major industrial state intended to discourage another from attacking a weak state would, moreover, encourage pre-emptive attacks in order to forestall rearmament, and this danger would inhibit states from employing such threats.

Democratic states would be particularly reluctant to offend domestic and foreign opinion with threats to break a universal disarmament treaty unless their own vital interests were unambiguously in jeopardy and unless there was a good chance of protecting these interests with military action if the threat of rearmament should prove insufficient. They might also have particular difficulty in demonstrating the credibility of such threats by partial mobilization. In any case, there could be little assurance that even a completely credible rearmament threat by a potentially powerful state trying to defend the territorial *status quo* could promise to bring enough timely force to bear upon the local situation to discourage a determined and potentially powerful aggressor from exploiting his local superiority, the remoteness of his major adversaries, and the advantages of striking first with the benefit of advance preparations for counterrearmament. Under these circumstances, it is more than likely that the threat of rearmament would only hasten the aggression.

In many ways, therefore, the limitations upon war potential as a deterrent in the disarmed world would be comparable to the limitations upon nuclear deterrence in the armed world. The onus of rearming, the difficulty of employing rearmed forces quickly and decisively in remote local conflicts, the threat of counterrearmament, and the risk of provoking pre-emptive action or of hastening aggression would all tend to inhibit defensive states from rearming against anything less than either the adversary's rearmament or major and direct military threats which could not be countered without rearmament. The credibility and utility of the threat of rearmament would be correspondingly depreciated, much as the Soviet possession of nuclear weapons is presumed to have depreciated the credibility of American nuclear threats.

Actually, war potential in a disarmed world would probably be considerably less effective than the United States's existing combination of nuclear forces and mobile conventional forces in preventing local aggression upon other states because war potential could not so quickly establish a military presence in some trouble spot as a buffer and, if necessary, as a trip-wire upon a force capable of sudden devastation. Thus rearmament would be a particularly cumbersome and ineffectual response to the quick, local, military *fait accompli*. The aggressor who in the nuclear age would hesitate to exploit a local military advantage for fear of precipitating sudden nuclear retaliation or escalation might well ignore threats of rearmament in the confidence that rearmament could not affect the local situation before victory had been won.

Thus it seems likely that, in the absence of effective peace-keeping machinery, general and complete disarmament would create disturbing imbalances of power and new inducements to war, which the major powers (as measured by population and industrial advancement) interested in promoting a safe and orderly world would be unable to counteract with internal security forces and war potential. If, nevertheless, a stable order gradually emerged in a disarmed world, it would probably be because a new system of alliances achieved a stable military equilibrium among states.

Disarmament might, in time, lead to the formation of new defensive alliances, as states which found themselves more vulnerable to aggression but which were no longer shielded by former protectors discovered common security interests. These alliances would amount to pledges of mutual assistance with internal and rearmed forces against potential aggressors. By the same token, new offensive alliances and new commitments to neutrality might arise. Conceivably, then, international politics might revert to a multipolar system of alliances and commitments comparable to the systems of the eighteenth and nineteenth centuries, and this system might be the foundation of a stable balance of power in a disarmed world. Ideally, the new balance would be managed, as was done after 1815, by a concert of power, that is, by a combination of major states of roughly equal power with a common interest in preserving the new international order.

The fulfillment of this possibility, however, would depend not only on the configuration of military power but also on the configuration of political interests—on the solidarity of states who needed and could provide mutual protection. The configuration of political interests in a disarmed world is quite unpredictable. It would probably be altered by the process of disarmament itself. It is a reasonable conjecture, however, that if the ideological contest were to persist in a disarmed world, it would significantly qualify pure considerations of military security in the formation of alliances. Furthermore, it would be remarkable if the extensive patterns of economic interdependence, of cultural and political relations, and of other forms of modern international communication were to create configurations of mutual national interest and concern which coincided with the required configurations of military security.

In any case, it is extremely doubtful that a new equilibrium based on basic realignments of power and interest would come about without numerous military contests, which usually created and sometimes maintained past military equilibriums. But whereas in the eighteenth century these military contests, according to prevailing historical interpretation, tended to preserve the system of alliances or were at least a function of that system, in the disarmed world they would tend to destroy it by precipitating rearmament. In the disarmed world without an effective international force, the balance of power among the great powers would depend critically, as in the nuclear age, upon threats and counterthreats of force which, if used, would probably destroy the balance; yet the inhibitions against using force against threats to vital interests in the disarmed world would be far less compelling than now. Thus the stable operations of a multipolar alliance system under general and complete disarmament would seem to require a combination of the political mobility of the past and the military stalemate of the present. This phenomenon is hard to envisage.

All the speculations above concern the effects of internal security forces and rearmament capacity upon the international power competition under general and complete disarmament. Finally, we must take account of the impact of paramilitary forces. Neither large numbers of forces in being nor rearmament would be needed to enable one state to incite and assist a foreign insurrection or wage some other form of "internal war." The state resisting the internal war, however, might be at a serious disadvantage unless it expanded its internal security forces or received outside military assistance in violation of the disarmament agreement. The capacity of friendly states to extend effective military assistance or simply to establish a military presence against paramilitary intervention would be substantially impaired under general and complete disarmament. Therefore, where internal unrest and the weakness of governments created the conditions for insurrection, internal war would offer the greatest political rewards at the least risk of arousing effective outside opposition from the standpoint of states with the doctrine and organization to exploit revolutionary opportunities.

Of course a disarmament treaty, in accordance with the prohibition of anything but internal security forces, might try to check paramilitary intervention by prohibiting shipments of armaments and armed forces to foreign countries, but in practice this prohibition would probably be much more effective against outside military assistance to the defending state than against the forces promoting the insurrection, especially if the target state were contiguous to the aggressor. In any case, there would seem to be no effective legal means of prohibiting the transfer from one country to another of light arms, and forces labeled as technicians, tourists, volunteers, returning students, and the like, as long as normal civilian trade and travel were permitted.

Taking into account all the effects of internal security forces, war potential, and paramilitary capabilities upon the configurations of military power and the nature of warfare in an effectively disarmed world, one can hazard certain generalizations about the

implications for international order of general and complete disarmament without an international military force. Effective disarmament would tend to increase the insecurity of the smaller,
less populous, and less industrialized states adjacent to large,
industrialized, expansionist powers and not adjacent to correspondingly strong powers interested in protecting them. As in
the armed world, the most vulnerable states would be the least
stable ones, and they would offer the most attractive opportunities for paramilitary intervention. The strong powers would be
more secure from attack and invasion from each other than in
the armed world, especially if they were separated by seas or by
other states. Yet general and complete disarmament might greatly
increase the capacity of even the smallest and weakest states to
seize, harass, or destroy foreign property, industrial facilities, and
lines of transportation and communication which were owned or
used by the strongest powers. It would, in any case, create many
significant disparities in military power among states with serious
conflicts of interest, and it is unlikely that these disparities could
be redressed or the resulting tensions mollified by a new pattern
of international alliances.

General and complete disarmament would eliminate the danger
of a catastrophically destructive surprise attack without a major
violation of the treaty, although it would probably increase the
danger of pre-emptive and preventive attacks among the states
with great war potential. It would also almost eliminate whatever
danger there may be now of unauthorized warfare resulting from
a technical or personal malfunction. On the other hand, it would
probably increase the incidence of local warfare among states
with little war potential and between these states and the more
powerful states. Without rearmament, general and complete
disarmament would greatly moderate the military escalation of
local conflicts, but it would not prevent escalation, which might
well lead to the more gradual escalation of war to catastrophic
dimensions as rearmament took place.

If these speculative generalizations are applied to the hypothetical context of the existing international political and ideological contest as projected into the foreseeable future, effective
general and complete disarmament would appear to be more

favorable to American interests than the armed world in some respects and less favorable in others. I base the favorable estimate, however, on the optimistic assumption that the United States and friendly powers with considerable war potential would be committed to mutual assistance against aggression and that these states would make an open policy of remaining organizationally and materially prepared to employ existing forces and to resort to rearmament in order to deter and counter military aggression and violations of the agreement.

Under these conditions, general and complete disarmament would almost eliminate the United States's vulnerability to direct attack, but it would greatly reduce the United States's capacity to protect its extensive overseas interests—in particular, the wide range of interests derived from the aim of containing Communist expansion, the general interest in preventing and limiting local wars which might expand and undermine the disarmament system, and the countless material interests dependent upon widespread trade and travel.

Despite the reduction of American power abroad, general and complete disarmament should greatly enhance the security of Western European states against Soviet aggression, but if the division of Berlin and Germany had not been satisfactorily resolved, disarmament would probably increase the danger of an explosive local war. In East Europe the removal of Russian forces (except, perhaps, for Soviet contingents in national internal security forces) would create an unstable situation, as the released pressures for internal political change and for the reorientation of foreign policies created serious tensions with the Soviet Union and threatened to provoke a reintroduction of Soviet forces. An equally volatile source of tension and war, however, would be the resurgence of political and ethnic conflicts among the East European states themselves.

General and complete disarmament without effective peacekeeping methods would increase the vulnerability to Communist encroachment of Middle Eastern and Asian countries close to Russia and China and to their satellites, since the capacity of the United States to project its power and offer military assistance to these countries would be greatly diminished relative to the

Communist states. Its huge population and its correspondingly large internal security forces would almost certainly improve China's chances of overwhelming contiguous Asian areas, although India might be a potential counterweight if it enjoyed an effective central government. The ability of the Soviet Union and China to extend their control beyond contiguous or nearby areas in a disarmed world would depend on their success in exploiting "wars of national liberation." There would undoubtedly be plenty of local wars, revolutions, and *coups d'état* to be exploited under this banner, but it is hard to predict the Communists' ability to gain control of the winning regimes. All that one can predict with any assurance is that, where the internal conditions are conducive to a pro-Communist revolution, the Communist states would find it much easier to establish a dependency without a conspicuous transfer of arms and armed forces than the United States would find resistance to a pro-Communist revolution or overthrowing a pro-Communist regime, with or without conspicuously violating a disarmament treaty.

All in all, as long as the major powers generally adhered to the provisions of a disarmament treaty, the minimum disadvantage that the United States might incur as a consequence of the new military environment—as compared to those it might suffer in the armed world—would probably be the greater opportunities offered to the Chinese Communists for expansion in Asia and to the Soviet Union for extending its control over border states in the Middle East. This disadvantage, however, might conceivably be a price worth paying in order to eliminate the strains of the arms race and the constant prospect of a war of sudden annihilation. The decisive advantage or disadvantage of general and complete disarmament may therefore lie in the likelihood and consequences of rearmament.

The Stability of General and Complete Disarmament

Rearmament might begin in any sector of the whole multifaceted process of weapons research, development, and production and in any aspect of the conscription and mobilization of manpower. One can be almost certain that there would be at least minor violations of an agreement that applied so many restrictions to the armed forces and war potential of so many states. Every violation, however, would not necessarily terminate the whole agreement in the eyes of every state. One must therefore consider the kinds of violations, both secret and overt, which would leave the disarmament agreement substantially in force, as well as the kinds of violations that would destroy it. One test of the stability of the agreement might be the frequency and the kinds of violations which could occur without destroying the mutual interest of the signatories in generally observing its restrictions.

The more comprehensive the restrictions in a disarmament treaty, the more liable to violation and the more unstable it would probably be. The disarmament restrictions proposed by the United States and the Soviet Union are exceedingly comprehensive and, if embodied in a treaty, would have to be exceedingly detailed. They would be imposed, moreover, in an area of national policy and action in which states have normally required maximum independence and flexibility: independence, because military power is central to their sovereignty; flexibility, because in the modern age the components and the international distribution of military power are continually changing in unpredictable ways.

Rearmament in violation of a disarmament treaty might occur in the absence of war—for example, to redress an imbalance in war potential or to prepare for an armed clash—or it might result from a war. In either case, the best deterrent to rearmament and the best means of limiting it and restoring the restrictions (short of preventive war) would be the capacity and will of other states to counterrearm, assuming, of course, that violations could be detected. Under general and complete disarmament, states with large populations and war potential could with relative ease and speed achieve a decisive military advantage by rearming. Therefore, prudent governments would constantly be prepared for rearmament, just as they must be constantly prepared for war in the armed world. They should be as vigilant against sudden rearmament as against attack. Any intensification of tensions among states or any dissatisfaction with the territorial and political *status quo* might lead a populous and economically advanced state, with its interests at stake, to rearm. Since international politics and the competition for power would not cease in a disarmed world, the resort to rearmament would always be immanent, if not imminent.

When rearmament could change the military balance so drastically and suddenly, perhaps as the result of a miscalculation of an adversary's intentions, prudent states would be prepared to undertake pre-emptive or preventive rearmament. Since there would be a great advantage in being the first to rearm, there would be a premium upon clandestine and surprise rearmament, and a state disposed to strike first in order to confront its adversaries with ultimatums backed by military superiority would have an inherent advantage over its adversaries.

The immense and increasing difficulty of distinguishing civilian from militarily useful technology (not to mention manpower) and the ease of converting the former into the latter would exacerbate suspicions of violation and tend to provoke counterviolation even in the absence of bad intentions. The rapid rate of technological innovation, so conspicuous since the middle of the nineteenth century, would compound this problem by continually rendering the detailed restrictions and the inspection procedures obsolete (even assuming that they would be periodically adjusted and renegotiated). The balance of rearmament capacities would be quite unstable in any case, since the chance of one state's making a militarily decisive technological breakthrough would be greater than in a heavily armed world. Even if a disarmament treaty could halt the invention, development, and production of militarily useful technology, it would be destabilizing simply because it would legally restrict the capacity of governments to adjust their most crucial element of power to meet unpredictable shifts of political interest and foreign policies among nations.

Among adversaries with little war potential but sizable populations there would probably be many occasions for prewar mobilization of armed forces, both offensively and defensively, beyond the treaty limits upon internal security forces. The illegal expansion of internal security forces would be particularly difficult to deter, not only because it would be difficult to detect and prove but also because it could be undertaken in the name of purely internal needs which fall within the prerogatives of national sovereignty. Nevertheless, this kind of rearmament would be less provocative and destabilizing than technological rearmament by the major industrial states. Here, too, states might significantly change the military balance under the guise of meeting civilian needs.

Thus in the ordinary vicissitudes of international politics in a disarmed world, there would appear to be many situations which might lead to rearmament short of an armed conflict. Yet the surest stimulus to rearmament would be the actual outbreak of war involving the vital interests of states with significant war potential. Some states would undoubtedly hesitate to violate a disarmament treaty on mere suspicion or even sure knowledge that other states were rearming unless they believed that they were an immediate target of attack. It is unlikely, however, that states with considerable war potential would be willing to lose a war or permit a friendly state to lose a war without rearming. Of course aggressors, anticipating this reaction, might first secretly rearm or prepare to rearm, attempt a quick victory before counterrearmament could have an effect, and then promise to disarm while threatening to precipitate a general rearmament race if the adversary rearmed. This stratagem, however, would not always work, and even if it did, the adversary would probably seize the first opportunity to rearm secretly in order to redress the loss or at least to be better prepared for the next assault.

If I am right in supposing that the frequency of warfare impinging upon the interests of the states with major war potential would tend to increase in the disarmed world, armed conflicts would be the most serious threat to the stability of a disarmament agreement. Yet perhaps even warfare between major powers would not under all circumstances lead to the complete nullifica-

tion of such an agreement. Therefore, in order to estimate the
role of military power in a disarmed world, one must, finally,
speculate about the consequences of rearmament.

The Consequences of Rearmament

I have said that not every violation of a treaty for general and
complete disarmament would necessarily destroy the whole body
of restrictions. Might not rearmament be limited and perhaps be
followed by disarmament, so that the agreement would remain
intact? Or would rearmament be more likely to touch off a rearmament race that would be so volatile as to destroy the whole
agreement and perhaps the signatories as well?

Like the escalation or limitation of war, the escalation or limitation of rearmament would depend upon the political and material
circumstances in which it occurred. Undoubtedly, a general and
complete disarmament treaty could survive numerous violations
and armed clashes among states which, even in the armed world,
posses in effect little more than internal security forces, providing that the states with great war potential were unwilling or
unable to intervene. Perhaps it could also survive some quick,
limited military actions by powerful states against weak ones.
Any rearmament or suspicion of rearmament among the states
endowed with major war potential and afflicted by serious conflicts of interest, and any warfare among these states or any
warfare impinging upon their interests, would be very likely to
produce an uncontrollably volatile arms race from which there
would be no return to disarmament.

The basic reasons for this volatility are that the states involved
would have immense unmobilized war potential, which they
could mobilize quickly, and that every increase in the mobilized
war potential by one power or the other could have a decisive
effect on the balance of military power among adversaries. This
being the case, there would be a great temptation to rearm and
strike first with the most devastating weapons. Furthermore,
sudden rearmament by any major power would drastically affect
the ratio of military power with many other states, which would

also be forced to rearm in a kind of chain effect. There would be no comparison between the severe tensions and insecurity created by this kind of arms race and the impact of any previous arms race in history.

To be sure, as in previous arms races the exacerbation of tensions and (if the arms race lasted long enough without producing catastrophic war) the necessary curtailment of other economic demands might lead to a peaceful settlement of the controversy that had caused the race. Even so, states which had become involved in wholesale violation of the restrictions would find it almost impossible to restore them. The fragile bonds of mutual confidence and reciprocal restraint in the disarmed world would have been irrevocably sundered. The experiment would be over. The rearming nations would then have no recourse but to grope their way back along the slope of rearmament until they reached again some point of relatively stable equilibrium at which they could feel confident of their security.

3.

NONMILITARY INSTRUMENTS OF POLICY IN A DISARMING AND DISARMED WORLD

Paul Y. Hammond

TWO COMMON substitutes for military capabilities in foreign policy, which are important for a disarming world, are economic power and world public opinion. Economic power, as used in this context, means power to grant or to deny commercial opportunities and economic assistance, trade, or aid. It can be exercised unilaterally or in concert by several states, one against one or several against one. A powerful influence in political relations, it is difficult to control without other instruments of power to support it. German economic penetration in Eastern Europe in the late nineteen thirties and Soviet Russian exploitation of the same area after World War II both depended in large measure upon military and political controls, as have the economic controls associated with imperial orders. Without these supporting instruments, economic power is unlikely to be capable of anything more than the imposition of a boycott dependent for its effectiveness upon almost complete unanimity of support among states and offering large material temptations to violation.

Colonial rule and the Marxist denunciation of it have sensitized many states to economic pressures, even those applied as incentives. Strings attached to United States economic aid, even those designed to forward long-term development, have repeatedly been denounced by the recipients as economic imperialism, as have withdrawals of such aid.[1] Attempts at concerted economic pressures have met comparable difficulties. In late 1963 and early 1964 Cuba breached the economic embargos fostered by the United States in several significant sectors, just as the undertaking seemed to be taking effect. United States economic pressures on the Soviet Union were similarly offset by Soviet efforts to establish trade links elsewhere through long-term credit arrangements. Both cases are indicative of the limits of influence and coercion through economic restrictions. Few states are, or must remain, dependent upon a single source for any important need. In looking for alternatives, small states have the advantage of small needs. Large states have the advantage of many resources to accomplish objectives. In any event, only a few breaches are needed to break the impact of an embargo.

Similar difficulties apply in the use of world public opinion as a constraint upon states. As a factor in maintenance of order as armed coercion declines, it must serve as a general limitation upon national power rather than an instrument. A difficulty arises in trying to bring it to bear upon specific issues. Theoretically, certain states might be able to marshal world opinion through such instruments of persuasion as manipulation of the assistance made possible through disarmament. Disarmament might provide major industrialized powers with great opportunities for carrying forward their foreign policies. On the other hand, disarmament would probably raise inordinately high expectations of largess among underdeveloped countries. According to a view endorsed by United Nations Secretary-General U Thant and held widely by others, the primary problem in the world is that of the improvement of the lot of the needy states. Officials and people

[1] See, e.g., Egyptian reaction to United States withdrawal of offer to help build Aswan dam (*New York Times*, July 25, 27, 1956); Cuban reaction to United States cut in sugar quota (termed "aggression") (*ibid.*, July 7, 8, 1960); Cambodia's explanation for severing economic and military ties with the U.S. (*ibid.*, November 13, 15, 20, 1963). In the last case, when the United States responded by canceling aid shipments of gasoline and jute sacks necessary for the export of Cambodian rice, Prince Sihanouk accused the United States of trying to "asphyxiate" Cambodia (*ibid.*, December 20, 1963).

in these states would regard a major disarming agreement as confirming this proposition and as justifying expectations of huge increases of assistance from the West and the Soviet bloc. They would probably translate their expectations into rights and any failure to fulfill those expectations into a denial of their rights. Attempts to manipulate levels of aid would therefore result in frictions and resentments likely to alienate their support. As these speculations imply, it would be improvident to count on world opinion as a mainstay either of United States national interests or of a common international order. One might anticipate a general pattern of good feeling in a disarming world. That supposition would eliminate many problems. In such a situation, world opinion might indeed constitute a formidable constraint on any state.

These comments discounting economic coercion and world opinion as substitutes for military power in earlier phases of disarmament suggest the inadequacy of these alternatives under conditions approaching general and complete disarmament. Yet to test the relevance of our experience in an armed world to a disarming and a disarmed world, one must take account of conditions conducive to or restrictive of success in the application of particular instruments of foreign policy.

An analytical model to serve as a basis for further exposition of the problems of substitute means in the exercise of political power should reflect four mutually interdependent variables: (1) the stages or conditions of disarmament itself; (2) instruments or means in foreign policy, distinguishable as (a) military means, (b) nonmilitary means, and (c) international organization politics; (3) national security interests; and (4) comparative advantages between the United States and (a) the Communist bloc or blocs, (b) allies of the United States, and (c) neutrals. The first variable is limited to conditions approaching general and complete disarmament, with little attention given to variations in conditions within that limit, apart from consideration of the difference between possession of an international military force that is not as yet unchallengeable and one that is unchallengeable.

The focus of this essay can now be stated as a question posed by the subdivisions of the second variable. What would happen to nonmilitary instruments (b) and to international organization politics (c) if military instruments of national security policy (a) were severely reduced through disarmament? The third variable, national security interests, has been left unstructured in order to reflect the intended emphasis on the second variable, as well as the difficulty of undertaking an analysis of it. For analytical convenience the fourth variable, comparative advantages, is structured with three subdivisions to reflect differences in both instruments and interests.

Instruments and interests are viewed primarily as American, but to confine discussion to American instruments and interests would be to disregard interactions among states as these variables change—interrelationships that deserve attention for the purpose of this essay. Consideration of the first variable, disarmament, is limited to the late phases of disarming as specified in the *Outline,* for example, in the beginning of Stage III. The first variable establishes an analytical setting for aspects relevant to the other three, as follows:

Effects on the third—namely, national security interests—under these conditions.

Changes in availability and utility of the second—namely, different instruments of foreign policy.

Effects of the changes in instruments and interests on the fourth—namely, comparative advantages.

Effects of changes in comparative advantage, in turn, on definitions of national security interest and the utility of instruments.

Elements in the Displacement of Military Means

Particular aspects of the displacement of military capabilities in the pursuit of state interest may now be considered one at a time without losing sight of relationships between the elements and of the hypothetical setting. Four will be discussed: trade-offs between military and nonmilitary instruments, relationship of interest variations to the efficacy of alternative means, comparative advantages in exploitation of bilateral means, and comparative advantages in the politics of peacekeeping.

First, however, there is an additional consideration. Problems addressed and solutions posed in radical arms control proposals are oriented to a long-term future and to a radical change in the *status quo.* They break away—often quite intentionally—from a widely accepted rational standard for analysis of policy. Such analysis involves two processes, a step-by-step comparison of all alternatives[2] and a discounting of speculations about the future to take account of their uncertainty. Such a standard obliges one to compare disarmament with other armament policies—presumably with all other possible armament policies—with respect to risks to national security. To do that would involve an inquiry quite beyond the scope of this study, which is concerned with peacekeeping, not with the alternatives to it. The following analysis concentrates on costs and risks of disarmament. So as not to ignore comparisons between these costs and risks and those of alternative courses, comparisons are drawn between present conditions of disarmament. Present conditions, however, are not the only alternative to disarmament deserving of systematic comparison.

Military-Nonmilitary Instrument Trade-Offs

On the basis of a record showing a great flair for achieving objectives by nonmilitary rather than military means, particularly in comparison with its major rivals both present and potential, the United States could undertake to participate in at least the initial stages of disarmament with considerable confidence in being able to hold its own even in face of unabated rivalry among

[2] Adopting the terminology of military or political gaming, Walter Millis argues against the need for such comparative analysis by claiming for disarmament studies the same license to hypothesize claimed for military and political gaming (Millis *et al., A World without War* [New York: Washington Square, 1961], pp. 53–69).

nations and could indeed expect competitive gains, at least at the outset.

Such a record is not in fact demonstrable. The United States has made extensive and varied use of military aid, alliances, and training relationships with other countries for promoting political and economic development, particularly in Latin America, Southeast Asia, and the Middle East. Reliance upon military personnel and methods, particularly to legitimize less popular forms of government, is in principle undesirable and in many cases imprudent. The value of United States military programs, however, is not negative, negligible, or even low. Reducing military aid would not necessarily result in reducing reliance on military personnel and power among the regimes affected. Most such regimes would be disposed to support their military forces at the expense of economic development and social welfare. Even the particular vice of wanting overly sophisticated weapons would probably not be corrected by cutting off American sources. Other countries would have modern weapons available and would find advantages in exporting them.

Second, cutting of ties between the United States and military forces of smaller powers would in many cases eliminate a restraining and constructive influence.[3]

Third, in many cases the military is a positive force in the country, not only for law and order but also in civil administration, action, and support of constitutional order. The American military establishment has been alert to opportunities to indoctrinate its foreign counterparts and trainees in liberal principles and wider civic roles.

Fourth, United States military aid has often been a device for promoting changes and imposing restrictions deemed essential to the success of economic assistance. However modest, these accomplishments might not otherwise have occurred.

In the light of these accomplishments, it would be irresponsible under present circumstances for the United States government to

[3] The best published summary of the case for military assistance along these lines is Amos A. Jordan, Jr., *Foreign Aid and the Defense of Southeast Asia* (New York: Praeger, 1962), chap. ii.

eliminate military aid in the expectation of finding other ways to achieve its objectives. That view was taken by the Draper committee in addressing itself to questions of emphasis between military and economic aid. The committee was unwilling to recommend any limitation upon the prerogative of government officials to decide each case on its merits.[4]

American military power has not rested exclusively upon military aid programs, even those in support of the comparatively successful North Atlantic Treaty Organization. The main justification for military assistance programs has been the supplementing of American military capabilities by relating United States strategic interests to those of recipient countries. Without the manifest ability and willingness of the United States to undertake operational military commitments, it is doubtful whether any governments along the geographical periphery of Soviet or Chinese hegemony would have accepted American military assistance. In cementing alliances and constraining adversaries, the United States has made extensive and varied use of its military posture and operational military capability. Much of United States influence in Europe, the Middle East, and Asia rests upon estimates of American willingness to use military force if necessary. These estimates rest in turn largely upon visible military posture.

Reciprocal effects from changes in military posture in the Soviet-American strategic confrontation are acknowledged on both sides. Both regard strategic nuclear capabilities as the vital core of military power. At a minimum, the principle of proportionality in disarmament would surely have to apply to such weaponry. Changes in a disarming world would probably pertain to the relationships of the United States and the Soviet Union to allies and neutrals more explicitly than to direct rivalry. Political consequences of disarmament for the two great powers should be measured in terms of the differences between them in availability and potency of alternative means for pursuing interests. Re-

[4] See especially the President's Committee to Study the United States Military Assistance Program, Final Report, *Conclusions Concerning the Mutual Security Program* (Washington, August 17, 1959), pp. 22–32.

ductions in military threats and inability to respond to them, if the responses can be be kept commensurate, would probably loosen American alliance relationships and reduce United States leadership. The meaning for United States policy would depend heavily upon the factors summarized above as interest variables, variables in comparative advantages, and variable possibilities of exploiting the politics of peacekeeping. It is fitting to examine the shift from military to nonmilitary methods by concentrating on the instruments themselves.

With the arbitrary constraints which are necessary to avoid extremely complex multiple-variant projections into radically different situations, the inquiries must be modest. I will consider three questions. The first is whether we can expect the United States to make less or more use of military instruments in the future.

What is said about trends in the utility of military instruments at least helps to delimit the problem. On the one hand, it is not evident that the trend is toward increasing expenditures on military instruments, whether judged in absolute terms or as a percentage of the gross national product, and quite without regard to the validity of the argument over whether we are engaged in a quantitative or qualitative arms race. On the other hand, no clear trend toward smaller arms expenditures and armed forces can be demonstrated which would justify the inference that the secular trend is toward disarmament without negotiated agreements. Unless present trends change, military expenditures are likely to remain bearable economically and politically for an indefinite future, but at the same time, relatively undiminished military forces and capabilities are likely to be considered useful and necessary by governments and their people.

A second inquiry, which concentrates on the potentialities of military power substitutes, is simply the examination of nonmilitary instruments for their adaptability. These instruments can be dealt with in an arbitrary five-fold classification: psychological, economic, technological, diplomatic, and political. By psychological I mean propaganda, cultural relations, psychological warfare, and prestige as a national asset. By economic I mean the management of material wealth as a resource or an incentive for the production of prestige, military rearmament potential, specific political persuasion or manipulation, and general socioeconomic (and hence political) transformations. By technological I refer to the special role which technical innovation plays in economic power, in particular socioeconomic transformations, and in military rearmament potential, national prestige, and potential national power breakthrough. By diplomatic I mean the manipulation of national commitments—using the term in its broad but traditional sense, not as a synonym of foreign policy. By political I mean the cultivation of domestic political support abroad through any means. All of these instruments lie within the grasp of individual national regimes; they do not include international approaches to peacekeeping, such as international law or an international military or police force. Here I shall deal with economic, psychological, and technical instruments, the first three types, leaving the fifth, political warfare and subversion, until later in this section. I shall omit consideration of the fourth, diplomacy, because it would depend so heavily upon the others and upon particular peace-keeping arrangements.

In a disarming world probably the most obvious great-power adaptation which does not involve either the threatened use of military power, the use of armed forces in an illegal manner, or the employment of internal security forces as military power would be the further exploitation of economic capabilities. Funds saved on arms could be transferred to other foreign policy uses, though undoubtedly some funds would have to go toward defraying the cost of international peacekeeping, which could become very expensive.

The comparative foreign policy advantage would probably favor the Russians if in both the United States and the Soviet Union the savings would go into paying for peacekeeping, increased domestic consumption, and increased expenditures on foreign economic policy. Increased rates of consumption in the two countries would probably be to the Soviet advantage. Substantial increase in private American consumption would have a negative impact on foreign public opinion. Increased United States consumption in the public sector, however—through expenditures on education, medicine, culture and the arts, roads, and so forth—would be likely to add to United States prestige abroad. On the other hand, any way in which the Russians increased their domestic consumption, whether on private or social expenditures, would boost the reputation of the U.S.S.R. for its Communist achievements and economic development.

On the other hand, it is difficult to see any important advantage accruing to either power from large proportional increases in the level of expenditure on foreign economic aid. In the past, both have had their discouragements with economic aid. So long as both remained active in the field, potential recipients would have the opportunity to play one country against the other. Whether or not the long-run interests of the U.S.S.R. are served by the development of relatively stable and independent national states, or whether economic aid contributes to this aim, the reallocation of resources from armaments to foreign economic aid should serve American purposes in the long run. However, as the experience with expenditures for economic assistance over the past fifteen years has made clear, this general congruence of interest is often inconsequential beside the more pressing interim and short-run problems of foreign policy, for which comparative advantage is more relevant, though unclear.

The psychological instruments of foreign policy—propaganda, cultural relations, psychological warfare, in fact any activities designed to enhance the national prestige—may be the subject of intensive concern on the part of government, as well as important determinants of the climate of opinion in which the interests of the United States will be pursued in foreign relations. But they are extremely difficult to use. Three factors which contribute to this deficiency are the difficulty of co-ordinating or controlling the flow of information abroad about the United States, the numerous sources of information available in other countries to heads of state and foreign offices even though much news is controlled for the public, and the difficulty of identifying, predicting, and controlling propaganda assets. An organized propaganda campaign may nevertheless serve a national purpose in particular circumstances. For example, it should be possible to kindle fears of arms agreement violations. Here, as elsewhere, however, the propaganda serves in a secondary capacity. Its function is largely to reinforce the effect of other instruments of policy.

Technological innovation may not itself be viewed as an appropriate instrument of foreign policy, but its wide ramifications make it important to foreign policy in an armed world, and, no doubt, in a disarming and disarmed world as well. Technological innovation has become a stimulus to national economic growth. It can play a significant role in the transformation of underdeveloped societies and economies, particularly when coupled with the implications for national prestige of pre-eminence in important technology. For example, a state which achieves superiority in a technology significant to the development of certain kinds of national economies can expect to be allowed or asked to train the major intellectual elites of the states involved, supplying them with its technicians and establishing permanent trade and technological connections which would assure it a considerable measure of political influence, if not outright control. Under certain circumstances it would not be unreasonable for a great power to commit major resources to the achievement of scientific and technical developments which would confer upon it just this kind of advantage.   •

At the same time, new developments in technology will persistently threaten to render the elements of an arms control agreement obsolete by conferring political advantages upon the state which has achieved them in ways which have not been proscribed or controlled under the agreement. No doubt establishing and enforcing the principle of disclosure of research and development work would help deal with the more obvious potential military applications from scientific innovations. But unless every aspect of research and development is inspected or unless none of it is secret, serious risks will be run that scientific innovations will confer surprising and substantial political advantages. Even agreements which cope adequately with the potential military applications of future research and development will not dispose of the whole problem of scientific innovation. If given sufficient attention, the development of "nonmilitary" scien-

tific application can be expected to yield important new methods
for asserting national purposes.

The problem here can be illustrated by the American *Outline*.
Its prohibition—eventually—of national armed forces includes
supporting functions, which probably means research, development, testing, engineering, production, storage, and maintenance
of military equipment. But what is military equipment? It is probable that negotiations and litigation could refine the meaning of
this term and that peace-keeping arrangements could cope with
the usual problems of inherent legal ambiguity. But they could
not eliminate major questions of ambiguity about the things
which, though they may not be military, nevertheless may vitally
affect national security or have military significance.

The trouble here is in the extraordinary ambiguity of the things
proscribed, whether they are identified as instruments of violence,
armed forces, or things military. The proscribed activity, after all,
is not confined to overt acts of war. The proscription runs also
against the preparations which give a nation the capability to
wage war. Since these preparations are integral to the society
and economy of the arming state, the problem of differentiation
posed is appalling. On the other hand the prohibition must be
kept severely limited if the functions and powers of the peace-
keeping force are to be kept limited. Even now it is probably
inappropriate to bring under the rubric of military weaponry or
to call instruments of violence some of the things that we do.
Not all of the technological capabilities now categorized as
chemical or biological weapons must be administered by uni-
formed forces under military discipline or be violent in their own
effects or be used to support violence or the threat of violence.
And this can be only the beginning. A state with rich resources
in scientific skills and productive capacity should be able to carry
out major scientific and engineering developments which would
have as one of their objectives the equipping of technical personnel (not "military" and not "armed") with instruments of
human behavioral control which are specifically designed to avoid
the prohibitions of an intelligently drafted disarmament agreement.

I do not mean to suggest that the legal arts have never dealt with appalling ambiguities before, but they have their limits. Here, the legal task is to define the limits of the functions and powers of a major governmental activity, which amounts in this case to nothing less than an international organ with a preponderance of military power. The prospects for exploiting this formidable ambiguity to produce highly unstable power relationships among major states and within the peace-keeping organs as well are serious, the implications for administrative determination and litigation from the outset of an arms agreement are enormous, and the possibilities of exploiting forms of national power which are not proscribed are extensive.

Variations in National Interests and National Means

Among the factors determining the extent to which nonmilitary instruments of foreign policy can be substituted for military ones under conditions expected to prevail with approaching general and complete disarmament, the schedule (the scope and character) of state interests is a major one. For advocates of unilateral disarmament, it is the dominant factor: it, more than anything else, will determine the transformation of the international system. But even the most pessimistic prognosis about disarmament must give prominence to changes in state interests. Under any set of assumptions general and complete disarmament would radically alter the national security interests of most states, or at least of the major ones. In analyzing the displacement of military instruments, therefore, it is necessary to examine their relationship to national interests.

National security interests can vary in several ways which are notable for the purposes of this essay; these include how vital the interest is, how competitive the pursuit of it is and how dependent it is upon military instruments. These variables go far toward determining the nature of the political relationships among states.

The level of tension among states in competition with each other can be measured by the vitality of the interests involved together with the competitiveness with which they are pursued. Competitive tension, in turn, is reflected in part in the geographical patterns of national security interests. Since the early nineteen forties the United States has usually defined its vital interests as extending across two major oceans, a prevailing geographical pattern which has reflected continuing tension over the security of the United States. The geographical manifestation of these interests has fluctuated considerably. Sometimes, as in the late nineteen forties, the line has been drawn short of any direct continental involvement in Asia. At other times, as in the early nineteen fifties, it has seemingly been extended to include certain of the European and Asian borders of the U.S.S.R. Never have these geographical delineations of state interest, either in their minimal or their maximal versions, been free from controversy.

This pattern of extended interests reaching into many sectors of the globe would probably be considerably restricted, at least during the latter stages of disarmament, when the reciprocal effects of shrinking military capabilities and the decline in public support for a foreign policy less oriented to military means would be reflected.[5] Yet perceived interests could not be expected automatically to shrink along with military capabilities. The geographically extended interests perceived by successive United States governments have not been created entirely by a concern with military threats. At least in part, they have been related to other factors, cultural or historical perhaps, or even juridical, but also to less ascribable considerations. If all manifestations of national military or coercive capabilities would shrink in proportion to disarmament, and interests would also, one could expect to see a stable international system of spheres of influence develop. Unfortunately (at least from the viewpoint of those who seek a stable order based on calculable interests), such consistency is not to be

[5] The greater support for military over nonmilitary foreign policy programs by the United States public is documented in Samuel P. Huntington, *The Common Defense* (New York: Columbia, 1961), pp. 242–48.

counted upon. While some state interests and capabilities can be expected to decline proportionately, others may remain unaltered, or even expand. Capabilities, similarly, cannot be expected to shrink in some neat geographical pattern. The nourishment of sustained insurrection in another country under conditions of substantial disarmament, for example, may urgently require closeness, even contiguity. On the other hand, the geographical requirements for fomenting military coups would probably not be so high. Coups could be generated or governments subverted from afar.

Neither pattern of capabilities is particularly reassuring. One can conceive of disarmament's resulting in a reduction in United States military power until the only capability left which could be consistently exercised would be the defense of the geographical nucleus of a "Fortress America," with the opponent at one's doorstep. This is a position which has great military disadvantages, quite apart from the severe political and economic restrictions which it could force upon the country. On the other hand, to counter this reduced position by vigorous and venturesome attacks upon areas geographically close to the opponent would be unstabilizing. Such behavior would be difficult to convert into an arrangement of mutual deterrence, which would be the only basis for a stable relationship under these circumstances.

American military aid and military posture in part depend upon the distinctions which they help to draw for the United States between its enemies, its allies, and neutrals. To the extent that competitive tensions decline, these differentiations and the military force which supports them become less essential because the moderation or constriction of American interests reduces the need for military instruments. Similarly, increases in tensions, which might occur if, for example, instabilities in hostile and competitive relationships grow, could expand and intensify interests and make necessary a greater dependence upon military instruments. Furthermore, the availability of military instruments could affect the level of competitive tension between states and the extent of need for military instruments in coping with that tension. Finally, the availability of military instruments in a disarmed world will depend, on the one hand, upon the effectiveness of the enforcement arrangements and, on the other, upon the skills and pressures applied to undermine such arrangements.

These propositions summarize a highly complex set of relationships between interests and a series of other previously identified factors which figure in a disarmament situation. They constitute an intricate set of interrelationships. In a sense, each is dependent upon the others. To the extent that this summary accurately depicts the factors upon which disarmament must depend, it is both encouraging and discouraging in its implications for disarmament. If one sees these intricate relationships in equilibrium, then any one of several moves could shift the equilibrium in a direction which would be more compatible with disarmament. Among other things, disarming itself could do that. It might generate the very changes which would assure its full and continued success. The trouble is that, as the earlier discussion in this section indicated, speculations on this subject can lead to quite the opposite conclusion—that disarming can lead to instabilities and tensions which could destroy some of the conditions on which its success seems to depend. The relationship of state interests to two conditions prominent in the propositional summary above should illuminate the functions which variations in national security interests have in the displacement of military by nonmilitary foreign policy instruments. The conditions are the level of competitive tension and the availability of military instruments. The discussion about them which follows deals with political warfare as an instrument of foreign policy.

The major problem of adaptation posed for both the United States and the U.S.S.R. in a disarming and disarmed world is how to maintain pre-eminence in world affairs while the military basis for that pre-eminence is diminishing. Since both nations will have interests to pursue, we should expect that their adaptations will be competitive. While tensions of certain kinds should decline, we should expect both Soviet and American foreign policy in a disarming world to be sensitive to trends in relative power and relative power potential. We should thus assume that tensions will build up over the turning points for trends. No doubt competition will be modified, but it may well not be moderated, for major political stakes will still remain to be competed for. In fact, in view of the past reluctance of both sides to engage in large-scale war, whether nuclear or not, the picture of international tension and competition might not change very much.

Interests, then, will depend in large measure on the intensity of the international competition; the competition, in turn, will affect the potency of certain instruments, in particular, complex ones like political warfare. The three instruments of foreign policy discussed in the preceding section—psychological, economic, and technological—all seem to offer some prospects for exploitation which could be sources of considerable instability and tension in great-power relations. If great-power competition remains intensive, so that the competitive pressures previously brought to bear through military capabilities are shifted to non-military applications, the nonmilitary instruments of foreign policy would be applied in the prosecution of an intense form of political warfare.

In a disarmed world great powers will want friends. Where they cannot win them with incentives and rewards, they will want to use threats and sanctions. It will be difficult to make very much use of direct pressures upon regimes from outside to influence their behavior, primarily for two reasons. First, outside pressures usually create internal support for the indigenous government as a nationalistic reaction. Second, pressures are usually sanctions, which are denials or threats of denial of something valued. We have already noted the difficulty of making sanctions effective. Threats of denial are plausible only if the threatener can cut off all practical sources of supply to his victim, a situation which seldom obtains for important wants unless the threat can be supported by armed coercion.

Internal pressures are quite a different matter. Political warfare, defined as a co-ordinated attack upon the national regime through indigenous political action in order to displace it with a new order, avoids both difficulties. Part of its method is to undermine the nationalist identification with the regime. Competitive counteractions, both competitive subversion and countersubversion in support of the regime, are possible. But they cannot gain immediate results in the way that aid or trade concessions granted competitively can. Their lead times are of necessity much greater. Any disarmament scheme which anticipates the use of peace-keeping devices should attempt to deal with political warfare, for it would undoubtedly be a major form of indirect aggression. The trouble is that dealing with it would not assure the surmounting of the formidable problems of definition and enforcement, which are the classical stumbling blocks to the effective prohibition of aggression.

Any disarmament agreement will establish a distinction between things which are proscribed and things which are not. Any distinction which serves as the basis for an enforceable proscription provides, in turn, the basis for ambiguity with which the legal processes of enforcement must cope. Whatever it is that a disarmament plan proscribes, it cannot be self-defining. In fact, the American disarmament plan contains severe ambiguities which have important implications for its utility.

Disarmament agreements proscribe or control things military, or things which can perpetrate violence, or things called armed forces. If we assume, with Locke, a nonviolent state of nature which has been corrupted by human cultivation, then disarmament may appear as a way out of the use of violence, and violence may be considered to be the thing proscribed. Peace-keeping plans which provide for enforcement, on the other hand, operate on quite different premises. Plainly, the American *Outline*, for instance, does not assume a peaceful state of nature or look forward to an unpoliced, disarmed world, for it proposes an international police force which would use and threaten the use of violence against states. It does not assume that all the incentives or all the opportunities to utilize violent coercion as an instrument of national foreign policy will be eliminated. Consequently, it makes violence available as an instrument of international peacekeeping. Furthermore, as in most schemes, the *Outline* expects national regimes to depend upon violence or the threat of it—in the form of police power—for the maintenance of internal order. Since organized violence is sanctioned for use in these two ways, it is usually also available for illegal exploitation. Because violence is often legitimate and is usually available, distinguishing the legal from the illegal in an internal order as provided in an arms agreement may be extraordinarily difficult, a fact which can be exploited by political warfare.

If the powers to govern conferred upon the international authority are to be kept limited, they must be given a precise delineation. Perhaps the most important determinant of the extent of these powers would be the distinction agreed upon between the things (violent and otherwise) which national governments may do and those which they may not, since the primary function of the authority would be to deal with that distinction. Quite obviously, the distinction is a highly sensitive one, for it concerns the limits of the powers and functions of an international organization which has the responsibility of enforcing an agreement intended to deprive nation-states of powers and capabilities which they have hitherto considered vital and which in any case they will still consider important.

States will want to influence the outcome of international actions which have the effect of determining what important functions they are prohibited from exercising. In the pursuit of their interests, they will also want to exploit the ambiguities inherent in the meaning of what is proscribed by the disarmament agreement.

By any rules of definition or jurisdiction, it will be impossible to prohibit political subversion, though some control over the more blatant efforts by one country to subvert the political order of another can be expected. One difficulty lies in distinguishing between internal political changes and those supported from outside the country. It will be in the nature of the international agreement that it will proscribe externally sponsored subversion. We should expect that it will not proscribe that internal subversion which is not dependent upon outside support, for to do so would be to guarantee without qualification the maintenance of existing regimes. As a practical matter, however, both rules may be considerably modified in practice. What is more important, political subversion might not be substantially affected by the prohibitions and the enforcement action which may apply to it in a legally based peace-keeping system, for it is already a clandestine activity. If it is sponsored by a foreign power, the foreigner usually has reasons for playing down his responsibility for it, among them the knowledge that the claim of legitimacy by the indigenous subversive forces will be undermined by the acknowledgment of substantial outside assistance. Internally, some or all of it will be clandestine.

Moreover, the inability to deal with clandestine political activity may be particularly disadvantageous to the United States, for it appears that subversive movements more often oppose United States interests than support them. Exactly why this is so may remain puzzling. It may be that subversive movements, if they are to be successful, require discipline, extreme personal motivation, and subordination, along with social alienation, a combination that does not readily mix with the moderate and pragmatic political behavior with which the United States would prefer to be associated. This may not be an adequate explanation. But we must not confuse the adequacy of the explanation with the extent of the evidence that radical movements, particularly communism, have been more successful than moderate ones in fomenting insurrection, revolution, and other forms of internal political violence.

The Comparative Advantages in the Exploitation of Bilateral Means

If we are to consider the implications of disarmament and peacekeeping for the instruments and interests of United States foreign policy, the discussion must eventually be put in terms of comparative advantages between the United States and other countries. The comparative approach is relevant because states compete (as well as co-operate) with each other in the pursuit of national security interests. It is necessary because no other method will adequately measure power or determine its import. Comparisons in this section will be confined to bilateral relationships and the bilateral aspects of regional security systems.

The major problem of adaptation for both the United States and the U.S.S.R. in a disarming and disarmed world will be how to maintain pre-eminence in world affairs while the military basis for that pre-eminence is diminishing. We should expect that for both states the pressure to adapt violence to nonmilitary foreign policy will be increased in order to increase the efficacy of those foreign policy instruments which are not proscribed by the disarmament agreement. We should expect the adaptive process to take full advantage of the ambiguities inherent in the distinction between what is and what is not proscribed by the disarmament agreement. In addition, I shall argue that the ambiguity of the distinction, the continued availability of instruments of violence, and their efficacy even at low levels of capability will assure that they will continue to play an important role even with disarmament and peace-keeping measures in full effect.

Both the Soviet Union and the United States rely heavily upon their military capabilities for their national security. The United States spends about 9 per cent of its gross national product for its military capabilities. It is estimated that the Soviet Union spends about the same absolute amount, which represents approximately 18 per cent of its gross national product. Reductions in armed forces would be reflected in reduced military budgets and hence in freed resources. With the changes in the allocation of resources thus made possible, a gain by one major power over the other would depend upon the comparative efficiency of the new allocations anticipated. The two sides would have approximately the same total amount to reallocate, although the Soviet Union would have about twice the percentage of its gross national product to reallocate.

One can conceive of the disarmament process setting similar forces loose in both societies, which would in turn produce extreme reductions in the level of total effort in behalf of foreign policy objectives. In the United States these forces would begin as the hopes and pacifist-isolationist sentiments aroused by the campaign to gain ratification for the disarmament treaty. As the threat from other major national military forces declined, the American public would expect the resources freed to go to domestic purposes. As American military power declined, the United States would lose interest in areas of the globe which it could not reach with its power. Rather than providing an occasion for a shift in the emphasis of foreign policy from military to nonmilitary instruments, the treaty could serve as evidence supporting a popular sentiment that foreign policy is no longer a serious concern. These reactions, if they were strong enough, would destroy most public support for foreign policy efforts, which would in turn impose severe limitations upon the capability of the national government to adapt to the changing circumstances of a disarming world.

It is not so likely that the Soviet reaction would take this form. Ratification of the treaty, for example, would not be an occasion for arousing domestic popular opinion, as it would be in the United States, although popular Soviet reaction after the fact of ratification could well take somewhat the same shape as the American reaction. Furthermore, because of the regime's control of propaganda and information sources, the Soviet government could be expected to cope more readily with this reaction. It could, nevertheless, be important. In Western eyes the Soviet public often seems to be somewhat unrealistically committed to a vision of a peaceful harmony of interests once the arms race has been stopped. In any event, the Soviet regime could face some difficulties with public opinion. Furthermore, the Soviet regime would have somewhat the same propensity as the United States to restrict its interests in accord with the reach of its power.

A more likely source of difficulty for the Russian government, however, would be the reallocating of a comparatively large arms budget to an economy that is on the verge, according to some analysts, of a consumption revolution. It could set loose the spiral of rising expectations of consumption and income which have plagued Western Europe and the United States in their efforts to maintain adequate levels of expenditures for foreign and national security policy.

The comparative adaptability of the Soviet Union and the United States to general and complete disarmament involves the capacity to make gross adjustments in the activities and commitments of the policy. Heavy dependence upon popular support for governmental actions is probably a disadvantage in wholesale adaptations which involve the international position of the state. Because the Soviet Union, in comparison with the United States, is freer to take initiatives in foreign affairs without first obtaining wide political clearances, and because of its greater control over the instruments of internal popular persuasion, the Russians have advantages in this quarter. Such advantages can be offset by many things, not the least of which could be the inefficiency of nonpopular, nondemocratic or nonliberal methods of mobilizing political support for programs of the regime. It is not clear, however, that the Russian political system is less efficient in this respect than the United States.

Finally, the Soviet Union has a general advantage over the United States in adapting to wholesale changes in foreign relations because of the breadth of the conception of public affairs in the Soviet Union. Because culture, mass communications, education, scientific research, all phases of economic activity, and most other aspects of society are considered within the scope of public policy and governmental action, whereas in the United States there are strong pressures against government regulations or control of many aspects of these activities, Soviet adaptability would be greater. It may be possible for the United States to exploit the limited character of its government in ways not possible for the Soviet Union, by methods which obscure or avoid governmental responsibility for actions taken to pursue national interests. While private armies may be out of the question, private research, propaganda, subversion, military training, and other activities may be more easily disassociated from government in the United States than would be possible in the Soviet Union. But the potential advantages here are small. What would be much more important in a competitive, disarmed world would be the style or *modus operandi* of the United States in government-to-government relations, which would probably be highly competitive and might very possibly be superior.

The Soviet Union has shown considerable ability to exploit political and military activities for which it avoids responsibility, despite the breadth of government authority. It has, as well, an advantage in the greater secrecy of its internal affairs, which makes clandestine activities easier. The ideological identification with communism and the Soviet example of forced-draft economic development are important additional assets for the U.S.S.R. in the prosecution of political warfare. The economic development model, however, may be a wasting asset simply because the passage of time brings other examples and more experience. In the ideological realm, racial affinity runs against the Russians as it does against the United States. The ideological connection with the indigenous political forces of other countries can be racist or Irredentist where racial and national affinities exist, but not for the Soviet Union and the United States when nonwhite races are involved.

A major, though perhaps rapidly wasting, advantage to the Soviet Union in political warfare has been its willingness to tolerate political chaos to achieve its objectives in foreign countries. A disarmament agreement would reduce this advantage, to the extent that internal chaos would be treated as a threat to the peace requiring intrusions which would counter the Soviet efforts. On the other hand, if, as the *Outline* stipulates, states will continue to have forces sufficient to maintain internal law and order, they cannot expect bolstering from peace-keeping agencies so long as the external sponsorship of internal chaos is not fully substantiated.

Communist subversive movements, variously motivated and sponsored by various Communist states, but principally by the U.S.S.R., are evidently now active and play a significant role in the internal politics of some underdeveloped states in every region. As Robert Osgood has suggested in another essay, because insurgency movements are most easily supported from contiguous states, in areas more remote from the United States than from the U.S.S.R. or its allies, such as South and Southeast Asia and the

Middle East, reductions in regular military forces should prove favorable to the U.S.S.R. or at least to indigenous communism. Elsewhere, where they are less patently a form of military operation, subversive movements use instead violence and terror combined with political methods in an effort to seize intact the levers of national power. In varying degrees of intensity, these methods are in use in most underdeveloped states.

Some of the constraints under which insurgency and subversive movements operate would be relaxed by disarmament arrangements. A major present constraint is the threat of counterinterventions by individual states. General disarmament with peacekeeping would severely reduce or eliminate this constraint. Under partial disarmament it would be very difficult to justify interventions in the form of overt national military operations to defend the political *status quo* of another state in the absence of convincing evidence of foreign support of insurgency or subversion: under complete disarmament the capability to intervene overtly would not exist. Removal of the threat of unilateral or bilateral covert intervention removes a constraint on the level of effort at which political warfare, covert or overt, can prudently be prosecuted. Presumably, it would be replaced by the constraints imposed by international peace-keeping measures. These could tighten or relax the limitations under which foreign support of insurgency and subversion could be prosecuted, but in any event they would become an important issue in the politics of peacekeeping. At the same time, with fewer alternative methods open, a considerable increase in efforts to exploit subversion and insurgency could be expected to occur. Under these circumstances, it is reasonable to expect the intense cultivation of economic, psychological and technological methods and capabilities through a co-ordinated strategy of political subversion, using persuasion and bribery, violence and terror, where appropriate, and always playing on the domestic weaknesses of the ruling elites. The objective need not be revolutionary overthrow, or even the peaceful absorption of the subversive movement. The threat of political subversion may be its major value in the diplomacy of its foreign sponsor.

The most direct United States answer to political warfare is now foreign military aid (the economic aid programs being usually addressed indirectly to this problem). While military aid could be modified in order to keep some of it going under the limitations of a disarmament agreement, the effectiveness of military aid programs would decline considerably with the reduction of the armed forces in both the United States and the state aided. The United States should be able to turn itself into a trainer of police forces and a supporter of law and order in other areas. It could undertake the development of countersubversion programs as well. In this role it would normally have the support of the government of the day, which could be a considerable advantage in conducting a program within the limits of general and complete disarmament. The prospects of constructive adaptation of United States methods, in short, are not insignificant, particularly if sufficient attention is paid them. The prospects of intensifying political subversion, on the other hand, are at least as large. Fewer initial adaptations will be required, and their clandestine character will continue to be an advantage in evading official peace-keeping efforts. A Soviet-American confrontation within the national political system of an underdeveloped country can be expected to play an important part in the international politics of a disarmed world, taxing the adaptive capacities of both national foreign policy efforts as well as of the international peace-keeping institutions.

The American rivalry with the Soviet Union, to the extent that it survives disarmament, can be expected to shift almost entirely to the pursuit of competitive interests in third states, particularly to the establishment of friendly regimes or the winning over of existing ones. Political warfare, we might expect, would be intensified in states which are not now members of either military bloc. In addition, the United States and the Soviet Union should be expected to intensify their competition over present bloc members, particularly in Europe and Latin America. First, Europe will remain, as it now is, the major political stake in the Soviet-American rivalry. Second, the Soviet and the Atlantic alliance systems are heavily dependent upon the military threat and military co-operation to hold them together. In both camps cohesion appears to be a wasting asset, to say the least. The United States may be more able than the Russians to adapt to more competitive and egalitarian forms of international relations than have obtained in either alliance system, but both powers have grounds for discouragement at their lack of success in coping with the changing forces already evident within their alliance systems.

The Comparative Advantages in the Politics of Peacekeeping

One of the major implications of any scheme which links general and complete disarmament to universal peacekeeping concerns the politics of peacekeeping. When the international military force becomes superior to national military forces, the most significant single political activity of any state seeking to advance its interests in the world arena will be the influencing of the politics of the international organization which controls the force. An important objective would be to win favorable disposition concerning the international military force. Experience with national military forces suggests that the exercise of formal legal powers is not the whole basis for controlling armed forces. It is nevertheless an important element in their control and is of particular importance for a projected international organization which would be charged with the supervision and control of a military force. For in the international system there could not be the reliance which national states place upon cultural factors, tradition, professional indoctrination, and legislative-executive rivalry to maintain civilian political control over the military. Instead, control would have to depend more heavily upon formal arrangements.

The trouble is that the lack of common background which makes it necessary to depend heavily upon formal legal arrangements for the control of the international force also makes it difficult to use formal methods successfully. For example, two critical and closely related requirements should be met in the establishment of peace-keeping institutions. First, it is necessary to limit the power of these institutions in order to assure that they will not become a vast superstate. Second, the functions of the international military force should be precisely defined ahead of time so that it will not become the major prize in world politics. Insofar as either need can be met, meeting it depends heavily upon the legal arts.

Ambiguity will be a large problem in these arrangements. Some of the implications of this fact have already been examined earlier in this essay—in particular, the fact that it is unlikely that states will be denied the use of instruments of violence. Here we are especially concerned with the implications for the direction and control of various peace-keeping activities—that their operation will not simply be a legal and administrative matter even with a high level of performance in the drafting of arrangements and the founding of institutions.

Both the disposition of the international military force and the choice and application of peace-keeping procedures associated with it will be matters of grave concern to the member states, even if nothing more is involved in the international peace-keeping system. For the United States, its own effectiveness in this new political forum will be of increasing importance as its options decline and the power of international force grows. How should we expect it to perform under these circumstances?

If, for example, the American *Outline* could be carried out, two probabilities are apparent for the conclusion of Stage III. First, the world disarmament order which had come about would represent the vested interests of many national states and more national regimes. And second, some national regimes, including in all probability the Soviet Union and Red China, and very likely the United States, would be highly enough motivated in the pursuit of their own objectives to test the system for what advantages it could bring them. This does not necessarily mean that they would be willing to defy an international police force or by some act shatter the whole disarmament order. It does mean that they would be willing to operate in the gray area between what is clearly proscribed and what is clearly permitted in the armament agreement. That would not be to challenge the whole order, but to challenge at the margin the efficacy of particular rules. Usually these challenges would themselves be ambiguous.

The prospects are that this kind of behavior would pay off enough to be justified. No doubt these prospects could be reduced by the refinement of peace-keeping techniques, but only to a limited degree. Disarmament would be a limited contract. We could have little assurance that peace-keeping techniques could dispose of legal ambiguities because the major ambiguity involves the limits of the agreement itself. Where ambiguity confers advantages on the other side, these advantages could be diminished if the United States and its allies were competing in their exploitations.

For quite another reason the United States might become involved very early in "competitive chiseling" as insurance against the risk that the disarmament agreement would be thrown aside at an early stage, where it would be possible to do so. For instance, it would be prudent for the United States to prepare to resume testing, to rearm, and to remobilize as quickly as possible in the event that the disarmament arrangements collapsed, and it might be prudent actually to proceed with these actions where the prohibition of them was unclear or as the enforcement of the prohibition was shown to be ineffective. Under these circumstances, who would gain the competitive advantage? Any international power competition, whether proscribed by the agreement or not, will be made at least partially illegitimate by the agreement. The inherent *sub rosa* character of such competition throws the advantage to the competitor who can most easily conceal his moves.

In the politics of an international organization, however, the United States need not assume that it would be at an inherent disadvantage. Admittedly, it might be at its best in comparison with the Soviet Union or with any of the nonparliamentary governments if the objective of its efforts was to influence parliamentary or legislative actions. But even its influence in administrative and adjudicatory behavior would be marshaled with at least as much skill as any other nation if the international organization provided a genuinely competitive political environment and if experience in competitive politics is determinative. However, to the extent that the politics of peacekeeping depended upon influence exercised through what I have termed political warfare, the American advantage would be less certain. Whether by political warfare we mean the relatively benevolent activities of cultural relations and propaganda or, at the other extreme, the more ruthless methods of insurrection and subversion, the closed systems of government with control of communications have considerable advantages in secrecy and manipulation.

In their relations with allies and neutrals both of the great powers could be expected to suffer dramatic losses of influence which would be apparent in the politics of peacekeeping. For both, bloc leadership depends not only upon interbloc tensions but upon the ability of the leader to provide military and economic support. The withdrawal of troops and the adjustment of objectives and methods to reflect the reduction in national military forces would in all probability alter radically, if not the membership of the Atlantic and East European blocs, then at least their domination by the United States and the Soviet Union, respectively. It may be, however, that for both this domination is passing away.

Similar trends can be anticipated in relations with neutrals and friends—trends, again, which are already apparent. In any situation short of extreme tension and competition, the Soviet Union and the United States could expect to find the neutrals and the nonaligned states persistently striving to shape the institutions of peacekeeping for their own purposes, which are likely to diverge increasingly from those of the great powers. That would be true particularly with respect to the uses of the peace-keeping institutions. Suppose we take the worst case: the United States and the Soviet Union are interested in competitive "cheating" and "chiseling" to gain whatever advantages they can out of those institutions without actually disrupting the general arrangements for disarmament. Under these circumstances, some underdeveloped countries would oppose the competition of the great powers because it would mean a diversion of great-power resources from development to armament. The pressure they would bring to bear might be an important force for disarmament. However, not all states have or will continue to have the same stakes in disarmament. Some will have no development assistance from the great powers to lose should the Soviet Union and the United States turn their attention to rearmament. They, and even some of those who do, might see in the rearmament of the industralized states a source of very substantial quantities of foreign exchange— quantities much greater than anything they could hope to glean from economic assistance programs for many years, as attested to by the experience of more than one state during the rearmament of the early nineteen fifties, with its favorable terms of trade.

These appear to be dismal prospects. It should be noted, however, that when these speculations are put together, they suggest the elements of a stable equilibrium which may hold some promise in its own right. The more intense the competition between the Soviet Union and the United States under disarmament with peacekeeping, the more they would involve other states in the Soviet-American rivalry and win control over the actions of the others in the politics of peacekeeping. The less intense the competition, the more independent the nonaligned (and probably the aligned) states would be, but each of the great powers would be more flexible in coping with the divergent purposes of the underdeveloped countries, and it would be less likely that the latter could successfully threaten the big powers with the disruption of great-power disarmament. But if this is a description of a stable equilibrium, the elements of stability are those found readily in the contemporary world.

For anyone who speculates about the prospects that would be opened up for the United States by disarmament, its present extensive reliance upon military instruments in foreign policy is the most persistent fact that must be coped with. We may want to argue that it ought not to be this way, that it could have been different, but this is the way it has been. In order to support the claim that it could have been different, it would be necessary to show reasons why, where, and in what respects it could have been different. Even if one were to accept the hostile stereotypes which portray American officialdom as unreasonably militaristic, the argument would not be over. It would still be necessary to show some reason to expect that more competent and flexible people would be in charge of United States foreign policy in a disarming and disarmed world. Even if the two caricatures of reality often associated with extreme pacifism—that belligerent and militaristic regimes are simply the product of large military establishments and that disarmament would reduce international tensions proportionately—were true, it would still be necessary to account for the fact that states, including the United States, have been belligerent when their military establishments have been small. The judgment that the officials or the regimes which have thus depended upon their military capabilities have been and are stupid or irrational may be appropriate, but even if that is so, that judgment alone provides no assurance that things will change.

The United States has shown some interest, but no great success, in shifting to nonmilitary instruments in its foreign policy, for example, in 1959 when there was concern in the United States Congress over what was thought to be excessive dependence on military aid in the foreign assistance program. If one could count on such a transformation of the international system under general and complete disarmament that the shift could be made very much easier, the fact that the United States has not yet substituted for its military capabilities more attractive foreign policy instruments should not make much difference. The speculations here and in other chapters of this study indicate that differences would not be so great as to make the shift that much easier, if at all. But are there steps which could be taken now, or over time, which would later put the United States in a better position to adapt to a disarming world?

One conceivable course of action, which would at once give the United States more grounds for confidence in its ability to adapt to a disarming world, would be to carry out some major unilateral innovations in foreign policy that would shift the burdens from military to other instruments. By this I do not mean that one should run the risks of unilateral disarmament. What would be sensible would be to develop new instruments or refine old ones in a major innovation, investing the same level of commitment as goes into the developmental aspects of new missile systems or moon shot projects. If that level of effort is not justifiable, either because of low expectations of success or lack of urgency, then general and complete disarmament may not be either.

The rigidity of the alliance policies of the United States does not augur well for adaptation to a disarming world in which the threat of a common enemy and the incentives of American military support have been severely diminished. Hence, another way to put the United States into a better position for disarmament might be to turn at least its Atlantic alliance into a political community by substantial concessions of authority and resources to its co-members. If successful, such a move could salvage the advantages of the western alliance system before they dissolved under the changing conditions of a disarming world. One should expect to encounter risks in this course of action comparable to those of protecting one's status through political maneuvering in a universal international organization, but presumably these risks would be encountered in a more manageable arena.

Both courses would substantially improve the United States's bargaining position in disarmament negotiations. By demonstrating its ability to follow constructive policies compatible with disarmament and favorable to its interest, these acts would increase the credibility of United States support for disarmament and bolster American confidence about future capabilities.

II

PEACE-KEEPING MEASURES AND THE PROCESS OF DISARMAMENT

4.

PEACEFUL SETTLEMENT
AND PEACEFUL CHANGE

Laurence W. Martin

TAKEN LITERALLY, the United States *Outline* insists, as a condition for general and complete disarmament, upon states abstaining from every form of violence, direct or indirect, and on their strict adherence to peaceful methods of settling international disputes. In a still more far-reaching way, by binding states to design and agree upon methods to assure that disputes are in fact settled, and settled justly, the *Outline* goes beyond mere suppression of violence and requires establishment of an international order providing for peaceful change. Thus in the second stage nations would "agree to such additional steps and arrangements as were necessary to assure the just and peaceful settlement of international disputes, whether legal or political," while in the third stage they would also "provide a basis for peaceful change in a disarmed world."[1]

This realistic insistence that positive steps will have to be taken if these highly ambitious goals are to be reached contrasts with the ostensible Soviet assumption that disarmament will make military solutions impossible and that therefore peaceful pro-

[1] *Outline*, Stage II, G, 1, a; Stage III, H, 1.

cedures will naturally and inevitably be increasingly employed.[2] According to the assumption underlying the American approach, even under disarmament nations will continue to be tempted by opportunities to win their way by coercing others, and sometimes this coercion may take violent forms. Yet even the smallest incidents of violence are regarded as endangering the stability of disarmament, for fear that they will grow in magnitude and ultimately provoke rearmament. Because violence, at present a common method of resolving disputes, must therefore be totally excluded, some effective alternative methods must be provided. Disputes must be resolved and not merely repressed indefinitely by peace-keeping enforcement or fear of rearmament. Otherwise, disarmament would entail the permanent freezing of many situations until the cumulative strain ultimately destroyed the whole system. This implies that, rather than disarmament's making war impossible, war must be made unnecessary if disarmament is to endure.

Theoretical reasoning of this kind is doubtless supplemented by the reflection that an insistence upon the outlawry of violent settlement without elaborate appearances of offering substitutes would imply a resignation to the *status quo* that would scarcely be popular in a world containing as much dissatisfaction as the

---

[2] In addition to Soviet refusals during negotiations to countenance American reiteration of the need to make sure that a disarmed world is a peaceful world (see USACDA, *Disarmament Document Series #303*, October 23, 1962, esp. p. 2), one may note the remarks of Y. Korovin, Corresponding Member of the Academy of Sciences, July 21, 1962:

A disarmed world will be not only rid of all the methods of settling international conflicts by force, but the means of peaceful settlement of disputes will acquire a new quality. Diplomatic negotiations and consultations at all levels (right up to the top), commissions of inquiry and conciliation, and mediation, arbitration and the international court will be quite different. The disappearance of the possibility of settling differences between states by force will inevitably enhance the importance of all kinds of peaceful legal procedures; instead of being optional many of them will become compulsory, and instead of casual, habitual. . . . The states will be faced with the following alternatives: either no solution of the disputes arising between them, or settlement by peaceful diplomatic and legal methods.

Quoted in Arthur Larson (ed.), *A Warless World* (New York: McGraw-Hill, 1963), pp. 182–83.

present one. Moreover, it would be unjustified to assume that the aspirations to change and justice in United States proposals do not also reflect genuine hopes that the disarmed international system would lead to an increasingly satisfactory world for all.

It is obvious, however, that American concern for making available procedures for peaceful change and settlement is not based simply on apprehension that many good causes will go unheard and unrewarded. Clearly, this preoccupation also reflects a lively fear that, under disarmament, states will have recourse to other methods, including low-level or covert military action, and that these, besides tending to undermine disarmament, are forms of struggle for which the United States is ill suited. More precisely, this fear arises from the belief that covert aggression and the exploitation of revolution and unrest are weapons particularly dear to Communist hearts, that the United States finds it difficult to meet such weapons in kind, and that therefore the United States might find itself the first to face the dilemma of either suffering a steady erosion of its interests or of escalating to overt military action and rearmament. Indeed, the Soviet conception of coexistence is an open avowal of such a threat, and, by examining the categories of dispute excluded from Chairman Khrushchev's proposals for the peaceful settlement of territorial disputes, for example, it is possible to gain a clear warning of the Soviet intention to exempt types of struggle profitable to them from the list of prohibited measures.[3] This, then, is presumably why, in the American *Outline*, references to peaceful settlement are closely

[3] Chairman Khrushchev asserted, for example, that "The peoples still under colonial domination are striving to achieve their freedom and independence by peaceful means. [If this is not possible] the oppressed peoples have no other choice but to take up arms themselves and this is their sacred right. . . . War bases, established in foreign territories alienated from other states, should be liquidated in the same way." Also ominous, perhaps, for American ideas of what is necessary to maintain order, was his remark concerning the unification of Germany, Korea, and Vietnam: "It goes without saying, however, that the question of reunification should be settled by the peoples of these countries and their governments themselves, without any interference . . . from the outside, and certainly without foreign military intervention—occupation, as is actually the case, for instance, in South Korea and South Vietnam" (*New York Times*, January 4, 1964, p. 2).

associated throughout with proposals for renunciation of subversion and indirect aggression and for a code of international
conduct. This close association between the rules of international
conduct and the procedures for peaceful settlement is obviously
not fortuitous but necessary. Definition of the acceptable manner
of peaceful settlement is, if only by implication, also definition of
the impermissible instruments of self-assertion.

The question of peaceful settlement, perhaps more than any
other, compels recognition of the truly vast implications of attempting to achieve general and complete disarmament. To make
provision for the universal peaceful settlement of disputes and for
effecting, also peacefully, all necessary adjustments to change,
be it political, economic, or ideological, would be to establish a
great deal of what we normally understand by a system of government. The responsibility for adjudicating disputes and, still
more, for adjusting social arrangements in the light of changed
circumstances is necessarily an expansive one that requires either
a legislative procedure or a judiciary that progressively takes on
legislative aspects. Instituting such arrangements on a global
scale would not be merely a fundamental procedural change: it
would do much to determine the future substantive political and
social order of the world. It is not to be wondered at, therefore,
that American proposals relegate these basic questions to further
study—study that is, indeed, to continue even after a treaty is
actually signed. For peaceful settlement poses questions more
vexing than the problems of phasing arms reduction. The arrangements for arms reduction, which are spelled out in considerable
detail in the *Outline,* while admittedly complex, involve merely
the elaboration of techniques to achieve a negative purpose on
which prior agreement in principle is assumed. Peaceful settlement, on the other hand, calls for techniques to achieve positive
and constructive action on purposes that not only may but must
be assumed to conflict.

Peaceful settlement thus takes us back inexorably to the underlying conflicts of which arms are the manifestation, symbol, and
instrument. Although there is some truth in the argument that
the nature of modern military technology makes the arms race an

autonomous source of danger,[4] it is impossible to sustain the argument that weapons are the sole source of conflict. Yet fear of weapons, particularly fear of major nuclear weapons, is the only identifiable basis for optimism that we in this age can overcome the many barriers that have hitherto defeated endeavors to achieve substantial general disarmament. The extent to which this limited consensus can be extrapolated down the scale of means of contention until all but peaceful means have been eliminated will determine the prospect of obtaining disarmament with adequate peacekeeping.

This consensus, narrow as it is, would have to support a system that went far beyond a set of purely negative mutual restraints on national actions. Even the task of repressing outbreaks of violence—perhaps even the task of policing disarmament—would alone almost certainly involve the increasing intervention of such international authorities as were established in the affairs and ultimately the internal affairs of states.[5] Covert aggression in particular, which is so frequently disguised as an internal affair of the afflicted nation, will inevitably require the authorities responsible for international order to judge the true nature of various internal events. Some of these events will be genuinely internal, and the international authorities will thus be passing upon the character of domestic revolutions and uprisings. From these it is a short step to judging the merits of domestic adversaries and to influencing the course of internal struggles; the Congo and Cyprus operations already provide suggestive illustrations. Another problem that will arise from revolutions will be the build-up of unofficial forces that, though not the creation of the government, may yet alarm neighbors as much as an official breach of the disarmed balance. After both the American and the Algerian civil wars, the large armies of the victorious side were regarded as a real threat by neighbors. Yet measures to

[4] It is, of course, also a source of security. For one view of the autonomous arms race, see Jerome B. Wiesner, "Forward," *Daedalus*, Fall, 1960, pp. 678ff.
[5] Cf. Charles Burton Marshall's essay, "Character and Mission of a United Nations Peace Force," in this volume.

curb the growth of these forces could only have resulted in intervention in the civil struggle.

Even if such breaches and supposed breaches of the rules of
conduct did not draw the international authorities into passing
judgments on a wide variety of internal and international issues,
the prescription of a capacity to ensure not merely peace but
peaceful change and not merely change but the just disposition
of disputes would inevitably and by definition take us across the
line from mere suppression of violence into positive action to
rearrange and improve international society. Plans to meet this
specification are designs to legislate on a world scale.[6] Whoever
has charge of this legislation can be assured of a busy occupation. New disputes will constantly arise, and there will indeed
be a new category of disputes, those concerned with the implementation of disarmament itself. If the disputes of the future are
hard to forecast, those of today are numerous and must be expected to persist. One of the great merits of recent approaches
to disarmament, in the eyes of some, is that they no longer require
that disarmament be preceded by political settlements.[7] This is

[6] Another illustration of the way in which the *Outline* would project us
into positive action beyond the mere dismantling of arms can be perceived
in the requirement that the international peace force guarantee the security
of all. Initially, the plan merely requires that disarmament be such that
"at no stage could any state or group of states obtain any military advantages" (*Outline* B. Principles, 2). Cf. "All measures of general and complete disarmament should be balanced so that at no stage of the implementation of the treaty would any State or group of States gain military
advantage and that security is ensured for all" (United Nations, *Joint Statement of Agreed Principles for Disarmament Negotiations* [A/4879, *September*
20, 1961]). Some states have advantages now, and others enjoy little security.
Thus the peace force has to go beyond demilitarizing the present balance
and achieve a new one, if states that are not now secure are to be so in
the future. To make South Vietnam secure, for example, is to recast the
balance of power and revise the political climate of Southeast Asia. In
reality, one suspects that the caveat against military advantage is intended
to refer only to Soviet-American relations during transitional stages. Even
here, however, it has more far-reaching implications than are at first
apparent.
    [7] The same spirit apparently underlies the postponement of difficult as-
pects of disarmament itself. Cf. David Cavers, "Disarmament as a Cumulative Process," (*Disarmament: Its Politics and Economics*, ed. S. Melman
[Boston: American Academy of Arts and Sciences, 1962], p. 33), praising

undoubtedly the only basis for analysis if it means recognition that a complete settlement of outstanding issues can never be achieved. Many have succumbed to the temptation to assume that this realization somehow proves that progress is possible without settling disputes. This remains to be seen. It may well prove the case that at least certain particularly acute disputes must be resolved before a climate favorable to disarmament is achieved. Be that as it may, a survey of existing disputes offers a sobering notion of the kinds of tasks a system of peaceful settlement and change must perform.

In estimating these tasks, too much attention has probably been paid in the literature of disarmament to Communist intentions and the Cold War, with a consequent tendency to imply that, could that struggle be mitigated, serious disputes would become rare. Nothing in history or political theory justifies this assumption. Rather, it seems reasonable to expect the indefinite continuation of sharp disputes of a type that can only be resolved at some considerable cost to one or both parties. There is a strong implication in the Anglo-American conception of politics that disputes are largely illusory, in the sense that reason can, at least theoretically, discover a solution beneficial to all parties or at least more beneficial than one reached by violence. Some of the phraseology of the American general and complete disarmament proposals could, indeed, be taken to reflect such hopes.

When Alice ran the Caucus race, the Dodo discovered that, happily, "*Everybody* has won and all must have prizes." In international politics, however, there are and will continue to be competitions from which some emerge winners and others losers. Contests in the prototype of zero-sum games do exist, not least because many diplomatic goals are irrational—dysfunctional—in terms of any reasonable concept of a world system. The law of comparative advantage does not extend to power and prestige.

---

the *Outline* proposals because "some of the matters on which agreement is most difficult may be left until the basic plan has been accepted and operations are well under way." This seems a two-edged principle and may in fact rest on a confusion between limited agreements and a limited degree of agreement on wider matters.

Who would venture a logical exposition of the concessions that would placate President Sukarno? Where is the logical compromise between Israel and those who would deny its existence? Nor is it easy to reconcile a faith in the increasing future amenability of governments to the kind of reasonable and mutually advantageous bargains that appeal to our mercantile view of foreign policy with the kind of charismatic, nationalist ruler that students of political development suggest will dominate most of the new nations of the world for the next few decades. Bargains undoubtedly will be struck, but not by sweet reason alone.

The *Outline*'s call for a study of procedures for peaceful settlement is therefore well advised, but it has to be accepted at the outset that is it not in the realm of procedures that great progress is likely to be made. Most admirable procedures have existed for years for those who wished to reach agreement. What is lacking is the will to use the procedures and accept the results in each and every case, either because of unwillingness to risk an unfavorable decision or, frequently, because the outcome of a particular procedure is only too clear in advance. This has long been apparent to all dispassionate students of the problem. As long ago as 1940 W. E. Rappard put the matter succinctly: "Either the parties to a dispute are anxious to avoid a rupture, and then, rules or no rules, a pacific solution can almost always be devised. Or one or both parties are bound to have their way at any cost, and thus the most perfected procedures offer no assured protections against war."[8]

As this remark itself suggests, procedures are by no means irrelevant. In marginal cases the availability of procedures, precedents, and pacificators may tip the balance. But while mechanisms may provide the methods of settlement when parties are willing to refrain from force, that willingness itself must rest on other sanctions and balances. Many international disputes are so trivial that the question of violence never arises. In more serious conflicts, peaceful settlements still occur when at least one of the antagonists decides that the issue is not worth a fight. Such a

[8] William E. Rappard, *The Quest for Peace* (Cambridge, Mass.: Harvard, 1940), p. 483.

result is achieved when a weaker party yields rather than face a hopeless contest; if the weaker party is plaintiff, the dispute may never even emerge. Evenly matched opponents may be deterred by doubt as to the outcome, including calculations of possible aid from allied or international forces. States confident of military victory may yet be restrained by contemplation of the costs of violence measured against the stakes. These costs are both material and intangible, the latter including the possible discredit that violence earns in domestic and foreign opinion, the internalized restraints felt by policymakers, and any stake a state may feel it has in continued respect for systems of international order and conciliation. Enthusiasts for peaceful change and settlement have long maintained that the costs of violence always outweigh the gains, hence the faith in clarificatory procedures to make the stakes and odds unmistakably clear. History shows, however, that so far the balance of considerations has frequently disposed nations to believe their interest would be served by violence.

What would become of these balances under general and complete disarmament? In its literal form the *Outline* offers a theoretically complete solution for the problem of denying profit to violence—if not for that of providing change—for it calls for a peace force "fully capable of insuring international security." This faces up to the fact that prohibitions of violence will not restrain all nations and must be forcibly supported. Such a capability ought to be taken to imply not merely adequate forces but a directing political will to wield them. Given the inevitable penetration of this force's purview into the affairs and internal affairs of nations, this political will becomes the nucleus of a world-wide authority. In today's economic and social circumstances it seems likely, however, that such an authority would rapidly extend its competence. The nineteenth-century political theorists' conception of an abstentionist policeman-government is hardly compatible with modern life and modern conceptions of what governments can do.

A political authority using a peace force to deter violence, to put it down when it occurs, and, if it takes seriously the requirement for justice and assured change, to force redress of grievances upon states against whom plaintiffs might otherwise be helpless would have to be capable of making a positive disposition of cases and even to anticipate and forestall general conditions that might give rise to contention. To do this in an atmosphere of legitimacy, the authority would have to embody, and be acknowledged to embody, a conception of the public interest of the orderly international community. Even a reasonably orderly system of traditional international law as we have known it seems to require a favorable political and ideological context.[9] This need for a conception of legitimacy based on some consensus as to the purposes of the society becomes more apparent when it is recognized that the conception must provide a basis for legitimizing not only change but also stability. A tolerable political order comprises more continuity than change. Peaceful settlement as a universal phenomenon therefore embraces denial of the plaintiff as well as his vindication. Peacefulness thus requires widespread reconciliation to the existing order, as well as, or more than, the provision of ways to alter it.[10]

Since there will be no recourse against this order—certainly not the recourse of self-help—it would be wise to make quite sure that we understand its nature before we commit ourselves. To put the question of whether the chances of agreement among the nations of the world on how to run such a constitutional order are good makes it virtually necessary to answer negatively. It demands a performance internationally that is rarely met within nations. The question forces renewed acknowledgment that a common fear of nuclear weapons and total war is, if deep, also a narrow basis for common action. Yet peaceful change in its full form calls for co-operation on the most fundamental matters. A peace force to deal with all disputes and to provide a world of change and justice, one that is not overworked by constant de-

[9] Cf. S. Hoffman, "International Systems and International War," *World Politics*, October, 1961, pp. 215ff.

[10] That is why such a comment as that of Arnold Toynbee, "A policy of accepting and promoting peaceful change is a necessary condition for the maintenance of a warless world" (quoted in Larson [ed.], *A Warless World*, p. 39), is a very partial statement of the truth and hence provides little or no guidance.

fiance and left stranded at each point of application (as most of our *ad hoc* forces so far have been) for lack of ability to resolve the underlying tensions, one that is neither tyrannical nor ineffective, would seem to call for a much greater consensus on the question of political order than we now enjoy.

It is all the more necessary, therefore, to discover what would be the prospects for ensuring peaceful settlement without an international force or with one that was less than omnicompetent. In what would be a world of states still essentially independent, still possessing military potential and residual security forces, resort to violence, great or small, would involve much the same calculation of balances as it does in the present world. There would, however, be substantial differences in detail arising from the disarmament agreement.

Most existing occasions for dispute would persist, though those that arise from armaments themselves—those over foreign bases for example—would be removed or modified. The instruments available for violent self-assertion would be vastly different from those that now exist, but they would by no means be absent. They would include elements of internal security forces, paramilitary forces, unofficial or revolutionary forces, subversive agents, and subvention to indigenous disruptive elements. Economic, propagandistic, and other nonviolent methods of aggression would also have to be taken into account.

The distribution of capacity to use these instruments would differ from the present balance of armed power. It would require long, careful, and perhaps then only partially successful research to predict what that distribution would be. It may be taken for granted, however, that it would result in substantial shifts in local and general balances of power. These shifts must be expected to subdue some disputes in which the plaintiff's capacity to act is reduced and to uncover others in which the disgruntled party finds itself newly endowed with the means to assert his wish. Moreover, in many existing disputes not only the power but also the interest of the parties would frequently be altered. Disarmament would therefore produce considerable shifts in spheres of interest and influence, the more so as the capacity of states to assist and co-operate with each other would be one of the elements of power that would be sharply modified. The period of disarmament would consequently be an unsettling one, somewhat comparable to postwar periods in which unfamiliar possibilities are explored.

In considering what moderating influences disarmament would bring to bear on those who might otherwise contemplate violent measures, it must first be acknowledged that the very readiness of nations to disarm might be taken to indicate a substantial basis of underlying agreement on wider issues. This might be so, but the possibility is too vague for useful speculation. Nothing in present approaches to disarmament justifies much reliance on this hope. It is admittedly possible that if we ever do get disarmament, national leaders will have had to commit their prestige to the system in order to justify it to their followers. This commitment, however, would at best be partial. Moreover, it seems certain that whatever the great powers may temporarily decide, many smaller powers, while overawed into agreeing to general and complete disarmament, would not have made a careful study of the relationship of this step to their own immediate situations and would, in any case, suffer little encroachment on the types of military power which they now control.

If disarmament could not be taken as proof of a general reconciliation of intentions, it is reasonable to assume that it would reflect a widespread fear of major war and that resort to violence would therefore be restrained, as now, by fear of escalation. Under disarmament escalation would initially lead toward rearmament rather than nuclear war. Little is known of the processes of escalation under such circumstances. Would the once-removed fear of nuclear war be as lively a deterrent as the present more immediate fear? Presumably, a decision to rearm would be a less dreadful one to take than the decision to employ nuclear weapons, but the inhibition would still be great, and the question would probably arise at lower levels of crisis. Would a sense of these inhibitions be distributed among the powers in the same proportion as present fears? Would fears that local outbreaks of violence might ripple out to the superpowers and involve all in catastrophe take the form they do today? Would such fears be more or less effective as brakes on provocative action? Would these expectations also be changed and the links from local behavior to great-power response be different?

If rearmament thus provides a clear threshold of escalation at a less terrible level than that of the initiation of nuclear operations, this fact may either reinforce or weaken the deterrent value of escalation. Indeed, could the threshold be so easily perceived? Denunciation of a treaty is one thing; clandestine rearmament is another. Study of these possibilities would lead into the question of which states are best able to make gains at levels of struggle below the threshold, to tolerate such gains on the part of opponents, to maintain a capacity for rearmament, and to pursue diplomacy in such a disarmed or "pre-rearmament" environment. Estimates of all these possibilities and of the fear of escalation itself may be expected to vary considerably with the passage of time. In such an environment, even a less than all-powerful peace force might well prove an important new element in calculations of power.

Assuming that a combination of a lack of arms, a peace force, a residual national capacity to resist aggression, and a fear of disrupting the disarmament agreement would create a climate in which resort to violence is not lightly undertaken, it remains to be seen whether we can develop rules and procedures that, by making prompt, efficient and ingenious solutions to disputes available, would reduce the likelihood of violence still further. Essentially, procedures for settling disputes perform three main functions: they clarify facts, they suggest solutions, and they lay down rulings. It seems unlikely that existing mechanisms could be much improved upon in these respects. Procedures also serve two other roles. They may be the vehicles by which third parties, whether states or organizations of states, bring pressure to bear to induce acceptance of a settlement, either by direct threat and inducement or by implicit indications of probable future alignment. Prearranged procedures may also encourage settlement by associating the prestige of the international community with the solution and the processes of solution. In this way, formal procedures may not only bring pressure to bear; they may also facilitate agreement by saving face for the contenders, enabling governments to present concessions as a service to world peace and relieving them, on occasion, of the fear that yielding will be taken as a general precedent for appeasement and will thereby encourage new demands.

All of these functions are direct services to settlement. Any of the various procedures may also serve the cause of peace simply by imposing delay. This is frequently the prime purpose of peace-observation missions, and such expedients may, in favorable circumstances, bring about a retreat from immediate action that hardens into a permanent deadlock—one of the commoner forms of "settlement," as many truce lines testify. Such settlements may be particularly useful where the dynamics of dispute acquire a rhythm of their own and where a break in cadence may thus arrest the progress toward violence. Such devices might very well be used with increasing frequency in an age acutely conscious of escalation and consequently anxious to consider carefully the possible ramifications of each incipient clash of arms.

It may well transpire that it is in this respect that constituting new arrangements and institutions would be most worth while, not because they offer truly novel expedients, but because their establishment would serve to associate an obligation to peaceful settlement more intimately with disarmament itself. Embodying a commitment to specific procedures for handling disputes in a treaty for general and complete disarmament would symbolize and serve as a constant reminder of the intimate connection between peaceful settlement and the stability of the disarmament system itself.[11] Undoubtedly, there is also a case for making the

[11] Such links could conceivably be counterproductive if they served to exaggerate minor violations by making it seem as if a serious challenge of principle had arisen. Moreover, it must be recognized that every commitment to procedures offers an added *locus standi* to parties to the agreement who wish to interfere in the affairs of others; they can claim that the procedures are not being followed or are being followed inexactly. One notes, for instance, that Chairman Khrushchev cited his proposals on peaceful settlement of territorial disputes as an explanation of his demonstration of concern with the Somalia-Ethiopia dispute.

facilities for some of these tried and tested procedures more readily available by preparation, so that they can keep pace with the accelerating tempo of modern diplomacy. Provision of ear-marked observation forces, of predefined procedures of intervention, and the explication of precedents may thus be worth while. It must be confessed, however, that a survey of recent peace-keeping operations leaves a more lively impression of their disparate nature than of the possibilities for regularization.

It has to be recognized that any procedures will be under a very heavy strain if all states are compelled to employ them. The more that such use is compulsory, the more the procedures will become entangled in the merits of particular issues and the ramifications of general quarrels. Moreover, there can be no doubt that an emphasis on peaceful settlement, particularly by devices employing third parties, introduces a bias into disputes, for agreement becomes increasingly highly rated for its own sake. Thus both parties are urged to concessions irrespective of the merits of their individual cases; indeed, the more reasonable or the weaker party is frequently subjected to the heavier pressure. In addition, any procedures which draw upon the judgment of the existing United Nations Secretariat or General Assembly would obviously have a particular bias on many contemporary issues.[12] To a large extent, the Congo and Cyprus peace-keeping operations constitute efforts to preserve peace by casting a cloak of legitimacy over the success of the stronger combination of internal forces and external support.

A discussion of measures to enforce peaceful settlement under disarmament should not be concluded without a consideration of the possible undesirable effects of making recourse to force impossible. Violence is presently the classical way to thrust

---

[12] As many observers have pointed out, it is not necessary to assume that these United Nations biases would always go against the United States. On the other hand, it has to be remembered that all United Nations behavior, whether it is what American observers call "responsible" or "irresponsible," has taken place in the context of the existing armed balance of power and as the result of strenuous American diplomacy. What the pattern would be under the drastically changed circumstances of disarmament is a vital and mist-shrouded question.

grievances onto the agenda of political action. This is true in extreme domestic cases; it is quite normal internationally. The relation between force and justice is not a simple one. Violence is so frequently the agent of injustice that it is easy to assume that the abolition of unilateral force is by definition a gain for the cause of justice. This is in reality far from axiomatic. Endemic violence is admittedly an unlikely climate for a flourishing justice, as it is when employed in self-defense or in revolt against oppression. The use of force by strong powers is not always directed against just causes,[13] while small powers with a legitimate grievance frequently draw attention to their plight by a hopeless but dramatic assault on their oppressors.

The persistent use of such methods may well produce intolerable dangers in a nuclear age. It is certainly conceivable, on the other hand, that disarmament as a remedy would perpetuate many injustices by depriving the sufferers of the means to make their grievances a "threat to the peace" by inhibiting them with a meticulous respect for keeping the peace or by suppressing them with a peace force that, while capable of quelling violence, lacks the ability to deal with the underlying situations. Thus not every extension of peacefulness is necessarily a gain for the other goals of justice and flexible adjustment to altered circumstances postulated in the proposals for general and complete disarmament. For this extension to be achieved, any satisfactory system of peaceful settlement must at least embrace a reliable equivalent for petition and writ of redress. The unfathomable implications of such devices return us again to the lack of international consensus as to the kind of social order to which such redress should be directed. In view of this lack, to what compulsory procedures is the United States now willing to bind itself for the active disposition of all complaints against itself?

Both because of the current political configuration of the world and because of the inherent difficulty of the task even in theoretical terms, it thus seems unlikely that the specification that disarmament be accompanied by a totally effective ban on

[13] Would we wish to multiply legal embarrassments to our Cuban blockade?

violence and by universally employed procedures for peaceful change and settlement can be met within the foreseeable future. If this conclusion were accepted, it would become necessary to ask whether the goal of disarmament should be abandoned or the specification relaxed. Everything suggests that general disarmament will have to coexist with injustices and continued low-level, covert armed struggle if it is to exist at all.

The answer to the question of whether it can so coexist will have to emerge from attempting the experiment. Whether the United States is willing to postulate this coexistence and embody it in its policy is a decision that may have to be made privately; in practice, it need not be made formally, for there is obviously no way in which adequate provision for peaceful settlement can ever be demonstrated or denied absolutely. Not even the most beautiful constitution will work if the political attitudes compatible with it are absent or disappear; even crazy contrivances can survive if the participants so will it. The decisions of 1789 created a constitution that worked, that later ceased to work, and that later worked again. The analyst can demonstrate the difficulties and estimate the odds; he cannot prove that the political attitudes will or will not emerge to make the scheme workable.

This means that the practical question we should ask ourselves about rules of conduct and peaceful settlement under a disarmament scheme is not whether we have absolute assurance they will work, but rather whether we are sufficiently reassured to accept the odds and proceed with the gamble. As I have tried to suggest in the preceding discussion, our answer should depend more on our material and moral preparedness for struggle in a disarmed world than on our minute appreciation of legal procedures and arbitral tribunals.

5.

LEGAL RESTRAINTS
ON COERCION

Robert W. Tucker

DISARMAMENT PROPOSALS may be distinguished by the emphasis they place on the peace-keeping measures that are to precede or to accompany disarmament.[1] At the one extreme, a disarmament plan may be addressed almost entirely to the disarmament process itself,[2] leaving aside conditions that have given, or are presumed to have given, rise to national military establishments. At the other extreme, a disarmament plan may be broadly addressed to the environment within which disarmament is to take place and seek deliberately to transform this environment, either in the process of or as a precondition to disarmament.

To be sure, the goals envisaged by both types of plans may be the same: both may hold out the eventual prospect, particularly

[1] In the following discussion the term disarmament is used not only in its literal sense, to imply the reduction or abolition of arms, but also in a broader sense, to include other measures that may form the content of an agreement on arms, e.g., limitation on the character, development, deployment, etc., of arms.

[2] The "disarmament process" may be understood to comprise the procedures agreed upon for reducing and restricting arms, as well as the means of disclosure and verification. It does not include those arrangements that may be provided, in addition to disclosure and verification, for ensuring that the arms agreement is observed. In a general sense, then, the term "peacekeeping" refers to all such arrangements and includes not only a system of sanctions to be employed in case of nonfulfillment of the agreement but also other measures designed to ensure that the parties will not have a strong incentive to break the agreement.

if they are proposals for general and complete disarmament, of an international society in which war is no longer the *ultima ratio* and in which the security of all states is assured. Moreover, to undertake a substantial reduction of arms—let alone comprehensive disarmament—would result in a number of changes in the international system quite apart from such peace-keeping measures as states may be able to agree upon in concluding a disarmament treaty.

Even so, a significant distinction remains to be made between disarmament proposals limited to the disarmament process itself and proposals that place disarmament within the broader framework of other and more comprehensive measures for the organization of peace and security.[3] Whereas the one assumes the continued reliance of states upon the traditional instruments of diplomacy, the other assumes that these instruments must be largely supplanted by new methods of resolving conflict and ensuring peace. Whereas the one assumes the continuance by and large of the institution of self-help, in which each state remains at liberty to protect its interests as best it can with the means at its disposal, the other assumes that the scope of self-help will be severely restricted. Whereas the former may accord only a very modest role to law, the latter must give to law a central role. For the latter type of plan is necessarily dependent upon the creation of a security system within which states would be effectively deprived of their traditional freedom not only to resort to armed force in the last resort but also to threaten seriously the security of their neighbors through other forms of coercion. Yet it is precisely because a centralized security system would have to be created for a society comprising very disparate and conflicting groups that these restraints on coercion would have to take a predominantly legal form and

---

[3] Even if the argument is granted that security is a condition of disarmament, it remains true—and particularly in the nuclear age—that disarmament is also a condition of security. Hence the phrase "other and more comprehensive security measures."

would have to be clearly defined.[4] They would have to take a predominantly legal form because the forces other than law that normally operate within stable domestic societies to restrain contending groups would remain—at least for a considerable period—weak and undeveloped.[5] They would have to be very clearly defined because of the weakness of those forces other than law which in domestic societies serve both to restrain contending groups and to give meaning to the law itself. The weakness of international law must be attributed not only to the absence of effective collective procedures for applying and enforcing this law but also to the weakness of those social forces other than law which largely give to the law its effectiveness. It is less commonly recognized, however, that in the absence of those forces "peace through law" can only be attained by giving to law[6] a role of importance in international society that it has rarely possessed in domestic society. And it is chiefly for this reason that the recurrent demand of "peace through law" either appears impossible to satisfy or seems to hold out novel dangers if, by some miracle, it were suddenly to be satisfied.

[4] There is no valid comparison, therefore, between such a system and the system of the United Nations Charter. If law is not given a central place in the Charter, it is because the centralization attempted in that instrument is made contingent upon the unanimity of the great powers. Given such unanimity, there is very little that the great powers cannot do according to the terms of the Charter, or, for that matter, without the Charter. Altogether different is a security system in which effective centralization is not made dependent upon great-power unanimity.

[5] It is, of course, the vitality of the forces other than law that make possible the "rule of law," that term being used in its broader sense. "The essence of the rule of law ideal," Julius Stone remarks, "lies . . . not in technical law as such, but rather in the supremacy of certain ethical convictions, certain rules of decency prevalent in the community, and in the psychological fact that those who are at the apex of power share those convictions and feel bound to conform to them" (*Quest for Survival: The Role of Law and Foreign Policy* [Cambridge, Mass.: Harvard, 1961], p. 4).

[6] And this can only mean giving it to those individuals competent to apply and enforce the law. The rule of law, it may be useful to recall, is still always the rule of men.

Illustrations of the two types of proposals alluded to above are afforded by current Soviet and American disarmament plans. It is apparent that the Soviet Union's draft treaty of March 15, 1962, on general and complete disarmament conforms to the first type of disarmament proposal. Throughout, the Soviet draft treaty is addressed almost entirely to the disarmament process itself and reflects the general position on disarmament consistently maintained by the Soviet Union since the nineteen twenties. The general tenor of the Soviet plan may be found in the statement in the preamble to the draft treaty which asserts the "fact" that general and complete disarmament under strict international control affords a "sure and practical way to fulfill mankind's age-old dream of ensuring perpetual and inviolable peace on earth." It is true that the Soviet draft treaty contains other peace-keeping measures, but, with the exception of a few general provisions on "peaceful coexistence," these other measures scarcely go beyond a reaffirmation of the United Nations Charter. Moreover, they reaffirm the Charter in a particular way. In calling for the "strengthening of the United Nations as the principal institution for the maintenance of peace," the Soviet plan points to the arresting of certain developments occurring within the United Nations since the early nineteen fifties—above all, the rise in importance of the General Assembly, together with the modest peace-keeping ventures undertaken by the Assembly— and a return to the "original Charter," with its almost exclusive emphasis upon the primacy of the Security Council. It is this original Charter—the Charter of the permanent members of the Security Council—that is to provide the scheme of international order and security for a disarming and ultimately for a disarmed world.

Thus the restraints that states are to observe in their mutual relations are, apart from the provisions on "peaceful coexistence," the restraints that are already imposed by the Charter. The principal restraint imposed by the Charter is, of course, the obligation contained in Article 2, Paragraph 4, that all members "shall refrain from the threat or use of force against the territorial integrity or political independence of any state, or in any other

manner inconsistent with the Purposes of the United Nations."[7]
So, too, the system provided in the Soviet plan for enforcing the
peace is substantially the system provided for in chapter vii of the
Charter, the sole deviation from this system being that in a
completely disarmed world the command of police (militia) units
placed at the disposal of the Security Council by the member
states is to be composed of "representatives of the three principal
groups of States existing in the world on the basis of equal representation" and to be exercised by "agreement among its members
representing all three groups of states."[8] Clearly indicative of the
Soviet position toward the peace-keeping institutions to attend
disarmament is the all-encompassing provision in the Soviet draft
treaty which reads: "All questions connected with the safeguarding of international peace and security which may arise in the
course of the implementation of the present Treaty, including
preventive and enforcement measures, shall be decided by the
Security Council in conformity with its powers under the United
Nations Charter."[9]

[7] It is interesting to note, however, that Article 3(b) of the Soviet draft
contains no qualification to the obligation not to resort to the threat or use of
force. Instead, it would obligate the parties "not to resort to the threat or
use of force to settle any international disputes that may arise, but to
use for this purpose the procedures provided for in the United Nations
Charter." This unqualified prohibition of force in the Soviet draft reflects the
interpretation that the Soviet Government has consistently sought to give to
Article 2, Paragraph 4, of the Charter.

[8] Article 18 of the Soviet draft treaty provides for the implementation of
Article 43 of the Charter during the initial and middle stages of disarmament, when states still possess regular military forces. Article 37 of the
Soviet draft provides that in the advanced stage of disarmament, after the
complete abolition of regular national military forces, states are obligated to
place at the disposal of the Security Council, on its request and again in
accordance with Article 43 of the Charter, "units from the contingents of
police (militia) retained by them, as well as to provide assistance and
facilities, including rights of passage." The Soviet plan distinguishes between the "strategic direction" of these contingents, which remains vested
in the Security Council, and their command, which is assigned to representatives composed of the three principal groups of states on the basis of
equal representation.

[9] Article 40. This provision in the Soviet draft occurs in Part V, which
deals with the structure and functions of the International Disarmament
Organization. It is preceded by the sentence, "The Organization shall deal

While the essence of the Soviet Union's draft treaty is disarmament within the framework of the "original Charter," the essence
of the peace-keeping proposals in the United States *Outline* is
disarmament within a transformed—and, ultimately, a radically
transformed—system of international security. The *Outline*, like
its Soviet counterpart, also reaffirms the obligations of the United
Nations Charter. The parties to a disarmament agreement would
undertake "to refrain . . . from the threat or use of force of any
type . . . contrary to the purpose and principles of the United
Nations Charter."[10] Still more generally, the *Outline* calls upon
the parties to a disarmament treaty "to support measures strengthening the structure, authority, and operation of the United
Nations so as to improve its capability to maintain international
peace and security."[11] But whereas a reaffirmation of the obligations of the Charter substantially exhausts the Soviet peace-
keeping proposals, it forms no more than a point of departure
for the American proposals. Throughout, the American peace-
keeping proposals reflect the general position that the existing
system of the Charter is inadequate for a disarmed as well as for
a disarming world—inadequate in the restraints imposed on the
coercive measures states are forbidden to employ, inadequate in
the arrangements provided for the peaceful settlement of dis-

---

with questions pertaining to the supervision of compliance by States with
their obligations under the present treaty." Article 42 of the Soviet draft
declares that one organ of the Organization, the Control Council, shall
promptly notify the United Nations Security Council "of any infringements
by the States party to the Treaty of their disarmament obligations under
the present Treaty." Presumably, then, the Control Council may decide
when the treaty has been violated and, according to Article 42, may do so
by a two-thirds majority vote. Great-power unanimity is required only at
the stage of preventive or enforcement action.

[10] *Outline,* Stage I, H, 1. Here again, what appears to the casual reader
as no more than a paraphrasing of the Charter appears much more significant to the careful reader. If the Soviet version of Article 2, Paragraph 4,
of the Charter omits the qualifications contained in this prohibition of force,
the American version of Article 2, Paragraph 4, adds a novel stipulation in
forbidding the threat or use of force "of any type." The American version
may therefore be interpreted to encompass not only armed force but other
forms of force or coercion (e.g., indirect aggression, subversion, etc.) which
may threaten the territorial integrity or independence of states.

[11] *Outline,* Stage I, H, 4.

putes, and inadequate in the mechanism intended to deal with breaches of the peace and acts of aggression.

The American peace-keeping proposals therefore represent the principal institutional reforms required for a disarming and disarmed world. The defects of the present international system are to be gradually corrected in the course of the various stages of disarmament. At the outset, the parties to the disarmament agreement would undertake to submit to the International Court of Justice all disputes arising over the interpretation or application of the treaty which have not been settled by other means. In view of the importance that a comprehensive disarmament agreement would evidently have, this proposal for compulsory adjudication affords a significant indication of the general tenor of the American plan. There is no real parallel to this proposal in the Charter of the United Nations.

More important still, the *Outline* requires in Stage I the "conclusion of an agreement for the establishment of a United Nations Peace Force in Stage II, including definitions of its purpose, mission, composition and strength, disposition, command and control, training, logistical support, financing, equipment and armaments."[12] The same provision also calls for an "examination of the feasibility of concluding promptly the agreements envisaged in Article 43 of the United Nations Charter."[13] These latter agreements are not seen as a possible alternative to, or substitute for, the United Nations peace force; instead, they are considered only as a possible interim arrangement, to be "examined for their feasibility," whereas the agreement for establishing the United Nations peace force is to be "concluded" prior to advancing from the initial stage of the treaty to the more advanced stages. The character of the proposed peace force is not further elaborated in the *Outline*. Nor has the character of this force been elaborated in the subsequent disarmament negotiations at Geneva. It is only reasonable to suppose, however, that in its composition and control the force would differ, and fundamentally so, from the forces envisaged in Article 43 of the United Nations Charter. Whereas the forces to be provided to the

[12] *Ibid.*, c.
[13] *Ibid.*, b.

United Nations through Article 43 of the Charter are clearly
national in composition, the proposed peace force is presumably
to be international in composition. Whereas control over the
forces provided through Article 43 of the Charter is exercised
by the Security Council, and is therefore subject to the veto,
control over the peace force is presumably to be free of the inhibiting effects of the veto. In a word, the peace force is intended
ultimately to constitute an effectively centralized international
force.

The very comprehensive security arrangements that character-
ize the American peace-keeping proposals are developed further
in Stage II of the *Outline*. As a result of studies undertaken
during Stage I, the parties are to agree "to such additional steps
and arrangements as were necessary to assure the just and peaceful settlement of international disputes, whether legal or political
in nature."[14] All legal disputes arising between the parties to
the treaty—and not only disputes which concern the interpretation or application of the treaty—are to be submitted to the compulsory jurisdiction of the International Court of Justice. In
addition, the parties are to adopt "such rules of international
conduct related to disarmament as might be necessary to begin
Stage III."[15] In particular, they are to agree to such rules as may
be necessary to "assure states against indirect aggression and
subversion."[16] There is no indication in the treaty outline of who
is to be entrusted with the critical task of interpreting and applying these rules of international conduct, just as there is no
indication in the *Outline* of who is to be entrusted with the competence to order an enforcement action by the peace force.
Here again, however, it is only reasonable to assume that this
task would not be entrusted either to the parties themselves or
to an international organ subject in its operation to the inhibiting
effects of the veto. Finally, the peace force, agreed upon in Stage
I, "would come into being within the first year of Stage II and

[14] *Ibid.*, Stage II, G, 1, a.
[15] *Ibid.*, 2, a.
[16] *Ibid.*, b.

would be progressively strengthened during Stage II."[17] And it is in Stage II that the parties who have not already done so are expected "to enact national legislation in support of the Treaty imposing legal obligations on individuals and organizations under their jurisdiction and providing appropriate penalties for non-compliance."[18]

In Stage III, as envisaged in the *Outline*, the Rubicon is finally crossed, since it is in this stage that the peace force would be strengthened "until it had sufficient armed forces and armaments so that no state could challenge it."[19] Before this point is reached, there is a covenant without a clearly effective international sword. After this point is reached, there is an international authority which, through its possession of an effective monopoly of force, is presumably able to coerce any state or any probable combination of states.

The broad implications that may be drawn from the American and Soviet proposals on the peace-keeping measures to accompany an agreement on general and complete disarmament are further confirmed by the exchanges that have marked disarmament negotiations until now.[20] The American position in these exchanges has been to insist upon the principle that any progress toward general and complete disarmament is dependent upon parallel progress in peacekeeping and progress along the lines indicated in the *Outline*. The general and complete disarmament of states, even though carried out within an effective system of verification, is not enough. Arthur Dean, in setting forth the American proposals on peacekeeping, has pointed out that

[17] *Ibid.*, 3.
[18] *Ibid.*, 5.
[19] *Ibid.*, Stage III, H, 3.
[20] These exchanges may be found in the verbatim record of the Geneva Conference of the Eighteen-Nation Committee on Disarmament (ENDC). A thorough account of the discussions on peacekeeping, covering the period from March, 1962, to July, 1962, may be found in Alan F. Neidle, "Peace-Keeping and Disarmament" (*The American Journal of International Law*, LVII [January, 1963], 46–72). As of March, 1964, no significant changes appear to have occurred in the basic position on peacekeeping of either the American or the Soviet governments.

since other forms of power would remain at the disposal of
nations to be employed in situations of conflict,

we must have an alternative realistic system for coping with
such differences and disputes as will inevitably arise. . . .
General and complete disarmament on the one hand and improved peace-keeping machinery on the other are but two
sides of the same coin. We cannot have one without the other.
Either we develop effective institutions for settling international
differences and keeping the peace, or we in effect abandon our
hopes for general and complete disarmament.[21]

The Soviet response to the American position has been that
disarmament—general and complete disarmament—is itself the
surest means of obtaining international peace and security:
"When the means of waging war are destroyed, when states
dispose of neither armies nor armaments, no one will be able
to apply force or the threat of force in international relations."[22]
Nevertheless, the Soviet position has not been one of denying,
in principle, any need for peace-keeping machinery, whether in
a disarming or in a disarmed world. It has rather been one of
insisting that such machinery already exists in the form of the
United Nations Charter and particularly in the powers conferred upon the Security Council by the Charter. Apart from
the adherence of states to the principles of "peaceful coexistence," what is necessary, and all that is necessary, is to strengthen
the principal organ of the United Nations, the Security Council.

[21] ENDC/P.V. 40, pp. 10–11. It is important to distinguish between the
argument that peace-keeping machinery is needed to control the "other
forms of power" that would remain at the disposal of nations in a disarmed
world and the argument that peace-keeping institutions—in particular, an
effective international force—are necessary to ensure against inadequacies in
the system of verification. If no known system of verification is entirely reliable, particularly at the advanced stages of general disarmament, peace-
keeping machinery is needed as a safeguard against the illegal accumulation
of arms. Even so, American spokesmen have made clear that even if a system of verification could be devised that would prove reliable at all stages
of the disarmament process, peace-keeping machinery would still be necessary to safeguard nations against other threats to their security, e.g., those
threats arising from indirect aggression and subversion.

[22] ENDC/P.V. 51, p. 12 (Zorin).

The American peace-keeping proposals are therefore viewed as a plan to subvert the Charter and the powers of the Security Council. Moreover, Soviet spokesmen have insisted that the American proposals are designed to delay indefinitely and thus to frustrate any real progress toward general and complete disarmament. Given the "profound differences'" that exist between states on what constitutes legitimate forms of persuasion, as opposed to illegitimate forms of coercion, how are they to agree on the "rules of international conduct related to disarmament'" emphasized in the American *Outline* and, in particular, on agreements assuring states of protection against "indirect aggression and subversion"? Finally, the peace-keeping measures in the United States *Outline* are seen by the Soviet Union as an attempt both to arrest the "natural historical process of the revolutionary transformation of society in accordance with the interests and wishes of the masses struggling for national and social emancipation" and to interfere in the domestic affairs of sovereign states. To the Soviets, the proposed "rules of international conduct relating to disarmament" provide the justification for such interference, and the United Nations peace force provides the military means for doing so.[23]

In comparing the Soviet and American peace-keeping proposals, there is at least one point that should raise little dispute.[24] Whereas the Soviet plan is simple and well defined, the American plan is complex and—beyond a statement of principle—largely undefined. The Soviet plan may be defective in principle and wholly unworkable in practice, but its simplicity can hardly be gainsaid. In effect, the Soviet position amounts to little more than the proposition that the order of a disarming and of a dis-

[23] ENDC/P.V. 17, p. 21; P.V. 22, p. 12; P.V. 50, p. 31; P.V. 55, pp. 56–58.

[24] An excellent discussion of the general issues raised in the following pages may be found in Hedley Bull, "Two Kinds of Arms Control" (*The Year Book of World Affairs,* ed. G. W. Keeton and Georg Schwartzenberger [New York: Praeger, 1963], pp. 150–70).

armed world must depend, as the international order has depended, upon the disposition of the great powers. The "original
Charter" is an almost perfect reflection of this proposition; hence
the Soviet insistence upon the need to return to and abide by the
original system of the Charter. To be sure, the pious hope is
added that in the course of disarming the great powers may
achieve a degree of agreement sufficient to permit their effective
co-operation in carrying out those functions assigned to them by
the Charter. But the Soviet plan does not depend upon the
realization of this hope, despite its apparent emphasis on the implementation of Article 43 of the Charter. It acknowledges, and
even presupposes, the prospect that in most of the present conflicts of interest between the great powers they shall retain their
traditional freedom of action—a freedom symbolized by their
right of veto in the Security Council. Disarmament must be undertaken, if it is to be undertaken at all, within the context of
great-power relations and despite the conflicts that continue to
mark these relations. It follows that what the great powers may
do they may also undo if the circumstances prompting their initial agreement should change.

The American peace-keeping proposals, on the other hand,
may be sound in principle, but they scarcely go beyond a rather
elaborate statement of principle. In substance, we are told that
comprehensive disarmament can occur only within an international society that has succeeded in establishing effective collective procedures for maintaining peace, ensuring security, and
providing for just and peaceful change. We are told very little,
however, about the actual design of the institutions that are to
operate in a disarmed world. Thus the provisions in the United
States *Outline* dealing with the proposed peace force affirm the
principle that the alternative to the institution of self-help is a
central authority possessed of an effective monopoly of force.
Whatever the general merits of this principle, it tells us nothing
about the composition and control of the projected United Nations peace force. So, too, with respect to the rules of international conduct related to disarmament, we are instructed in a
general principle but we are not given much guidance on the

possible content of these rules. Instead, we are told that if states are ever to disarm they may be expected to do so only as a result of prior agreement on rules which protect their legitimate interests while providing adequate means for the peaceful and just settlement of disputes. Once again, whatever the merits of this position in the abstract, it does not itself afford much indication of the content of the rules that are to restrain the behavior of states and to determine the actions of the international peace-keeping authority.

If the American proposals are very much wanting in significant detail, are they nevertheless sound in principle? That principle, we may remind ourselves, is that comprehensive disarmament and the development of effective international institutions for keeping the peace are but two sides of the same coin, and that progress in the one must be attended by a parallel degree of progress in the other. The point has been made on a number of occasions that the principle on which the American proposals are based is by no means novel and has been advocated in previous disarmament negotiations. Presumably, then, the American position today follows the French argument of the interwar period, an argument commonly characterized by the phrase "security before disarmament." More accurately, the French contended that disarmament is impossible—or, if possible, undesirable—without a parallel organization of international security. Disarmament must be in proportion to the degree of security attained by means other than those traditionally employed by states: the problem of disarmament is the problem of the effective international organization of peace. Substitute the terms "security" and "organization of peace" for "peacekeeping," and the American position echoes the French arguments of a generation ago.[25]

[25] The French position is of course reflected in the provisions of the Covenant of the League of Nations. It is also seen as early as 1922 in a resolution (Resolution XIV) adopted by the Assembly of the League, where it is declared that "in the present state of the world many governments would be unable to accept the responsibility for a serious reduction of armaments unless they received in exchange a satisfactory guarantee of the safety of their country" (see United Nations, General Assembly, *Historical Survey of*

It is by no means a criticism of the American position, and the principle from which it proceeds, that the possibility of comprehensive disarmament is virtually precluded from the start. It is necessary to acknowledge, however, that the peace-keeping proposals in the United States *Outline* do appear to have this result. They call for nothing less than the kind of consensus that can be found only in cohesive and well-ordered domestic societies. Thus the restraints on coercion that states are expected to agree to, in the form of legal norms, are not simply an incidental feature of the American proposals but, along with the creation of a United Nations peace force, evidently form the very core of these proposals. Indeed, they are in a sense more important than even the satisfactory design of a United Nations peace force, since it is clear that agreement on them is a vital precondition not to the bare establishment of such a force but to endowing it with an effective monopoly of force. Yet it is apparent that a satisfactory agreement on these rules, which would in large measure define the essential features of the new international order, presupposes a degree of consensus that even the European states of the nineteenth century were very far from achieving. It seems redundant to observe that there is much less prospect today of states achieving such a consensus.[26]

---

the *Activities of the League of Nations Regarding the Questions of Disarmament 1920–1937* [A/AC. 50/2, June 18, 1951]). The resolution coupled a defensive treaty of mutual guarantee, open to all states, with the commitment to reduce armaments according to a general plan. In the literature on disarmament the French argument was perhaps first made explicit in Salvador de Madariaga, *Disarmament* (New York: Coward-McCann, 1929), p. 218: "There is only one way of solving the problem of disarmament, and that is by considering it, in the admirable French saying, as the organization of peace." See also the memorandum by George Scelle and Rene Cassin, "French Opinion and the Problem of Collective Security" (*Collective Security*, ed. M. Bourquin [Paris: International Institute of Intellectual Co-operation, 1936], pp. 66ff).

[26] Nevertheless, illusions persist on this very simple—though vital—point. They are reflected, for example, in Grenville Clark and Louis B. Sohn's *World Peace through World Law* (2d ed. rev.; Cambridge, Mass.: Harvard, 1960). Clark and Sohn are at pains to emphasize that their proposals deal only with the "limited field of war prevention." Although they have devised a very complex institutional structure for ensuring world peace through an effective system of enforceable world law, they have virtually

Then, too, the point must be emphasized that it is one thing to define the various forms of aggression for a society the members of which continue to rely primarily upon methods of self-redress, and quite another thing to define those uses of power to be considered as illegitimate for a society in which the scope of self-redress has been severely restricted. If states have been unable in the past to agree upon a definition of aggression, this failure is not only due to the absence of the kind of consensus referred to above. It is also due to the fact that attempts to define aggression have been made within a society affording no reliable assurance to its members that their respective rights will be protected and that their demands for change will be given due consideration.[27] In the absence of institutions capable of giving such assurance, the reluctance to define aggression may typify both a *status quo* power and the state that desires change. At the same time, the attempt to provide for these institutions can only prove feasible if the norms that are to govern their actions are very clearly and comprehensively defined. For in the absence of that consensus, which grows out of shared traditions and common values, the danger of arbitrary action by the law-applying and enforcing organs must prove very real. It is quite understandable, then, that in the United States *Outline* considerable emphasis is placed on the "rules of international conduct related to disarmament" which are to restrain the behavior of states in a disarmed world and to determine the ac-

---

nothing to say about the rules to be enforced by this system regarding coercion, beyond the present injunctions of the United Nations Charter. At the outset the authors declare that "the world law against international violence must be explicitly stated in constitutional and statutory form" (p. xvi). Nowhere in their study, however, do they suggest what specific content this world law might take, but simply repeat the broad—and disputed—injunctions against force contained in the Charter. We must assume, then, either that they consider more specific restraints on coercion unnecessary in establishing an effective international force or that, once a force is established, the devising of such restraints would not prove to be a critically important—though in the present circumstances a virtually impossible—task. Unfortunately, there is no warrant for either assumption.

[27] On this issue, and related issues as well, see Stone, *Aggression and World Order: A Critique of United Nations Theories of Aggression* (Stanford: University of California, 1958).

tions of the United Nations peace force. Yet the very attempt to define these rules with any real precision and in any detail is bound to be frustrated from the outset by the absence of the kind of consensus their successful formulation must require.

Similar considerations apply to the requirement in the *Outline* calling for agreement upon such rules and arrangements as are necessary to assure the "just and peaceful settlement of international disputes." The virtue of this requirement is that it reflects an awareness of the need to provide for change in addition to the need for order and security. The same obstacles in the way of achieving agreement on illegitimate forms of coercion must frustrate the attempt to provide for collective procedures assuring both just and peaceful change. Quite apart from the absence of a meaningful consensus today on what constitutes "just change," there is the inherent difficulty of attempting to give legal form to those ends—much less assuring them—toward which a society is to evolve. Only rarely do domestic societies make this attempt—at any rate, they rarely make this attempt through the formal instrument of law. What they do attempt, with varying success, is to provide a reasonably workable mechanism for effecting change. That mechanism—in democratic societies, the principle of majority rule—may itself be a significant part of men's conception of a tolerably just society. Still, it does not so much define the direction of change as it does the manner in which change is to take place. How satisfactory and effective it may prove to be will depend upon the wisdom and sense of restraint with which men employ it, and this will in turn ultimately depend upon a moral consensus that is always far more the creator than the creature of law. Given the profound moral schisms that mark the contemporary international society, it is absurd to imagine that a workable mechanism for assuring the just and peaceful settlement of international disputes can presently be found by devising ingenious schemes for weighted voting in the General Assembly or, even worse, by creation of an international equity tribunal.[28]

[28] Both types of schemes are elaborated at length in Clark and Sohn, *World Peace through World Law.*

These observations indicate the imposing obstacles in the way of general disarmament. They clearly do not invalidate the assumptions on which the American peace-keeping proposals are based. There may not be the slightest prospect that the substance of these proposals will be acted upon. This, however, may be less a criticism of them than a commentary on the adverse environment that inhibits their implementation. It may be true that the peace-keeping institutions called for in the *Outline* are not a self-evident requirement for a disarmed world. It is possible to conceive of a world in which, despite the continued absence of effective collective procedures for maintaining peace and security, nations have abandoned their arms and have come to rely instead upon methods of self-help other than armed force. At the same time, to conceive of such a world requires us to break from past experience. There may be no logical reason for assuming that, in the absence of those institutions which have brought peace and security to domestic societies, nations will not disarm or, even if they do not disarm, will not remain disarmed despite the persistence of profound conflicts of interest. If history, however, is considered relevant in this respect, there is good reason to assume they will do neither. An assumption that has almost the whole of past experience in its support is not easy to criticize, let alone to reject. This is not to say that such an assumption cannot be criticized, and even rejected, but simply that a heavy burden must rest upon those who attempt to do so.

Moreover, the American proposals are not simply dependent—or even primarily dependent—upon the assumption that past experience must remain the guide in the present as well as in the foreseeable future. After all, it is possible to question the relevance of this experience if only for the reason that it is drawn from the record of "peacekeeping" within domestic societies. It does not follow that the experience of peacekeeping within domestic societies has a necessary applicability to the problem of peacekeeping in international society, that whatever the alternatives, international disarmament can or should proceed only by following this experience, and that regardless of circumstance it is undesirable to undertake general disarmament in the absence of those peace-keeping institutions characteristic of the state. Nor do the American proposals really appear to assume the contrary. What they do clearly assume is that quite apart from the experience of domestic societies, the risks implicit in any comprehensive disarmament scheme that is not attended by the kind of peace-keeping institutions outlined in the American plan outweigh the risks of no disarmament at all. That assumption may or may not be true. Whether or not it is true, it and not the assumption that the kind of peace-keeping institutions outlined in the American plan are somehow inherent in any possible plan for general and complete disarmament, is the critical assumption on which the American position rests.[29]

Whereas the American position assumes that without the development of effective collective procedures for ensuring peace and security the risks of general disarmament must prove too great, the Soviet position necessarily assumes (if we are to view it seriously) that the risks implicit in the present arms competition outweigh the risks of disarming in a world where nations would nevertheless continue to rely upon methods of self-help. The American plan evidently implies the end of a system dominated by these methods.

[29] A detailed analysis of this assumption is undertaken elsewhere in these essays. Here it is sufficient to note that, apart from the problem of verification, this assumption appears to rest primarily on the conviction that in a disarmed world the means of self-help other than armed force would be inadequate in defending allies against forms of coercion which fall short of armed force. The other side of this conviction is that the United States would probably prove particularly inept in employing these forms of coercion and would thereby be placed at a grave disadvantage. In this situation, the alternatives would be either to abandon one's allies—and, consequently, one's influence in many areas—or to break the disarmament agreement and to rearm. The former alternative would presumably result in turning over much of the world to the Communist states. The latter alternative would result in a new arms race. Even if it is assumed that public opinion could be quickly brought around to support this drastic step—an assumption that may well be questioned—it is argued that the new arms race would very likely prove more unstable and less controllable in its effects than the present situation, if only for the reason that we have come to know a good deal about the present arms race and the means required for keeping it under reasonable control. In an arms race beginning from a condition of general disarmament, however, we would be confronted with an essentially novel situation and one that would be likely to prove much less amenable to control.

How can agreement be reached on the norms a world authority is to apply and enforce so long as states remain divided into basically antagonistic social and political systems? Who would apply and enforce this law with impartiality even if agreement on its content could somehow be reached? In view of the apparently insurmountable difficulties indicated by these questions, the insistence that general disarmament must be attended by a basic reform of the present system is therefore seen by the Soviets to deny the possibility of general disarmament. If nations are ever to abandon their arms, though the basic conflicts that gave rise to these arms remain, it will only be through the present system and not as a result of its deliberate transformation. It follows from the Soviet view that, apart from denying themselves the capacity to resort directly to armed violence, in a disarmed world states will continue to rely upon the traditional instruments of diplomacy. Moreover, implicit in the Soviet position is the possibility that states may always break the disarmament agreement and rearm. The threat of military force will therefore remain one of the instruments of diplomacy. Hence war itself will remain the *ultima ratio of* diplomacy, though at one stage removed.[30]

[30] It must be made clear that the above interpretation of the Soviet position assumes—and, admittedly, it is a very large assumption—that a reliable system of verification can be devised and accepted by the parties to a general disarmament agreement. If this assumption is invalid, the Soviet position makes no sense whatever. It is possible to argue that in a disarmed world nations might continue to rely upon methods of self-help without incurring inordinate risks if it is assumed that the illegal accumulation of arms could not be undertaken surreptitiously. It is equally possible to argue that, given certain kinds of arms, the absence of a reliable inspection system and the consequent possibility of cheating would not prove incompatible with a system of self-help. But it is scarcely possible to employ the latter argument with respect to nuclear weapons, for the nature of these weapons is such that their sole possession by a nation, though only in limited quantity, may well confer upon the possessor what is in effect a virtual monopoly of force. If there is no reliable way of ensuring that the parties to a general disarmament agreement have carried out their obligations at every stage, the risks of disarming in a world where nations continue to rely upon methods of self-help would be inordinately great. These risks could be reduced to acceptable proportions only by the peace-keeping institutions called for in the American plan.

There is a distinctly limited utility in further analyzing these radically divergent approaches to the problem of peacekeeping in a disarmed world. So long as a consideration of the problem of peacekeeping remains tied to the vision of general and complete disarmament, the controversies thus engendered over the order a disarmed world should have are likely to prove sterile and inconclusive for the reason that the vision of a disarmed world, whether with or without effective collective procedures for keeping the peace, represents too sharp a break from our experience. This being so, peace-keeping proposals for such a world almost of necessity partake of the same unreality as the world they presuppose. Much more useful, it would seem, is an inquiry into the problem of peacekeeping in a partially disarmed world. It may of course be seriously questioned whether even partial disarmament, if it is to proceed beyond a mere token reduction of arms, can at present be considered a serious prospect. Whatever the position taken on this issue, it is at least clear that nothing beyond partial disarmament can be meaningfully considered, given the character of contemporary international society.

The view could be taken that the peace-keeping requirements of partial disarmament must be seen in terms of the peace-keeping requirements of general disarmament, and that the peace-keeping measures necessary for general disarmament are in principle also necessary for partial disarmament, though in the case of partial disarmament such measures would of course be of a more modest character. It is apparent that this view of the relationship between disarmament and peacekeeping is valid only if the process of disarmament itself is seen as a continuum marked by no radical breaks and, consequently, if the systematic changes effected by disarmament are seen to occur fairly evenly throughout the disarmament process. Put in its simplest terms, a 50 per cent reduction in the present level of armaments would therefore represent, both quantitatively and qualitatively, a kind of halfway station between the present world and a disarmed world. Similarly, the peace-keeping measures attending this 50 per cent reduction would represent a kind of halfway station between the institutions of the present international system and the institutional requirements of a disarmed world. If, however, the process of disarmament is not seen as a continuum, then it evidently does not follow that the peace-keeping measures required for partial disarmament are simply a modest version of the peace-keeping measures required for general disarmament. It may instead follow that there is really no meaningful parallel at all between the two situations and that any insistence upon finding such a parallel in terms of the problem of peacekeeping would only serve as an unnecessary hindrance to achieving partial disarmament.

There does appear to be a rather general conviction among students of disarmament that the process of disarmament cannot be seen to follow a continuum with systemic consequences roughly proportionate to the quantity of arms reduction. Instead, there is agreement that in the absence of certain compensatory measures the consequences of a given percentage cut in armaments, and particularly in strategic arms, may vary, and vary considerably, depending upon the point in the scale of arms at which the cut is made. Although a substantial reduction of strategic weapons—let us say from 30 to 50 per cent of present levels—might not give rise to any marked increase of instability, a reduction of 80 to 90 per cent of levels of such weapons would almost certainly have this result. Moroever, as the upper ranges of strategic disarmament are reached, the resulting instability might well increase so sharply as to bear almost no relation at all to the corresponding percentage cut in armaments. Thus there is a point beyond which a further reduction in strategic weapons is very likely to give rise to acute fears of successful evasion, and perhaps of surprise attack, unless the system of verification is generally felt to be quite reliable. And even if the verification system is considered reliable, there may be a marked increase of instability at very low levels of strategic weapons. Similarly, there is a point beyond which any further reduction in conventional arms will sharply diminish, if not simply preclude, the possibility of taking effective though limited action in the defense of one's allies or, more generally, of taking many of the limited pacificatory measures that great powers have traditionally taken. Precisely where

these points must be located and how far-reaching may be the
effects of passing beyond them are matters about which a good
deal of controversy and uncertainty persists. But there seems
little doubt that there are such points and that they represent dis-
continuities in the disarmament process.[31]

There is a further consideration that must prompt us to view
with skepticism the position that progress in disarmament cannot
proceed without parallel progress in the development of peace-
keeping institutions. If the process—or progress—of disarmament
cannot be seen as a continuum having evenly distributed effects,
there is perhaps even less warrant for considering the development of peacekeeping in a similar manner. Indeed, it may be
argued that in the case of peacekeeping we are more nearly faced
with an either/or proposition than we are in the case of arms
reduction and that this disparity between the two creates a
special difficulty. If the systemic effects of arms reduction are
uneven when taken as a whole, there are still segments of this
whole in which the effects are likely to prove quite even in their
progression. Even where these effects are quite uneven in terms
of a given quantity—or a given percentage cut—of arms reduction,
there still does not appear to be a literal point of no return, a
point at which the system is suddenly and for all practical purposes irrevocably transformed into something altogether different.

In the case of peacekeeping, however, there does appear to be
such a point. It is not reached when nations have merely agreed
in principle to submit to certain collective procedures for the
peaceful resolution of their differences, or even when they have
taken some of the initial steps required to implement such agreement. It is reached when they no longer possess the independent
military power to resist these collective procedures effectively.
In the *Outline* it occurs in the final stage of general and complete

[31] The peace-keeping proposals in the *Outline* need not and should not be
seen as denying the above view. The peace-keeping measures that are proposed for the initial stages of disarmament should be understood simply in
terms of a preparation for the ultimate goal of general and complete disarmament. If the American peace-keeping proposals are interpreted in this
manner, it does not follow that these proposals are necessarily relevant to
the problem of partial disarmament.

disarmament, when the United Nations peace force has "sufficient armed forces and armaments so that no state could challenge it." Before this point has been reached, the projected peace force can be, at best, merely one power among other powers. Even this prospect seems fanciful, however, if we only assume a world in which the great powers would still retain military forces at one-third of their present levels. In such a world the peace force would have to be a very substantial one to have even a moderating role in great-power conflicts, let alone a decisive influence. Unless the great powers were to go well beyond what might reasonably be considered as partial disarmament, the peace force, even if established, would in all likelihood have no more than a marginal effect on the present system. Nor is it likely that, in the absence of a centralized peace force possessing a preponderance of military power-in-being, states would place much confidence in the other peace-keeping measures they may have been able to agree upon. Even if they were able to agree upon "rules of international conduct related to [partial] disarmament," these rules would still have to be interpreted and applied by a competent third party if they were not to give rise to the same difficulties that have so regularly arisen in the past when the interpretation of rules of conduct has been left to the interested parties. The effectiveness of third-party judgment, and the willingness of states to submit to third-party judgment, will surely depend in large measure upon the expectation that force is so organized as to assure states that third-party judgment, once given, will be enforced.[32] In the absence of this assurance (that is, in the absence of a centralized monopoly of force), the international society must be expected to remain one characterized in all important respects by the dominance of self-help.

---

[32] No doubt the notorious unwillingness of states to submit their disputes to third-party judgment has also been due to reasons other than the absence of such assurance. It would be foolish, however, to underestimate the significance of this consideration.

Once these considerations are accepted, it follows that the problem of peacekeeping in a partially disarmed world will at best differ from the problem of peacekeeping in the present world. We may therefore put aside those institutional changes which, if effected, would mean the end of the system of self-help or even the serious modification of this system. There remains the possibility of peace-keeping measures that are clearly compatible with a system in which self-help would continue to dominate. In particular, it is possible to insist that an agreement on partial disarmament be attended by agreement of the parties on "rules of international conduct related to partial disarmament." The purpose of these rules would presumably have to be that of imposing additional restraints on state conduct, that is, of imposing restraints on state conduct in addition to the restraints already imposed by the United Nations Charter and customary international law. Still another and related purpose might be to resolve existing controversy and uncertainty over those restraints already imposed upon states, particularly those restraints imposed by the Charter.

If we are to consider the desirability of insisting upon additional rules of international conduct as a condition of partial disarmament, we must begin by asking ourselves what are the existing legal restraints on the coercive measures states may employ in their mutual relations and what makes these restraints effective or, as the case may be, ineffective. The principal restraints laid down by the Charter are to be found in Article 2, Paragraphs 3 and 4. Article 2, Paragraph 3, obligates member states to "settle their international disputes by peaceful means in such a manner that international peace and security, and justice, are not endangered." And Article 2, Paragraph 4, of the Charter declares that the members "shall refrain in their international relations from the threat or use of force against the territorial integrity or political independence of any state, or in any other manner inconsistent with the purposes of the United Nations." To these two principles, which have been termed the fundamental law of the Charter, must be added the provision reserving to the member states the right of individual and collective self-defense. Thus Article 51 provides that:

Nothing in the present Charter shall impair the inherent right of individual or collective self-defense if an armed attack occurs against a Member of the United Nations, until the Security Council has taken the measures necessary to maintain international peace and security. Measures taken by Members in the exercise of this right of self-defense shall be immediately reported to the Security Council and shall not in any way affect the authority and responsibility of the Security Council under the present Charter to take at any time such action as it deems necessary in order to maintain or restore international peace and security.

The difficulty is not in identifying the provisions of the Charter which limit the coercive measures states may employ in their international relations but in determining the precise scope of these provisions, and particularly the scope of the right of self-defense. It is the latter question that continues to occasion controversy and that requires some elaboration and comment. According to one view, the restrictive view, the effect of Article 2, Paragraphs 3 and 4, is to forbid any threat or use of force—and certainly any threat or use of armed force—on the part of the member states except where expressly permitted by some other provision of the Charter. In this view, the fact that the broad injunction in Article 2, Paragraph 4, to refrain from the threat or use of force is immediately followed by the words "against the territorial integrity or political independence of any state" is not interpreted to qualify the comprehensive character of the general prohibition of force. It is argued that the terms "territorial integrity" and "political independence" are but synonyms for territorial inviolability and that, in any event, it is scarcely possible to employ armed force against a state without affecting either its territorial integrity or its political independence.[33]

[33] Thus: "Territorial integrity, especially where coupled with 'political independence,' is synonymous with territorial inviolability" (Lassa Oppenheim, *International Law*, ed. H. Lauterpacht, Vol. II: *Disputes, War and Neutrality* [7th ed.; New York: McKay, 1952], p. 154). ". . . it is hardly possible to use armed force against another state without violating its territorial integrity or political independence" (Hans Kelsen, *Collective Security under International Law* [Washington: Government Printing Office, 1957], p. 62). In addition, there is much to be said for the argument that "the phrase 'political independence and territorial integrity' has been used on

Moreover, Article 2, Paragraph 4, does not simply forbid the threat or use of force against the territorial integrity or political independence of any state, but forbids force "in any other manner inconsistent with the Purposes of the United Nations." Thus the threat or use of force against the territorial integrity or political independence of a state is only one manner (though not the only manner) that is inconsistent with the purpose of the United Nations. The principal purpose of the Organization is, as Article 1, Paragraph 1, declares, to maintain international peace and security through the taking of "effective collective measures." Any use of force which has not the character of a collective measure in the sense of Article 1, Paragraph 1, is therefore forbidden by the Charter unless expressly permitted as an exception to Article 2, Paragraph 4. Apart from such effective collective measures as are taken in accordance with the decisions of competent United Nations organs, Article 51 provides—for all practical purposes[34]—the only exception to the general prohibition of Article 2, Paragraph 4. The effect of Article 51, however, is to limit the right to employ force in self-defense to the one case of a prior armed attack. The words "if an armed attack occurs" are therefore deemed critical in determining the scope of self-defense afforded by Article 51 of the Charter, and they are interpreted to forbid the taking of anticipatory measures of self-defense. It is true that Article 51 also speaks of an "inherent" right of self-defense. But the significance of this term (if, indeed, it possesses any significance at all) is, at best, obscure. In any event, it cannot detract from the general prohibition laid down in Article 2, Paragraph 4, and the otherwise apparent requirement in Article 51 that self-defense may only be exercised in response

---

many occasions to epitomize the total of legal rights which a State has" (I. Brownlie, "The Use of Force in Self-Defense," *British Year Book of International Law,* ed. H. Waldock and R. Y. Jennings, Vol. XXXVII [London: Oxford University Press, 1961], p. 235). Finally, it should be recalled that when the Charter was drafted the intended purpose of the phrase "territorial integrity or political independence" was not to qualify or to restrict the general prohibition of Article 2, Paragraph 4, but rather to give more specific guarantees to the small states.

[34] I.e., excluding Articles 107 and 53.

to an armed attack. In sum, this view holds that self-defense provides the one exception to the general prohibition on force in the Charter and that this exception is in turn restricted to the sole contingency of a prior armed attack.[35]

In opposition to the restrictive view, it has been argued that Article 51 must be seen as a reservation rather than as a grant. What Article 51 makes clear, then, is that measures of individual or collective self-defense against an armed attack are permitted members (in the absence of effective intervention by the Security Council) regardless of the restraints laid down elsewhere in the Charter. But beyond this, the right of self-defense as determined by customary international law remains unimpaired, save where it is restricted by Charter provisions other than Article 51.[36] In this respect Article 2, Paragraphs 3 and 4, is not interpreted to impose substantive restraints on the customary right of self-defense. Thus it is contended that, by definition, force employed in legitimate self-defense (i.e., legitimate according to the customary law) cannot be directed against the territorial integrity or political independence of a state, else it would cease to be legitimate self-defense.[37] Nor is there any compelling reason why the

[35] The restrictive view outlined appears to have received a substantial measure of support in the attitude taken by a majority of states in the General Assembly of the United Nations. Cf. R. Higgins, "The Legal Limits to the Use of Force by Sovereign States: United Nations Practice," *British Year Book of International Law,* Vol. XXXVII (1961), pp. 297–308. It is easy to overestimate, however, both the significance and the clarity of these expressions on the part of governments in the course of General Assembly debates.

[36] Thus: "The form of Article 51 as a reservation rather than grant is critical. Within the limits of Article 51 the license of self-defence is reserved even if some other provision of the Charter apparently forbids it. Beyond these limits self-defence by all States still depends on customary international law as modified . . . by any specific prohibitions elsewhere in the Charter" (Stone, *Legal Controls of International Conflict* [New York: Rinehart, 1954], p. 244).

[37] "Action undertaken for the purpose of, and limited to, the defense of a State's political independence, territorial integrity, the lives and property of its nationals (and even to protect its economic independence) cannot by definition involve a threat or use of force 'against the territorial integrity or political independence' of any other state" (D. W. Bowett, *Self-Defense in International Law* [New York: Praeger, 1958], p. 185).

exercise of self-defense, if taken in conformity with the customary law, should be considered as a use of force "inconsistent
with the Purposes of the United Nations," for these purposes, and
the obligations they presumably imply, are themselves dependent
on the assumption that the system of collective security established in the Charter will prove effective in practice. At the
very least, it is doubtful what precise obligations for members
can be read into Article 1 once this assumption is invalidated. In
effect, this view not only asserts that the customary right of self-
defense remains substantially unimpaired by the Charter, but it
comes very close to asserting that in the absence of those "effective collective measures" which form the core of the Charter, and indeed its *raison d'être*, the member states may once
again employ the traditional measures of self-help, including the
use of armed force, in the protection of their interests.[38]

Still another view that appears in almost equally sharp contrast
to the restrictive view outlined above may be noted. It has been
argued that even if the restrictive interpretation of Article 2,
Paragraph 4, is accepted and Article 51 is found to provide the
one exception to the general prohibition of force, it still does
not follow that the conclusion drawn by the restrictive view is
correct, for these conclusions respecting the scope of the right of
self-defense evidently depend upon a particular interpretation
of Article 51, and this interpretation must be seriously questioned.
It is possible, however, to interpret Article 51 as itself preserving the substance of the customary right of self-defense.[39]

---

[38] Cf. Stone, *Aggression and World Order,* pp. 92–103. ". . . any implied
prohibition on Members to use force seems conditioned on the assumption
that effective collective measures can be taken under the Charter to bring
about adjustment or settlement 'in conformity with the principles of justice
and international law.' It is certainly not self-evident what obligations (if
any) are imported where *no* such effective collective measures are available
for the remedy of just grievances" (p. 96). In effect, Professor Stone argues
not only for the continued validity of the customary right of self-defense
but for the continued validity of the right of self-help generally in the absence of the "effective collective measures" projected in the Charter.

[39] The view under immediate consideration may be distinguished from
the preceding view in that it does not look upon Article 51 as a reservation
rather than as a grant. In this respect, then, it tends to agree with the re-

Article 51 declares that nothing in the Charter shall impair the "inherent right of individual or collective self-defense." The term "inherent" may be understood not merely to express a theoretical view of the drafters that the right of self-defense is a natural right but to reflect an intention to preserve the customary right of self-defense, subject, of course, to effective intervention by the Security Council. The broad effect of Article 51, then, is to make clear that in the absence of effective action by the Council this customary right remains unimpaired. To be sure, there is still a need to explain the words "if an armed attack occurs," which immediately follow upon the words "Nothing in the present Charter shall impair the inherent right of individual or collective self-defense. . . ." It is contended, however, that the word "if" may be understood to express a hypothesis rather than a condition and therefore simply emphasizes one possible circumstance in which the right of self-defense may be exercised; it need not be interpreted to exhaust, and probably was not intended to exhaust, all of the possible circumstances in which the right of self-defense might still be exercised.[40]

strictive view in considering Article 51 as an exception—a restriction—to the general prohibition of Article 2, Paragraph 4. The difference arises primarily in the interpretation of Article 51 itself, and not necessarily in the interpretation of Article 2, Paragraph 4, or the relationship between the latter provision and Article 51. On the other hand, the practical difference between the two views which oppose the restrictive interpretation of self-defense in the Charter may be quite modest, in that both argue in effect for the continued validity of the customary right of self-defense. It is true that one view presses even beyond self-defense and argues that in the absence of the effective collective measures promised by the Charter, states may regain the customary right of self-help generally. Even here, however, the difference may not prove very great, if only the customary right of self-defense is broadly interpreted. As will presently be seen, there has always been a strong tendency to make the customary right of self-defense very nearly synonymous, for all practical purposes, with the right of self-help.

[40] See James L. Brierly, *The Law of Nations: An Introduction to the International Law of Peace,* ed. Humphrey Waldock (London: Oxford University Press, 1963), pp. 416–20. All sides in this controversy over the scope of the right of self-defense under the Charter have of course appealed to the *travaux préparatoires* in support of their respective arguments. But the *travaux préparatoires* are not without a good deal of ambiguity, and for this reason alone the appeal to them can hardly prove decisive. It is true

There remains the task of commenting on the substantive issues, raised by these divergent views. It should be apparent that acceptance of the restrictive view would still not remove all of the uncertainty attending the right of self-defense permitted by the Charter. In limiting the right to use force in self-defense to the sole contingency of an armed attack, it is still necessary to determine what constitutes an armed attack. Thus Article 51 does not require that an armed attack be "direct" before it may be responded to with forcible measures of self-defense. There is no apparent reason, when considering the terms of Article 51, for refusing to consider the indirect employment of force by one state against another state as constituting an armed attack. It has been argued that the consequence of including indirect uses of armed force within the concept of armed attack is to expand

---

that the Committee which dealt with Article 2, Paragraph 4, declared that "the use of arms in legitimate self-defense remains admitted and unimpaired." But this statement merely raises the question as to what was intended by the "legitimate self-defense" which was presumably to remain unimpaired. If this statement is read to imply the preservation of the customary right of self-defense, it is not easy to square with the terms of Article 2, Paragraph 4. Nor is it easy—considering the notorious vagueness of the customary right of self-defense—to reconcile with the intent to impose strict limits on the measures of self-help permitted to the member states. It should also be noted that the same Committee went on to declare that the use of force "remains legitimate only to back up the decisions of the Organization at the start of a controversy or during its solution in the way that the Organization itself ordains."

With respect to Article 51, attention is frequently called to the fact that this provision was inserted in the Charter to accommodate regional security arrangements—particularly the inter-American system then foreshadowed by the Act of Chapultepec—with the highly centralized system of the Charter. Article 51 guaranteed the parties to such an arrangement that in the absence of Security Council intervention because of the veto the members of a regional security arrangement—or, for that matter, a mutual assistance pact—would nevertheless have the right to come to the collective defense of an attacked state. From this history the conclusion is often drawn that Article 51 was not intended to narrow further the customary right of self-defense but only to make quite clear that nothing in the Charter precluded a right to use force in self- or collective defense in the absence of effective Security Council intervention and that therefore the words "if an armed attack occurs" merely emphasize one contingency with which the drafters were particularly concerned. If this is true, the wording of Article 51 betrays a curious way of realizing this alleged intent, despite the ingenious suggestion that the word "if" should be read as a hypothesis rather than as a condition.

this concept to a point where it may well become almost mean-ingless as a legal restraint and that the only alternative is to con-fine its meaning to armed force directly employed by a state. The argument is not without merit. Even so, it finds little sup-port in the wording of Article 51. Nor can it be denied that a state's political independence may be jeopardized by such in-direct uses of armed force.

The principal criticism made of the restrictive view is not, of course, that it fails to remove all of the uncertainty attending the concept of armed attack, and consequently the uncertainty that must continue to surround the definition of the right of self-defense. It is rather that the restrictive view is unreasonable in that the requirements it lays down for the exercise of force in self-defense would, if adhered to, defeat the essential purpose of this right. To require that an armed attack must have actually begun before the right of self-defense may be exercised is to exceed even the requirements for exercising self-defense im-posed by most municipal legal systems, which permit acts in self-defense not only against an actual danger but also against one that is imminent. The restrictive view, it is argued, would therefore place more rigid requirements on the right to exercise self-defense precisely in those circumstances where this right must continue to afford the principal basis for security. More-over, this insistence upon restricting the right of self-defense beyond that required by municipal law is particularly objec-tionable given the character of modern weapons. The speed of modern weapons may leave no time for the attacked state to take adequate measures of self-defense, and the destructive power of these weapons, once they have been employed, may leave very little to defend.

The more general objection to the restrictive view, however, is simply that a state may be unable to preserve its vital inter-ests—and, above all, its political independence—if the use of force in self-defense is only legitimate where the measures used to endanger the state's interests take the form of an armed at-tack. The measures that may jeopardize a state's independence need not involve armed force, especially not the overt employment of armed force, though they may nevertheless be unlawful. The result of denying to states the right to respond to such unlawful measures by employing, if necessary, forcible measures in self-defense may well result in turning the right of political independence into little more than a sham. Nor is it useful here to draw a parallel between the state and international society. Within the state a right of self-defense is denied the individual short of an armed attack or the imminent threat of armed attack precisely because the individual may seek and receive protection against other unlawful acts endangering his vital—and legally protected—interests. The same assurance evidently does not obtain for states in international society. To require of states what is required of individuals within the state is to ignore the disparate circumstances that make the employment of armed force a reasonable condition for the exercise of self-defense in the one case and an unreasonable condition in the other case.

These criticisms of the restrictive view are surely not without considerable merit. It is much easier to make them, however, than it is to suggest an alternative that is not equally vulnerable to criticism. Admittedly, it appears paradoxical that the restrictive view, in denying the legitimacy of anticipatory acts of self-defense, would go beyond the requirements even of municipal law. In large part, the explanation of this apparent paradox must be found in those very conditions which normally attend the exercise of self-defense in international society, conditions which from one point of view so clearly seem to require a right to take anticipatory acts of self-defense. It is necessary to recall that within the state the right of self-defense is severely controlled. Although when acting in self-defense the individual must exercise a right of self-judgment, that right is merely provisional: in exercising that right, the individual acts at his peril, for his act of self-judgment is always subject to later review and impartial adjudication. This assurance of later review and impartial adjudication prevents the abuse of a right to take measures of self-defense against an imminent and not only an actual danger. The absence of this assurance in international society must give rise to the danger of abuse when the scope of the right to self-defense is extended to include anticipatory acts of self-defense. Critics of the restrictive view cannot have it both ways: the same conditions that do indeed lend support to the argument for permitting anticipatory acts of self-defense in international society also point to the very considerable dangers of granting such a right.[41]

Nor does the nature of modern weapons substantially alter this conclusion. If the speed and destructive power of modern weapons may defeat the purpose of self-defense in the absence of a right to take anticipatory measures against an imminent attack, it is these same characteristics that must also render a right to take anticipatory measures particularly dangerous and subject to grave abuse.

Apart from the issue of anticipatory self-defense, if the restrictive view of self-defense under the Charter is considered generally inadequate and unacceptable, what is the alternative? The broad response given this question has been to insist that the customary right to employ force in self-defense must be presumed to remain valid. Even if this position is accepted in principle, however, there remains the critically important task of determining the contents of the customary right of self-defense. What are the rights for the protection of which a state under the customary law may legitimately resort to forcible measures of self-defense? To the extent that the answer given this question is

[41] These dangers would be mitigated, if not removed altogether, given the assurance that alleged measures of self-defense taken by states would always be subject to later investigation and adjudication. In a frequently cited passage of its judgment, the Nuremberg Tribunal declared that "whether action taken under the claim of self-defense was in fact aggressive or defensive must ultimately be subject to investigation and adjudication if international law is ever to be enforced." But this and similar statements merely amount to the assertion that many of the difficulties and dangers attending the claim of anticipatory self-defense—and the exercise of self-defense generally—would not arise in international society if this society were only organized in a manner approximating the state. While undoubtedly true, the assertion is evidently no solution of the difficult issues which form the core of the controversy considered in these pages, issues which persist precisely because there are no effectively centralized procedures for investigating and adjudicating alleged measures of self-defense taken by states. In the absence of such procedures, to which the subjects of international law are obligated to submit, the right of self-judgment exercised by states is very likely to prove permanent rather than, as in the state, merely provisional.

vague and uncertain today, it faithfully mirrors the vagueness and uncertainty that have always marked attempts to define and limit the customary right of self-defense. Indeed, despite repeated affirmation of a customary right of self-defense, it is doubtful whether this right ever amounted to much more than a rather vague principle of political morality that could be and was used to justify quite disparate actions by states. It is not surprising that discussions of this right are frequently difficult to distinguish from an affirmation of a right of self-preservation, that is, the right of a state to take any action it considers necessary to protect itself against an actual or threatened injury to its vital interests. In turn, the right of self-preservation has never been easy to distinguish from the classical plea of necessity, nor is it surprising that many contemporary analyses of the right of self-defense result, in effect, in the affirmation of the same broad right of self-preservation. In both cases, the result has come very close to the affirmation of a "right" that must make difficult the possibility of drawing a meaningful distinction, even in principle, between the unlawful use of force by a state and its lawful exercise in self-defense.[42]

[42] The essential characteristic of the so-called right of self-preservation has always been the virtually unlimited freedom it gives to a state to act contrary to any norm of international law, and thus to violate any right of another state if such action is deemed necessary for its own preservation. Thus a state can resort to preventive measures of a forcible nature if they are necessary for self-preservation, in order to maintain or restore a balance of power. That the state against which the action is directed has actually violated or directly and immediately threatened to violate a right of the state acting for self-preservation is not required. The behavior of the state against which acts of self-preservation are directed may not be forbidden by international law. Even so, if this behavior jeopardizes another state's vital interests, and above all those interests on which its security depends, the latter may presumably take such measures as it considers necessary in the circumstances, including armed force. A recent illustration of the reaffirmation of the right of self-preservation, in the sense discussed above, is afforded by a former Secretary of State in discussing the Cuban quarantine: "I must conclude that the propriety of the Cuban quarantine is not a legal issue. The power, position and prestige of the United States had been challenged by another state; and law simply does not deal with such questions of ultimate power—power that comes close to the sources of sovereignty. . . . No law can destroy the state creating the law. The survival of states is not a matter of law" (Remarks by the Honorable Dean Acheson, *Proceedings of the American Society of International Law at Its Fifty-Seventh Annual Meeting* [Washington, D.C., 1963], p. 14).

According to the prevailing interpretation of the customary right of self-defense, the resort to forcible measures in self-defense is legitimate not only to protect the state's territorial integrity, its "physical person," against direct attack; self-defense is equally legitimate when resorted to for the protection of those interests which collectively comprise the nation's security and consequently its "existence," in the broader sense of political independence, and which may be endangered by measures other than armed force. Since uncertainty has always prevailed with respect to the scope of the rights—the legally protected interests—which presumably comprise the nation's security and independence, equal uncertainty has always prevailed with respect to the scope of the right of self-defense. This is one reason why the claim of self-defense, even when strictly limited to the protection of legal rights against delictual conduct, comes very close in practice to the much more general claim by states of a right to take forcible measures of self-redress in response to acts violative of their legally protected interests, though these acts may not endanger the state's security or independence.[43] Nor is

[43] Thus D. W. Bowett (*Self-Defense in International Law*, pp. 9, 24, 29, 270–71), while emphasizing that the precondition for the exercise of self-defense is delictual conduct by another state, and that it is this precondition which distinguishes self-defense from the "right" of self-preservation, defines the rights for which self-defense may be exercised as those rights essential to the security of the state. They include, in Bowett's view, the right of territorial integrity, the right of political independence, the right of protection over nationals, and certain economic rights. It will be apparent that these rights cover a very broad range of possible actions and, in effect, come quite close to a general claim of self-help—i.e., the right to respond, if necessary, with forcible measures against acts violative of a state's legally protected interests. Even so, Bowett's list can scarcely be regarded as authoritative. Many writers have in fact maintained that the right of self-defense in the customary law extends to the protection of the whole of a state's legally protected interests, thereby making the right of self-defense in effect identical with the right of self-help. Thus, John Westlake defined the customary right of self-defense to "include all violation of the legal rights of itself or of its subjects, whether by the offending state or by its subjects without due repression by it, or ample compensation when the nature of the case admits compensation" (*International Law* [Cambridge: Cambridge University Press, 1904], Vol. I, p. 299). Westlake's failure to make a clear distinction between self-defense and self-help found expression in the claims frequently put forward by governments. It is quite true that some writers sought to place limits on the scope of the rights in the protection of which self-defense could presumably be exercised. But there

this uncertainty over the scope of the customary right of self-defense dispelled by the frequent assertion that the right of political independence may be defined in terms of the supposedly correlative duty of nonintervention, i.e., the duty to refrain from the dictatorial or forcible interference in the affairs of another state. Even if it is assumed that the duty of nonintervention provides sufficient guarantee of the right of political independence, no clear agreement exists on the scope of the duty of nonintervention in the customary law. It is clear that not all forcible interference in the domestic or foreign affairs of another state has been or is today regarded as constituting illegitimate acts of intervention. In particular, measures of self-defense taken by a state may represent forcible interference in the affairs of the state against which these measures are directed, although they are nevertheless legitimate. But if the scope of the duty of nonintervention is largely dependent upon the determination of the right of self-defense, one uncertainty is made dependent for its clarification upon yet another uncertainty. To assert that the content of the right of political independence may be found in the correlative duty of nonintervention is simply to shift the problem, not to resolve it.

There is, of course, the further consideration that a state's independence may be impaired by the behavior of another state, although the latter does not employ force or even the threat of force. To the extent that intervention is held to encompass only those acts of interference in the affairs of another state that take an imperative or dictatorial form and involve the use or threat of force, the duty of nonintervention becomes irrelevant in dealing with behavior that may nevertheless effectively jeopardize political independence. Here, again, if the protection of the right of political independence is nevertheless held to justify the resort

---

is little, if indeed any, warrant for the contention today that these expressions prove the existence of a right of self-defense in the customary law limited to the protection of territorial integrity and political independence, or, for that matter, the protection of nationals, etc. Here, as elsewhere, the customary right of self-defense is characterized by vagueness and uncertainty, and it is probably impossible to make out a persuasive case for choosing any one of the varying views presented by writers on the subject.

to forcible measures of self-defense, and if the right of independence is given a sufficiently broad interpretation, the result must
be to enlarge the scope of self-defense to a point where it is
difficult to distinguish from the much more general claim of the
state to possess the competence to take measures of self-redress
(including, if necessary, forcible measures of self-help) as a
reaction to a wide range of acts of other states which violate its
rights under international law.

In the immediately preceding discussion, it has been assumed
that the acts in response to which self-defense is presumably
legitimate according to the customary law are acts clearly contrary to international law, i.e., are international delicts. Measures
of self-defense are permitted, then, in response to unlawful acts
which, at the same time, endanger another state's territorial integrity or political independence (or, if one prefers, the security
upon which independence rests). It is clear, however, that there
are a number of acts which may effectively jeopardize a state's
independence or security but which, nevertheless, are not specifically forbidden by international law. This is true, for example, of
at least some of the more novel methods of impairing a state's
independence through so-called "indirect aggression." A state's
political independence may even be endangered through the
economic pressures to which it is subjected by another state,
though these measures of economic coercion may not themselves
be expressly forbidden by international law. Perhaps the most
dramatic illustration in recent years of the general point under
consideration was the discovery in October, 1962, that the Soviet
Union was secretly establishing strategic missile sites on the
island of Cuba. The action of the Soviet government was interpreted by the United States, as well as by the Organization of
American States, as constituting a threat to the peace and security—and, accordingly, to the political independence—of the states
comprising the Western Hemisphere. The resort to forcible
measures, designed to prevent the further shipment to Cuba
of missiles and aircraft having an offensive capability as well as
to compel the withdrawal of such weapons as were already on
the island, was thereby justified. Yet it is clear that in sending

these weapons the Soviet government acted with the consent and co-operation of the Cuban government. There is no rule of general international law that specifically forbids a state from giving arms to another state or from establishing military bases in the territory of another state, whether openly or in a clandestine manner, so long as this is done with the latter state's consent. Nor is there any principle of general international law that forbids a state from attempting to alter the military balance of power in its favor, so long as this is done through actions which do not themselves violate the rights of other states. To the extent that the forcible measures taken by the United States in response to the action of the Soviet government are nevertheless justified as legitimate measures of self-defense (and it is believed that this is the most plausible basis for their legal justification[44]), they afford a striking example of the claim that forcible measures of self-defense may be taken in response to acts which are not at least *prima facie* unlawful.

It may, of course, be argued that such acts of coercion as threaten the security, and thereby the political independence, of other states are unlawful even though they are not specifically forbidden by international law. This is the evident implication of the claim that a state has the legal right to take forcible measures of self-defense, if necessary, against any and all acts which endanger its political independence. If this argument is once granted, it is difficult to see wherein it differs from the traditional claim of a "right" to self-preservation, a claim that is now generally rejected, presumably because it may be used and has been used to justify almost any action taken by a state.[45] If the

[44] The American government did not attempt, however, to base its actions upon the right of self-defense.

[45] Thus the authors of a recent study of self-defense point out that claims of self-defense "are claims to exercise highly intense coercion in response to what is alleged to be unlawfully initiated coercion" (Myres S. McDougal and Florentino P. Feliciano, *Law and Minimum World Public Order* [New Haven, Conn.: Yale, 1961], p. 209). The legally protected interests (or values) for the protection of which measures of self-defense may be undertaken are summarized as "territorial integrity and political independence." Political independence is defined, however, as that "freedom of decision-making or self-direction customarily demanded by state officials. Impair-

substantive rights on behalf of which force may be presently employed remain both expansive and ill-defined, if all that can be said with assurance is that in some vague manner these rights encompass the security and independence of the state, how does this constitute an improvement over the traditional and presently discredited claim to a "right" of self-preservation? If it is no less difficult to define the "rights'" essential to a state's security and independence than it is to define the "vital interests" of a state, can a meaningful distinction be drawn between a principle of political morality establishing "vital interests" as the criterion for the resort to force and an allegedly legal principle requiring that force used in self-defense must follow the violation or threatened violation of "rights"? That a right to use force has been transformed from a principle of political morality into a principle of law is not very significant if the ambiguities that marked the former principle continue to mark the latter principle as well. It is not easy to see what material difference this transformation makes as long as the "rights" states may still protect by force, if necessary, are not rigidly circumscribed and the acts in response to which the right of self-defense may be invoked are not restrictively defined.

There remain, it is true, other restraints that presumably govern the exercise of the customary right of self-defense. Thus the

---

ment of 'political independence,' as an attack upon the institutional arrangements of authority and control in the target state, thus involves substantial curtailment of the freedom of decision-making through effective and drastic reduction of the number of alternative policies open at tolerable costs to the officials of that state" (p. 177). Presumably, then, measures of self-defense are legitimate in response to acts of coercion by another state which impair or threaten to impair this "freedom of decision-making" of the target state, provided only that such measures are necessary in the circumstances and proportionate to the danger. Nor is it necessary that the acts in response to which measures of self-defense are undertaken be specifically forbidden by international law. They are unlawful, on his view, even if their only effect is to endanger a state's political independence. It is difficult to see any substantial difference between this view of self-defense and the older—and frankly political—doctrine of self-preservation. Professor McDougal confirms this conclusion in his remarks on the Cuban quarantine (Cf. "The Soviet-Cuban Quarantine and Self-Defense," *American Journal of International Law*, LVII [July, 1963], 597ff).

danger that gives rise to the right of self-defense must be immediate and of such a nature as to leave no reasonable possibility
for recourse to alternative means of protection. In addition, the
use of force in self-defense must prove reasonable, and it may
prove reasonable only if it is proportionate to the end of protecting those interests (rights) that are endangered. The use of
force in excess of this purpose is forbidden, since action taken
in self-defense is held to have a strictly preventive character.

The conclusion is frequently suggested that the effect of these
restraints is to ensure that self-defense will be a strictly limited
and regulated right under the customary law. But this conclusion
can be accepted only with respect to the actual exercise of the
right of self-defense, for the restraints in question still leave
largely unaffected (and undetermined) the vital issue of the
rights on behalf of which, and the acts in response to which,
forcible measures of self-defense may be undertaken.[46] Even so,
it may be doubted whether the effect of these restraints is such
as to ensure that self-defense is a strictly limited and regulated
right under the customary law. The degree of necessity held to
justify measures of self-defense must largely depend upon the
immediacy of the danger posed to the state. The immediacy of
the danger, however, need not and, it is generally claimed, cannot be gauged simply in terms of overt action of an injurious
nature: it is precisely the purpose of self-defense to prevent, if

[46] It is significant that in the classic case—the Caroline—in which the
requirements of necessity and proportionality were articulated, and which
is commonly cited in discussions of self-defense, no real guidance is afforded
with respect either to the rights on behalf of which or the acts in response
to which self-defense may be exercised. In this statement on the requirements of self-defense, the American Secretary of State, Daniel Webster,
declared that there must be shown "a necessity of self-defense, instant,
overwhelming, leaving no choice of means and no moment of deliberation,"
and, moreover, that the action must involve "nothing unreasonable or excessive, since the act justified by the necessity of self-defense must be
limited by that necessity and kept clearly within it." No clear distinction
appears in Webster's statement between a right of self-defense and a much
broader "right" of self-preservation. If anything, the implication is that
Webster was referring to a "right" of self-preservation. There is no insistence that measures of self-defense must be preceded by, and taken in
response to, acts violative of a state's international rights.

possible, such injurious action. This being so, the danger held to justify the taking not only of preventive but of anticipatory measures of self-defense will depend upon an interpretation of the significance of behavior that falls short of being overt and unambigious. Moreover, if the uncertainty to be tolerated before preventive measures are resorted to must be related to the nature of the danger posed, the nature of the danger will depend not only upon the *animus* thus far manifested by the other party, but also upon the means of injury the other party has at its disposal.[47] Hence the nature and immediacy of the danger that may serve to justify forcible measures of self-defense, and particularly anticipatory measures of self-defense, cannot reasonably be divorced from the technology of war. Presumably, as the latter changes, so those conditions held to constitute the degree of necessity required for the exercise of self-defense will change. Although it has never been easy to determine the degree of necessity needed to justify the resort to measures of self-defense, the difficulties attending such determination, and the opportunities afforded for abuse, are perhaps greater today than ever.

So, too, the principle of proportionality has never been free from substantial uncertainty in application. In its abstract formulation, the principle of proportionality requires that acts taken in self-defense must be proportionate to the danger threatened and that they must not exceed in manner or in purpose the necessity provoking them. Many writers have assumed that acts taken in self-defense must therefore be strictly limited to repelling the

[47] Thus in defining the Cuban "quarantine" as a legitimate measure of self-defense, many writers have urged that the nature of the danger posed by the Soviet action must be found both in Soviet intentions in placing missiles in Cuba and in the character of the weapons themselves. Soviet intentions are presumably deduced from past Soviet behavior and from the clandestine manner in which the missiles were brought to Cuba. This behavior, it is argued, indicates an intent to use the missiles to threaten the security and independence of the American states. It is concluded that when this presumed intent is coupled with the potential destructive power of the missiles, the necessity of the "quarantine" as a legitimate measure of self-defense is apparent. Whatever the position taken toward this argument, it is quite clear that the meaning of "necessity" on which it relies is not the necessity of the Caroline case ("instant, overwhelming, leaving no choice of means and no moment of deliberation").

immediate danger. But the preventive purpose of self-defense does not preclude an interpretation of the principle of proportionality to permit action directed to removing the danger, on the ground that a right of self-defense is without substance if it does not permit removal of the danger which initially justified the resort to measures of self-defense.[48] If the former interpretation is accepted, difficulties in placing meaningful limitations on the exercise of self-defense will still remain. But these difficulties may prove relatively insignificant by comparison with those emerging from the latter interpretation. When has the danger that allegedly justified the resort to force in self-defense been removed? An attack may be repelled, or a threatened attack may be prevented, but the danger may persist. The state

[48] The issue of proportionality arose in the Suez crisis of 1956. In attacking Egypt, Israel justified her action as a legitimate measure of self-defense, taken in response to a continuous series of armed raids on Israeli territory by *fedayeen* bands based in Egypt and in anticipation of what was alleged to be an impending attack on Israel by Egyptian forces. Quite apart from the issue of anticipatory self-defense raised by the Israeli action, the obvious and acknowledged intent of the Israeli penetration of Egyptian territory was to destroy the *fedayeen* bases in Egypt—i.e., to remove at least one of the sources of danger that was alleged to justify the resort to forcible measures of self-defense. In condemning the Israeli action, the General Assembly demonstrated not only a reluctance to acknowledge the legitimacy of forcible measures in anticipation of an armed attack; it also indicated that it considered the action disproportionate and unreasonable in relation to the acts (i.e., the *fedayeen* raids) which had provoked the Israeli attack. Yet there is much to be said for the position that, in view of the support given these raids by the Egyptian Government and their continuous character, the Israeli action was without purpose or reason unless directed to the end of removing this source of danger. In this respect, it is interesting to compare the position taken by Israel in 1956 and the position taken by the United States in the Cuban crisis in 1962. Much has been made of the proportionality and reasonableness of the Cuban "quarantine" in view of the considerable danger allegedly posed by the establishment of Soviet missile bases in Cuba. It should be noted, however, that the declared policy of the United States Government was not only to stop the further shipment of "offensive weapons" to Cuba but to compel the withdrawal of such weapons as were already on the island, and to do so by *any and all means* that might prove necessary. The proportionality and reasonableness of the American position can hardly be judged exclusively in terms of the measures that were actually taken; it must also be judged in terms of the measures threatened if the "quarantine" proved ineffective and the "offensive weapons" already on the island were not removed.

that claims that it is acting solely in self-defense may nevertheless insist that the danger has not passed so long as those circumstances which gave rise to the exercise of self-defense persist.
It may also insist that, given the circumstances attending the
exercise of self-defense by states, it is only reasonable to permit
the removal of the danger which initially justified the resort to
measures of self-defense. Within domestic societies the state
guarantees that a danger once repelled will be removed, hence
the justification for the severe restriction of measures taken in
self-defense is apparent. In the international society this assurance obviously cannot be given to states, and thus an equally
severe restriction of measures taken in self-defense may prove
unreasonable, in that it may defeat the essential purpose for
which measures of self-defense are permitted in the first place.
The argument is not without merit. Yet if it is once accepted,
what are the practical limits to the exercise of self-defense?

These considerations should not be taken as a denial of the
argument that serious dangers inhere in any attempt to circum-
scribe rigidly the rights that a state may protect through forcible
measures of self-defense. Nor should they be taken to imply
that a restrictive view of the acts in response to which the right
of self-defense may be exercised will prove adequate in protecting states against possible forms of conduct that may endanger
their security and independence. On the contrary, it is clear that
there remain certain kinds of behavior that are not forbidden
to states by international law, though their effects may jeopardize
the security of the states against which they are directed. The
ambiguity that has always surrounded the right of political independence, and continues to surround that right today, reflects
the fact that a state's independence may be threatened by measures that nevertheless cannot be characterized as unlawful.
Indeed, the traditional claim of states to a "right" of self-preservation, though frequently used to justify aggressive behavior, also
reflects the fact that security might prove dependent upon the
protection of interests which are left unprotected, or inadequately
protected, by law.

Yet the obvious objections that may be made to the restrictive view of self-defense should not obscure the equally obvious objection that may be made to the view which insists upon the continued validity—and the desirability of the continued validity—of what is presumed to be the customary right of self-defense. If the structural characteristics that mark international society, and would continue to mark it when partially disarmed, suggest the dangers inherent in the restrictive view of the right of self-defense, they also suggest the dangers inherent in the view that would not limit self-defense to the right of responding to force with force. However reasonable and justified the extension of self-defense beyond these narrow limits may appear when applied to the relations of states, it is those very circumstances in which the right of self-defense must be applied that make any extension hazardous.[49]

[49] The present uncertainty and controversy over the scope of the right of self-defense is also closely related to the more general issue of the desirability—and viability—of restricting the use of force as a means of self-help in the absence of an effectively centralized system of collective security. Indeed, it is clear that the tendency to expand the scope of self-defense is in part the result of denying to states the right to take forcible measures of self-help, if necessary, in response to acts which violate their legally protected interests even though they may not involve the threat or use of force. If it is difficult to reconcile Article 2, Paragraph 4, of the United Nations Charter with what is commonly presumed to be the customary right of self-defense, it is still more difficult to reconcile this provision with the customary right to take forcible measures of self-help (i.e., armed reprisals). Although the meaning of the term "force" in Article 2, Paragraph 4, remains the subject of some uncertainty, it is at least clear that it comprises armed force of any kind. Whatever the position taken with respect to the issues considered in previous pages, unless the right of self-defense is to be made practically identical with the right of self-help, it is equally clear that Article 2, Paragraph 4, forbids a state to take forcible measures of self-help in response to unlawful and injurious action so long as such action does not itself consist in the threat or use of armed force and does not immediately threaten the injured state's territorial integrity or political independence. The above formulation leaves open, then, the question considered in previous pages: whether Article 2, Paragraph 4, may be interpreted to permit states to take forcible measures of self-defense against unlawful acts which jeopardize their territorial integrity or political independence although they take a form other than that of armed attack. A distinction is therefore drawn in relation to Article 2, Paragraph 4, between self-defense and self-help generally. Whereas this provision of the Charter

Moreover, it does appear that the restrictive view of the right to employ force in self-defense is the view that has come to enjoy increasing support. When all has been said and done, and when the exceptional instances to the contrary have been duly noted, the conclusion that emerges is that there is one relatively clear and effective restraint presently imposed upon states, i.e., the rule forbidding the direct and overt use of armed force against other states save in response to a similar use of force. To say this, however, is not to suggest that the other forms of coercion which states may employ are therefore permitted at present. It still remains true that according to the customary law (and, it may be argued, according to the law of the Charter) many acts of so-called "indirect aggression" are forbidden. Thus the active, though indirect, support by a state of revolutionary forces fighting against the government of another state, the arming by a state of organized bands for offensive purposes against another state, the sending by a state of "volunteers" to engage in hostilities against the government of another state, the support and encouragement by a state of terrorist and subversive activities in another state are actions that are in principle still forbidden by international law. At the same time, it is equally clear that the law forbidding these actions has not been as effective as the rule forbidding the overt use of armed force. Indeed, it is this relative ineffectiveness of the law forbidding intervention even though it may take an indirect form that has

---

may be interpreted as compatible with the customary right of self-defense—though this is not the interpretation accepted here—it cannot be interpreted as compatible with the customary right (or, as some writers prefer, the liberty) of states to take forcible measures of self-help in response to unlawful action that either does not itself take the form of armed force or does not jeopardize another state's territorial integrity or political independence. It must be admitted, however, that in view of the vagueness with which the customary right of self-defense is defined, the utility of this distinction may be easily questioned. Quite different is the further question: are forcible measures of self-help permitted by Article 2, Paragraph 4, if they are taken in response to a *forcible denial of rights*, even though these rights may not involve territorial integrity or political independence? An affirmative response to this question appears to have been taken by the International Court of Justice in the Corfu Channel case (International Court of Justice, *Reports* [1949], p. 4).

prompted the view that the law itself is in the process of change and that certain types of intervention which had previously been considered unlawful are presently acquiring a new status. On occasion, the term "quasi-legitimate" has been employed to describe this novel status, a term which, if it is not to be understood simply as a euphemism for acts considered lawful, must be understood to indicate a status of uncertainty. If the continued validity of legal restraints is ultimately dependent upon their effectiveness (and in international law this would appear to be the case), it is not easy to reject this view. To the extent that the conviction has grown that armed force may no longer be directly employed in response to intervention that takes an indirect form, this view must receive still further support.[50]

It is another matter to speculate on the reasons that have led to this increasingly significant distinction between the direct and the indirect use of force, a distinction that roughly corresponds to the distinction between interstate war and domestic war.[51] International lawyers are prone to the distinction between the relative clarity of the one use of force and the vagueness and ambiguity attending the other. Whereas the overt resort to armed force across international boundaries is generally thought to be susceptible to objective and persuasive determination, the indirect resort to force is considered to be much less so. It is presumably this inherent vagueness of the standards which are applied to determine indirect aggression or subversion, as well as the difficulties of proof in a particular instance, that are there-

[50] This conviction and the decreasing effectiveness of the norms forbidding certain forms of intervention are evidently closely related. A legal restraint the violation of which cannot be responded to by armed force if necessary is not likely to prove very effective. It does not follow from the restrictive interpretation of the Charter that since indirect aggression and subversion cannot be responded to with force, these forms of coercion are thereby permitted. It does follow, however, that if this interpretation is accepted, the principal sanction contributing to the effectiveness of norms forbidding indirect aggression and subversion has disappeared.

[51] For a good discussion of the latter distinction, and of the reasons prompting intervention in domestic war, see Samuel P. Huntington, "Patterns of Violence in World Politics" (*Changing Patterns of Military Politics*, ed. Samuel P. Huntington [New York: Free Press, 1962]); also Huntington's Institute for Defense Analyses, Study Memorandum, "Instability at the Non-Strategic Level of Conflict" (1961).

fore held to account in part for the relative ineffectiveness of
the law forbidding the external support of domestic change by
forcible means.

The difficulties alleged to attend the determination of indirect
aggression and subversion are nevertheless a theme that frequently lends itself to exaggeration.[52] Although it is quite true
that these difficulties will normally prove greater than the difficulties involved in establishing the fact of overt aggression, the
distinction increasingly made between the two forms of coercion
must surely be attributed to other and more significant reasons.
Perhaps the principal reason is simply that intervention by indirect methods normally constitutes a more limited and controllable form of coercion than does the direct method of intervention.[53] Not only do indirect forms of coercion appear more
prudent in terms of the nature and scope of the commitment they
involve, and the public reaction they provoke, but they also
permit a response that is more readily limited than the response to the direct use of force. If change is inevitable, and is
always in part coercive, it is at least desirable that it should come
through methods that are less destabilizing and less destructive

[52] Thus one international jurist, in discussing the difficulties of regulating
indirect aggression and subversion, writes: "There are difficulties of vague
standards. When is support illegal, how much, what kind? There are the
difficulties of proof that particular assistance is being given. Most important
are the difficulties of seeking to assert or develop a role for law against the
interests and resistance of a major power, whether the Soviet Union or
Communist China, in the society we know today" (Louis Henkin, "Force,
Intervention, and Neutrality in Contemporary International Law," *Proceedings of the American Society of International Law*, p. 168). These difficulties of vague standards and of proof are by no means unique to indirect
aggression and subversion, however. In part, at least, they also attend the
determination that the use of force constitutes an "armed attack." Moreover, one must clearly separate ineffectiveness resulting from vague standards and difficulties of proof from ineffectiveness arising from a reluctance
or simply a refusal to conform to certain norms, no matter how clear the
standards these norms set out. If a large number of states insist upon resorting to indirect aggression and subversion, though for professedly different purposes, that is surely sufficient reason to explain the ineffectiveness
of norms forbidding these forms of coercion.

[53] On this and related points, see George Modelski, *The International
Politics of Internal Wars* (Princeton, N. J.: Princeton Center of Inter-
national Studies, Woodrow Wilson School of Public and International
Affairs, 1961).

than traditional interstate violence threatens to be in the nuclear age. It may be true that there are circumstances in which the independence of states may be destroyed as effectively by indirect aggression and subversion as by the overt use of military force. Experience indicates, however, that the possibility of effective resistance normally remains greater in the case of indirect aggression and subversion. Then, too, there is the conviction that indirect aggression and subversion will rarely prove successful when employed against a government that has the support and confidence of the public it claims to represent. Thus it is argued that if a legal—and moral—distinction is increasingly drawn between indirect and direct forces of coercion the justification for this distinction may be found in the greater dependence of indirect forms of coercion, if they are to prove successful, upon the support of the population. Guerrilla warfare and related forms of insurrection represent, in this view, a tolerable approximation of trial by ballot, even though one or both sides may receive the support of outside powers.[54]

The principal conclusions suggested by the preceding analysis may be briefly summarized. Despite the persistence of controversy, there is a growing consensus that the overt employment

---

[54] "Guerrilla wars," one advocate of this view declares, "ultimately rest for their success upon the support of the population. . . . This makes them probably as true an expression of the underlying 'general will' of those concerned as any form of political expression. . . . There seems to be a kind of general acceptance of their outcome as representing a closer approach to the goals of freedom and justice than do the outcomes of the great international wars" (Walter Millis et al., A World without War [New York: Washington Square, 1961], pp. 42–43; also Millis and James Real, The Abolition of War [New York: Macmillan, 1963]). In guerrilla warfare, no less than in the great international wars, however, victory is ultimately determined by relative military strength, and coercion remains the primary instrument for obtaining consent. To equate the outcome of such contests with justice may therefore prove no less objectionable than to equate the outcome of traditional interstate violence with justice. Nevertheless, the view persists that a moral distinction must be drawn between the two. The real basis for that view, it would seem, rests upon the assessment of the greater destructiveness of traditional interstate war.

of force is presently forbidden to states except in self-defense against an armed attack. It is clear that given the circumstances in which it must be applied this restriction of the right to employ force is open to serious objection. Nevertheless, the conviction remains that the use of force is, in principle, forbidden save in response to the use of force. It does not follow that other forms of coercion, and particularly those forms which involve the indirect use of force, are thereby permitted. The principal dispute that the provisions of the Charter have occasioned it not as to whether these forms of coercion are forbidden to states but as to whether they may be responded to by the overt employment of force. At the same time, it must be admitted that the effectiveness of the norms forbidding states from resorting to acts of indirect aggression and subversion is largely dependent upon the sanctions that may be legitimately employed in response to such acts. To the extent that the legitimacy of employing force directly is held to be conditioned by the requirement of a direct armed attack, the effectiveness of the norms forbidding indirect aggression and subversion must decline.

If one condition of an agreement on partial disarmament is a prior agreement upon additional rules of international conduct, these rules must either reaffirm and clarify existing, though no longer very effective, restraints or they must impose new restraints. It is difficult to estimate the degree to which insistence upon these additional rules would impede the prospects for achieving an agreement on partial disarmament, but it is scarcely open to question that the prospects of partial disarmament would be seriously impeded. There is no reason to assume that the attempt to reach agreement on these rules would prove any easier than the abortive attempts to reach agreement on what constitutes aggression. The same considerations that have prevented agreement on a definition of aggression can be expected to frustrate agreement on the rules of international conduct to attend partial disarmament. Whether the attempt is made to render more precise present restraints on state conduct or to devise novel restraints, the inevitable result must be to lay bare the nerve root of present-day antagonisms.

Moreover, it should be kept in mind that even if the parties to a partial disarmament agreement were able to agree upon additional rules of international conduct these rules would still be interpreted and applied by the interested parties. We cannot assume that an agreement on partial disarmament will be attended by the creation of central institutions that will possess the competence to interpret, apply, and enforce these rules. Partial disarmament will not constitute a departure from the present international system. On the contrary, it evidently presupposes the continuance of this system. It may, of course, be argued that if the rules of the disarmament agreement are given precise and detailed form, a deterrent of sorts may be erected against forms of intervention that do not presently exist. Guidance may thereby be afforded states—and the appropriate organs of the United Nations—that they do not presently possess. Against this argument, however, must be set the consideration that the difficulty of reaching agreement on additional rules of international conduct will be proportionate to the attempt to articulate these rules in any detail and with any precision. The same consideration must be set against the position that abrogation of a partial disarmament agreement will be made easier if there are relatively clear and detailed rules of conduct the violation of which may be readily ascertained.[55] And quite apart from the imposing obstacles in the way of reaching agreement on such clear and detailed rules, it may be doubted whether the presence of these rules would appreciably facilitate the task of justifying before world opinion the abrogation of the disarmament agreement.[56]

[55] The above passage in the text assumes that the principal sanction to be invoked against violations of such rules of conduct as are made an integral part of a disarmament agreement will be the abrogation of the agreement. There is no reason to assume that states would reverse the evolution discussed in preceding pages and legitimize the use of force as a sanction against the violation of these rules.

[56] Past experience does not afford much ground for optimism here. In recent years, the ineffectiveness and confusion of public opinion when reacting to indirect aggression and subversion has become a commonplace. The reason for this ineffectiveness and confusion, however, is often obscured. Thus one recent writer attributes this confusion to the absence of "recognized principles to help maintain objective standards," and declares

It does not follow from these considerations that a partial disarmament agreement can be kept or should be kept if the parties to it fail to observe certain restraints. What does follow is that to insist upon defining these restraints as a condition for entering into a partial disarmament agreement is to pose an unnecessary obstacle to partial disarmament. If it is once acknowledged that a partially disarmed world would still resemble the present world in all essential respects, there is no reason to expect that the forces prompting indirect forms of intervention in the present world will not continue to be operative in a partially disarmed world. The answer to the question of whether this nation should enter into an agreement providing for partial disarmament ought not to be conditioned by prior agreement on rules of international conduct defining and prohibiting indirect aggression and subversion. Even if it did prove possible to reach an agreement of sorts on these rules, given the international system in which they must be expected to operate, it would be folly to obtain them at the price of sacrificing or even diminishing any relative balance of military capabilities. To say this is not to rule out the prospect of partial disarmament; it is merely to say that the desirability and the viability of such an agreement should not be tied to a code of behavior on which we have little reason to expect states to agree and which we have still less reason to expect them to observe.

---

that "where no clear principles are recognized assessment [of aggression] will tend to be swayed by ideological or national predilections" (Evan Luard, *Peace and Opinion* [London: Oxford University Press, 1962], pp. 53–55). Yet it is precisely these disparate and conflicting predilections that must account for the absence of clear and recognized principles to help maintain objective standards. Without these predilections, which reflect the profound divisions in world public opinion, there would be little difficulty either in achieving reasonably clear principles or in maintaining objective standards of judgment. No doubt, there are instances of alleged aggression sufficiently ambiguous to confuse, and to divide, an otherwise united public opinion. But the real difficulty is obscured by putting the matter in this way. Luard assumes a latent consensus on "aggression" that stands only in need of the proper instruments—and above all clarification—in order to express itself. Experience indicates, however, that this consensus simply does not exist. There is no conceivable rule—or rules—that will unite public opinion in alleged cases of indirect aggression and subversion, regardless of whether these cases involve Cuba, Algeria, Angola, or Vietnam.

6.

CHARACTER AND MISSION OF A UNITED NATIONS PEACE FORCE

Charles Burton Marshall

The Project in Broad Compass

A PRINCIPAL ELEMENT of the United States government's conception of general and complete disarmament pertains to establishment and development of a force not identified with any national governing entity, subject to control by an all-embracing international collectivity, and charged with missions of global scope in connection with peacekeeping. The purpose of this essay is to examine what might be entailed, as conditions and as consequences, in establishing such a force. The discussion focuses quite explicitly on terms in the *Outline.* Other sources, including proposals and discussions of forces of a kindred type, are referred to for details concerning conceivable forms and conditions for the undertaking.

As set forth in the *Outline,* such a force would be brought into existence over a span of years. The process of realizing it would be linked, stage by stage, with a progressive diminution of all forces under national control. At a transforming juncture, national forces would have been scaled down to a level at which their projection of any threat beyond the borders of their respective domains would be rendered impossible. Concomitantly, the global force would be increased to such a level as to place it beyond effective challenge by any other force existing. The course would not be one of simply doing away with forces capable of deployment over a wide range. It would involve an amalgam of such forces into an all-encompassing monopoly—a coercive institution of scope and relative, if not absolute, power heretofore never achieved.

The lines of development would be essentially interdependent. The final step in reducing nationally controlled forces to a level commensurate with internal security requirements would be contingent upon a solid and immediate prospect of achievement of an efficacious global force. Fulfillment of the design for the global force, moreover, would be dependent upon diminution of nationally controlled forces.

A question, necessarily hypothetical, is in order concerning the appropriateness for their respective missions of the world peace force and of forces to be permitted under national control. The criteria in the *Outline* are limited to quantitative and technical considerations expressed in highly general terms. With respect to the world peace force, the key words in the *Outline* are: "sufficient armed forces and armaments that no state could challenge it" and "equipped with agreed types of armaments necessary to ensure that the United Nations can effectively deter any threat or use of arms."[1] The counterpart terms in the *Outline* regarding the forces that states are permitted to retain under their own direction are "agreed requirements for nonnuclear armaments of agreed types for national forces required to maintain internal order and protect the personal security of citizens." States would be required to disband "organizational arrangements comprising and supporting their national military establishment."[2]

Relevant qualities in each instance are simply postulated. Their feasibility and ascertainability are assumed. The terms necessary for fulfillment are left to be worked out by international accord. For the moment, questions of the adequacy of a purely quantifying and technical expression of attributes may be passed over, along with questions regarding the practicability,

[1] *Outline,* Stage III, H, 3; A. Objectives, 4.
[2] *Ibid.,* B, 1.

probability, or even desirability of the relevant contemplated developments. The focus here is on the broad missions of the force and its presumable character in the light of its missions and on the requirements and consequences inferrible from its missions and character.

A mission accorded the projected peace force with respect to maintenance of order and security among states, as explicitly expressed in the *Outline,* would be enormously inclusive and complex. In addition, however, the force would have duties to perform with respect to security within component states. Because this aspect of the matter is only implicitly indicated in the project, and because it is fundamental to comprehension of the idea of the peace force, elucidation is called for. To that purpose, it is necessary to make clear the transformation of the character of states envisaged in the project.

The Transformation of States

A decision to move into and past the transforming stage would involve both resolution of will and ascertainment of fact on the part of governments concerned acting in their single discretion but also as a group. A number of antecedent choices would have to have been made, and relevant actions taken, to take the course to that decisive stage.

Rather than speculating upon procedure, the purpose here is to examine the sorts of questions likely to require answer at the seat of judgment. As a precondition to the final step, or, more accurately, as a constituent part of it, the governments would have to register themselves as satisfied on two interrelated propositions: first, a solid and immediate prospect of the scaling down of forces retained under individual state control, case by case, to a level that would provide no surplus over requirements for domestic security; second, a concomitant transfer of overwhelming superiority to the world peace force. Clearly—and this point requires no argument—the determination would be both subjective and objective: the governments' wills would be resolved in response to their appraisal of relevant realities, but the relevant realities would in major part flow from their combined wills.

For the moment, the focus is on the first of the two propositions. The forces permitted to retain national identity and to be at the disposition of individual governments would be limited to agreed requirements and would be of agreed types, with the referent apropos of requirements and types to be the function of maintaining internal order and protecting the security of citizens. Capability for sustaining the internal security of states would have been removed from the autonomous jurisdiction of states.

One might speculate on a possibility of *pro forma* ascertainment, with each government's estimate of its own requirements and its related inventory of equipment and related manpower to be accepted as conclusive by the others. The supposition does not withstand analysis. Fulfillment of the paramountcy accorded the central forces would be measurable only in relation to capabilities to be retained by states individually or cumulatively.

As an auxiliary postulate, however, one might premise the irresistibility of the universal force by assuming it to have been vested with a monopoly of prodigious instruments such as nuclear weapons, thereby rendering uncritical the amounts of weapons of less destructive efficacy and the related trained manpower to be retained by individual states. This line of argument requires overlooking the reference to agreed requirements and to provisions in the project calling for states to disband "organizational arrangements comprising and supporting their national military establishment." It requires one to hypothesize huge improvidence on the part of the participating governments in creating a world security force capable of effective action only at highest levels of destruction—a characteristic far more likely to inhibit authorized use of the force than to intimidate potential challengers.

One might speculate also on a possibility of limiting the term of general concern in retained security capabilities to the moment of decision, after which the matter would revert to the autonomous jurisdiction of the respective states. This notion of lifting internal security requirements of states to the center of world concern only for a moment and then permitting them to subside immediately into concerns for each state to settle in its own way also fails of credibility. Factors simply do not shift so arbitrarily from importance to indifference.

The inference is clear. Limitation upon internal security capabilities to an agreed level of requirements would be a continuing and integral part of the pattern of general obligation in the disarmament undertaking. Establishment of that level, case by case, would be a matter for international authority not just initially and once but thenceforth and continuously. The limitation would be part of a contract underlying a global governing apparatus. Confinement within those limits would be an essential aspect of adherence to the whole scheme and subject, therefore, to the process of verification and enforcement underlying the disarmament program as a whole. Any question of upward revision of restriction settled on at the outset would be international business on a par with the question of setting limits in the first instance.

The constituent states would have yielded their autonomy with respect to allocation of resources as between the uses of civil enjoyment and provision for coercion. The autonomy thus surrendered would relate not only to power to decide, within the limits of the resources available, upon provision of forces for launching or repelling attack as counters in relations with other states but would extend as well to the discretion of any government as to requirements for maintaining the internal regime.

The point is basic and highly important—it is one deserving to be acknowledged for what it is rather than minimized euphemistically. The implications are made clearer by taking into account the nature of internal security requirements, which are implicitly predicated as fixed and predictable in the United States disarmament project but which are in reality elastic and unpredictable.

Predictability and Internal Order

How far ahead could the internal security requirements of any particular political society be divined? The question is not disposed of by postulating the efficacy of international arrangements for interdicting all factors playing upon such a society from beyond its borders. That sweeping assumption is scarcely demonstrable at best, but in order to forward the argument here, relevant doubts may be discounted. An array of imponderables would still remain.

To place the matter in perspective, it is in point to take account of the meanings of the key term "internal order" used in connection with standards and limits predicated for forces to be retained under the control of individual states. The phrase implies reliable conditions in human relations throughout the country concerned—a sense conveyed in an auxiliary phrase about "the personal security of citizens." Beyond that sense, the term embraces the idea of continuity of regime. Order may be said to obtain within a civil society when succession to places of authority is reliably controlled by rules, rather than subject to determination by forcible means. In an ordered society, those holding title to power would be enabled, as well as constrained, to convey that power to successors determined under the same basic licit arrangements by which the holders in their turn received it.

Those holding high magisterial positions under any orderly system of governance, moreover, must take heed of questions of continuity and descent. Faculties for deciding on allocation of means to ensure continuity of the system itself are an integral element in any governing system, a necessary constituent of the power to lay down the law. Divested of power to assure the means of survival, a system of government would lose a main prop of authority—an element of internal sovereignty, to use an overworked abstraction.

These observations do not imply a possibility of an absolute guarantee of survival for a system of government. Perhaps no regime could ever close off all possibilities, at least logical possibilities, of being overthrown by revolt or revolution. Nevertheless, the concept of order—and this is the main point—entails a licit and reliable descent of authority, as distinguished from violent disjunctions and overturns in the system of rulership.

Whether with respect to order in the sense of assurance of the personal security of persons or in the sense of assured continuity of the system of government, internal security requirements, stated in amounts or types, vary in relation to the mores prevailing within a society. They vary in relation to factors of urban concentration and rural dispersion. They vary in relation, moreover, to factors of identity and confidence operative between a regime and its populace. They are affected by degrees of confidence assumed by regimes, or accorded by their populaces, with respect to their legitimacy. They vary between circumstances of political tension and oppression and those of free consensus. They vary in relation to stress or contentment with respect to conditions of production and distribution, social unrest or placidity, and in relation to factors of ethnic and cultural homogeneity or diversity and circumstances of disturbance or adjustment among ethnic groups. They are affected by factors of morale and competence within the security forces themselves. All these considerations—and many others of indisputable relevance—may be summed up as inherent and persistent variables in any political society. The point requires no labored argument. One needs only to ask himself about the validity of a ten-year projection of internal security requirements for the United States drawn up, say, in the year 1855.

Variability of internal security requirements leads logically to a consideration of the role of military establishments in regard to internal security, the implications of abolishing such establishments under national control, and the bearing of the topic on the mission of the projected United Nations peace force.

Division of Functions Regarding Internal Order

This facet of the subject entails a recital of some elementary, even obvious, points concerning organization of coercion in relation to maintenance of order and statehood. The delineation is necessarily highly generalized, focusing on essences rather than details and eliding empirical distinctions between unitary and federal systems and among states of varying degrees of civic development in the contemporary world.

A basic division of functions with respect to the apparatus of coercion is generally characteristic of advanced states. The origins trace back to a stage of development when groups first settled down in permanent identification with delimited portions of the earth's surface and used them as sites for accumulating goods and established fixed habitations and passed them along from one generation to another. The concept of "state"—as suggested by its "static" implication—is rooted in the idea of fixed position. It represents the established order within an area, with diversity beyond the perimeter.

Basically, the relevant division of function lies between the establishment of a span of jurisdiction and control on the one hand and the exercise of control or jurisdiction within the established span on the other: between external security and internal security. These are distinguishable but not absolutely separable functions.

Military functions pertain to establishment of spans of control. They are concerned with securing, in the first instance, dominion over land or water, as the case might be, and in modern circumstances over air space as well; with holding perimeters against other forces competing for access to or mastery over all or part of the range concerned; and with expanding perimeters as opportune or necessary under the spur of ambition, advantage, or survival.

In our nomenclature, the generic term with respect to enforcing order within an established span of jurisdiction is "police"— derived, obviously, from the Greek term for "city," reflecting the institution known as the Greek city state, and cognate with such terms as "polish," "politics," "polity," and the like, associated with the handling of general affairs among a people living in proximity, interdependent, highly involved in each other's existence, and needing a pervasive and constantly operative scheme of order to administer the conditions of their common life.

Military and police institutions share many characteristics, some of them superficial only. Each type is customarily called a force, a term denoting coercion, directed energy, and a body of men prepared for action. Their specialty centers on weapons and their use. Uniform dress and distinguishing emblems to differentiate members from the general run of people are a normal requirement on duty. Each such institution—certainly, at least, in a constitutional order—is under rigorous restrictions regarding the occasions and purposes for bringing its specialty to bear in action. Their structures are tightly hierarchic. Each is more highly organized than other institutions of society in general.

Yet contrasting characteristics are also relevant. The rigor of organization and authority is generally more pervasive within a military establishment. Systems of tutelage and internal surveillance are more highly developed. Autonomous standards of privilege and courtesy are particular traits. Military organizations have separate codes of rules enforceable through an autonomous system of adjudication and punishment effected by magisterial systems of their own. Prerogative to deploy elements in what has been called systematic nomadism is part of the scheme of authority in the usual case. The obligation of service between a member and the military establishment is dissolvable only at the state's consent; that is, a member cannot quit at his option but must be absolved from duty. Such are the characteristics distinguishing a military establishment as a sort of state within a state.[3]

A police establishment is committed to its mission continuously. At all times it is deployed and operating within its assigned area. It acts on a basis of delegated discretion. Its activities on behalf of internal order, therefore, may be said to be of an administrative character. A military establishment represents, in contrast, a latent power under normal circumstances. Its mission is reserved. A military establishment exists in some degree of readiness, but it is not in action with respect to its mission except under extraordinary circumstances. Then it takes the field not on a basis of delegated discretion but properly in response to a specific com-

[3] S. E. Finer, *The Man on Horseback* (New York: Praeger, 1962), pp. 6–13.

mand or authorization representing an exercise of prerogative basic and central to the existence and maintenance of a state.

The prerogative to call military forces into action has to do not only with levying war against external enemies but also with maintenance of a state's span of jurisdiction against internal challenge as well. Military forces are a part, even if normally an abeyant part, of the internal security arrangements of a state. Police forces are calculated to be able to cope with predictable challenges to internal security. Military forces are a reserve capability for use when a challenge exceeds the capabilities of police establishments, whether because of some extraordinarily formidable character in the challenge or because of some factor of disaffection within the police apparatus. The concept here invoked is not merely theoretical. In an instance still fresh in American national experience, a thousand score of troops were called out to enforce the right of one individual to attend a university.

Thus one of the potentials for maintaining order within a state is military power. Disorder within a state's span of jurisdiction may take on proportions that challenge the integrity and continuity of the state's existence. In such an extremity, the relevance of military power to the maintenance of internal order becomes patent. Even in normal times, when military power is only an abeyant factor, the fact of its existence and the prospect of its availability in an exigency are a presumable, if incalculable, factor in support of internal security.

Discussion on the point here has been directed to the role of military power within political systems characterized by a high level of institutional development. In contrasting cases, military establishments are often dominant factors rather than subordinate elements in patterns of rulership. In some extreme instances (recent events in various African states come readily to mind) unbridled military establishments may even be an aggravating factor in discontinuity and disorder. In others, a degree of corporateness and effectiveness within the military apparatus may supply the principal and virtually the only basis for holding a so-called nation together. Such phenomena do not offset the main argument here concerning the basic role of military power within autonomous states.

The project for abolishing military capabilities of states thus has deep implications for their existence and for the character of authority within them. The prerogative to interpose forces in exigency beyond those forces provided in the police establishment for coping with challenges to internal security would pass from the hands of state authority and be vested in an organ external to each state.

Limitation of forces under control of any state to internal security requirements might be so construed as to permit each government to maintain armed bodies in some modest excess of constant requirements as a means for coping with emergencies. Some such thought is reflected in the *Outline*. This approach would raise a question of how to prevent use of such forces to threaten the security of neighboring areas. Neighboring areas, too, might have, as counters to such threats, forces of their own in excess of calculable internal security needs. This line of thought would tend to perpetuate in some degree the relationship which the *Outline* would seek to transform. Such a problem and the related necessity of dealing with it appear to have been anticipated in the *Outline*, which apparently envisages a system of continuous surveillance and reporting on positioning and operations of internal security forces.[4] The point supports a conclu-

---

[4] This conclusion is warranted by a careful reading. Indeed, no alternative interpretation seems adducible. After completion of disarmament, "The Parties . . . would apply to national forces required to maintain internal order and protect the personal security of citizens those applicable measures concerning the reduction of the risk of war that had been applied to national armed forces in Stages I and II" (*Outline*, Stage III, F, 2). Moreover, the International Disarmament Organization "would be strengthened . . . to ensure its capacity . . . to verify. . . ." This strengthening would be accomplished through extension of arrangements given in *ibid.*, G. Relevant provisions for Stage II simply refer to "extending and improving the measures undertaken in Stage I . . ." (*ibid.*, Stage II, E). Hence it is necessary here to refer only to Stage I. The measures are expressed as follows:

Specified Parties to the Treaty would give advance notification of major military movements and maneuvers to other Parties to the Treaty and to the International Disarmament Organization. Specific arrangements

sion concerning the subordination of internal security to international jurisdiction.

The basic intention would be to eliminate national forces in excess of the requirements for internal order, which are assumed to be predictable and passed upon by international authority. In the event of exigencies requiring forces in excess of allowed levels to cope with internal violence and threats to public order, each state would be left in the position of a petitioner for assistance from a source beyond its own control. Those having a determinative voice in withholding or making available such assistance from outside would be cast in the role of the ultimate arbiters of order within each state. The forces from outside, if made available, would operate under a chain of command external to the state concerned. The doctrine under which the force would operate would presumably be beyond determination by the state affected. The same would be true of personnel constituting the outside force.

It is fitting now to take account of some of the considerations relevant to establishing and maintaining such a force as envisaged.

---

relating to this commitment, including the scale of movements and maneuvers to be reported and the information to be transmitted, would be agreed. [Moreover,] Specified Parties to the Treaty would permit observation posts to be established at agreed locations, including major ports, railway centers, motor highways, river crossings, and air bases to report on concentrations and movements of military forces. The number of such posts could be progressively expanded in each successive step of Stage I. Specific arrangements relating to such observation posts, including the location and staffing of posts, the methods of receiving and reporting information, and the schedule for installation of posts would be agreed.   (*Ibid.*, Stage I, F, 1, 2.)

The *Outline* says further, in relation to Stage I: "Assurance that agreed levels of armaments and armed forces were not exceeded and that activities limited or prohibited by the Treaty were not being conducted clandestinely would be provided by the International Disarmament Organization through agreed arrangements which would have the effect of providing that the extent of inspection during any step or stage would be related to the amount of disarmament being undertaken and to the degree of risk to the Parties to the Treaty of possible violations . . ." (*ibid.*, G, 2, c).

Material Bases of the Projected Peace Force

Constituent governments acting to create a new framework of force would presumably have to be convinced in high degree of its prospective reliability before divesting themselves of control of military forces of their own and subordinating themselves to the new arrangement. A condition of the reliability of the new arrangement would be the good faith of all significant parties in subordinating themselves. The problems posed by interdependency between these two considerations are not logically more difficult than those involved in any proposition of forming a new frame of government by contract. The essential thing here is to recognize the process as that of forming a world state of sorts.

The matter of reliability of the new arrangement would include, apart from assurances against the likelihood of misuse of the peace force, assurances of the force's capability and disposition to meet its responsibilities. By a proviso "that no state could challenge it," the *Outline* predicates an overwhelmingly effective force, but the only index to its efficacy—a phrase regarding "sufficient forces and armaments"—is a quantitative and technical description reflecting what has been aptly characterized as a typical civilian fallacy in measuring military strength.[5] In all probability, the technical and quantitative aspects of putting such a force together would be the simplest part of the process—though its simplicity would only be relative to the difficulties of the rest.

The force would require mobility and technical proficiency of the highest order and would have to be immediately available when summoned to action to meet manifold and far-ranging responsibilities. It would necessarily be a fighting force capable of exerting coercive power with overwhelming effect—that is, to a degree calculated to prevail—at any level of armed activity against whatever adversaries it might be called upon to meet in

[5] Frederick Martin Stern, *The Citizen Army* (New York: St. Martin's, 1957), p. 4.

any environment whatever.[6] It would have to be, in sum, a sophisticated, versatile, multifarious force. Besides requiring at operating levels great subtleties of doctrine and an extraordinary degree of corporate identity and morale, it would need at staff levels a mastery of higher logistics and a huge proficiency in military and industrial mobilization. The matter of industrial and technical underpinnings for such a force is especially important. In this respect, the *Outline* affords small illumination, presenting not so much a formula as an invitation to governments to attempt a formula. Implicitly, however, it points to an intricate question of how to begin.

The requirements indicated, in connection with the reduction of force levels to internal security requirements, include action by participating governments "to cause to be disbanded organizational arrangements comprising and supporting their national military establishment, and terminate the employment of civilian personnel associated with the foregoing," dismantlement or conversion to peaceful uses of bases and facilities beyond those permitted to be retained for internal security purposes, and closure of all military research, development, production, and testing except as permitted by international agreement for purposes of maintaining internal security.[7]

Obviously, however, lore and technology relevant to military matters are in the hands of national governments. The international collectivity could scarcely start from scratch in fashioning

[6] This point seems adequately clear, notwithstanding a tendency among some to meet questions of how to fit United Nations contingents for unmeasured responsibilities by imagining the problem of force to have been obviated and the way thus opened for immaculate order. For example, one such writer predicates such a moral authority for the United Nations as to enable a force under its aegis to prevail by symbols—its efficacy in its arm bands rather than its arms (see William P. Frye, *A United Nations Peace Force* [New York: Oceana, 1957], p. 91). The context shows this idea to have been a generalization overdrawn from the single case of the United Nations Emergency Force interposed between Israel and Egypt. Assumptions of a world so transformed, whether or not deserving of systematic rebuttal, are certainly beyond its reach.

[7] *Outline*, Stage III, B, 1, 2.

a military mechanism of the limitless scope and supreme proficiency intended. It would fall to participants to contribute to
aggrandizement of the force. Presumably, although this is not
explicit in the *Outline*, the process would have to be that of
conveyance, by the participants to the world collectivity, of
ownership, control, and operation of considerable portions of
their domains, their concentrations of relevant professional
talents, and their scientific and industrial complexes. At least,
this would be incumbent upon participants having such endow-
ments. The new military collectivity would have to have something to draw upon. It is scarcely plausible for nations at once
to extirpate military resources and to proliferate military strength
in combination.[8]

Something equivalent to a global defense ministry would have
to be founded, since retention of such agencies by individual
states would be forbidden. Implicitly, the establishment would
include a multifarious staff system of its own, research and development systems, access to and control of patents and manufactur-
ing systems, contractive powers, procurement processes, systems
for settling accounts, and the like, along with cantonments, training ranges, aviation complexes, depot systems, transport arteries,
port facilities, and vessels of its own or enforceable accesses to
them, and many other such properties of a cogent military capability. All of these would necessarily be operative within and

[8] A quite different set of hypotheses is employed, however, in one relevant work. The portion of nationals permissible from any one state would
be limited to 3 per cent of the force. Nationals of the twelve most populous
states—namely, China, the Soviet Union, India, the United States, Indonesia, Pakistan, Germany, Brazil, the United Kingdom, France, Nigeria,
Japan, and Italy—would be barred from service in the top command. Bas-
ing of any portion of the force in the aforementioned countries would be
forbidden. Implicitly, these provisions would amount to a wholesale re-
alignment of military capability. Militarily significant and resourceful areas
would be ordained to become militarily insignificant, and vice versa. No
empirical evidence to support the practicability of the proposal is adduced,
however (Grenville Clark and Louis B. Sohn, *World Peace through World
Law* [2d ed.; Cambridge, Mass.: Harvard, 1960], pp. xxix–xxxii).

located within the territory of presently independent states.[9] They would have to be exempt from interference by such states. Otherwise, obviously, the apparatus would be subject to impediment and interruption. Its efficacy would not then be a calculable surety. The force would lack the measure of absolute reliability postulated as a central characteristic.[10]

Tracing out the ramifications, one sees clearly, in general conformation if not explicitly in detail, the outlines of a world government. The point may be elaborated by considering, in addition to quantitative and technical aspects of the projected peace force, the more subtle requirements in terms of men to compose the force.

Manpower and Command in a Global Peace Force

Planning for a global peace force adequate for its manifold duties, while at the same time amenable to control by some collective authority, must entail appreciation of the nature of command and its interrelation with the character of the force commanded. Not a great deal on the subject is available in the

[9] Again, note should be taken of a proposal (*ibid.*, p. xxx) for locating "main bases . . . on easily defensible islands or peninsulas." The proposal has been elaborated with a suggestion of Trinidad, Madeira, Iceland, Malta, Cyprus, Zanzibar, and Ceylon as locations (Louis B. Sohn, in Arthur B. Larson [ed.], *A Warless World* [New York: McGraw-Hill, 1963], p. 5). Reasons for such anxiety about security in positioning a force supposed to be inherently paramount do not need to be speculated upon here. The main point of doubt concerns something else. A world peace force, if realized, would be a central reality, not a marginal and abeyant one. Of far greater apparent practicality—if such a quality may be invoked in respect of so hypothetical an exercise—is the idea of deliberately positioning such a peace force within the large industrial countries. See Thomas C. Shelling in Bloomfield, *op. cit.*, p. 227.

[10] On reading this part of the manuscript, some persons have suggested, as an alternative possibility, retention by various states of facilities essential to the material underpinnings of the global peace force, subject to an obligation to limit operations to those authorized and directed by the world collectivity. The idea amounts to a distinction without a real difference. Agency is not equatable with autonomy. In any event, the contemplated peace force is to be beyond challenge by any state. Implicitly this would mean placing it beyond possibility of being hamstrung by any state's withholding facilities.

general literature on the idea of a world peace force. For the most part, the writing is characterized by expansiveness of imagination amounting to romance, as anyone with appreciable military experience and some grasp of factors of diversity in the world would note. A sort of omnicompetence for governments and their negotiators is predicated. Cultural factors would become completely malleable on a premise of an absolutely new day in world affairs, and statesmen would be enabled to perform prodigies of combination heretofore unachievable. Heterogeneity would fall into ranks, and a homogeneous force would thereupon be ready to march. Ethnic antipathies and factors of diversity respecting language, nutritional habits, religious practices, and innumerable taboos would fade into inconsequentiality. Deficiencies in talent would somehow be redressed. Thus men from primitive societies would be fitted to constitute and to operate a complex, versatile, modernized force fit to serve in any climate and amid populations of any cultural level. The maximum admixture of ethnic and lingual groups in ranks and even alienism between officers and men would be cultivated as positive bases for morale rather than as conditions for chaos. Men would assign years of their lives to rotation among remote garrisons.

Such suppositions and propositions, drawn from the literature of disarmament, reflect what has been already described as a typical civilian fallacy of regarding military organizations in technical terms only.[11] This outlook, preoccupied with categories

[11] It seems pointless to churn at length through ideas contained in the largely fantastical literature on the subject. Essays of Schelling and Henry V. Dicks, respectively (*ibid.*, pp. 212–56), are of some considerable value, however, as endeavors to come to terms with problems inherent in such an undertaking. They avoid the fallacy of assuming that the world and all factors relevant to creating such a force can be made over to suit statesmen's designs. In contrast, little of relevant value appears in Clark and Sohn, *World Peace through World Law.* The work is interesting chiefly as an illustration of what has been called the civilian fallacy. This sort of fallacy has been aptly described by an authority in Gestalt psychology. From structural similarities between one heart and another, it construes a community among hearts and overlooks the ties functionally binding a heart to a pair of lungs in a relationship infinitely closer than any conceivable one between one heart and another (Wolfgang Köhler, *Gestalt Psychology* [New York: Liveright, 1929], p. 351, cited by Robert S. Lynd, *Knowledge for What?* [Princeton: Princeton University Press, 1948], p. 12).

rather than functional realities and noting structural parallels between one national force and another, construes military life as a genus of culture and imagines unlimited possibilities of combination. Components are treated as fungible, like mechanical parts. By this line of thought, a peace force would be susceptible of assemblage from components of national forces according to whatever design statesmen might determine. A force could be made multinational in whatever degree matched the authors' desires.

Such exercises in imagination have small bearing on practical problems. Planners for a world peace force could surely count on no exemption from the requirements relevant to the human equation that would be inherent in setting up a cogent military body. To assume such exemption would be equivalent to planning a ship in disregard of factors of seaworthiness.

Some guidance for such planners is provided by the *Outline*. The document calls for examination anew of the feasibility of giving effect to Article 43 of the Charter. A stipulation for the new force to "be supplied agreed manpower by states" might be construed as a scheme both to prorate participation and to authorize conscription for the purpose envisaged.[12] The language might accommodate preservation of symbolic national identities of troops, but it would be consistent also with conglomerate forces. The point is relatively inconsequential. The peace force is clearly anticipated as one inclusive apparatus. National command structures would be things of the past. Organization, support, and tempering of the force would be international business.

As a point for emphasis, the endeavor to create a force on such a motif of admixture, should it ever materialize, would be a departure from experience. No certain precedent indicating feasibility is adducible. Forces operating under the United Nations or, in earlier times, the League of Nations have not been in such a pattern but have consisted rather of temporarily and contingently

[12] This last interpretation is consistent with a ban on conscription expressed elsewhere in the *Outline*: "The parties . . . would halt all military conscription . . . inconsistent with the foregoing measures," which include the provision regarding supply of agreed manpower for the peace force (*Outline*, Stage III, B, 3).

assigned units of national military establishments. The French Foreign Legion is sometimes cited as a model, but the instance proves inapposite when examined in detail.[13]

The problem is put in better proportion by including among criteria of reliability such considerations as identity, common doctrine and motivation, and amenability to command and control, in addition to the relatively easy factors of magnitude and technical adequacy. One must see a way through these problems before being justified in any appreciable degree of confidence in the practicability of the whole idea of a global peace force. Without a plausible formula for bringing governments into concord on such sensitive and basic considerations, one could scarcely be said to have even the beginning of a plan.

Faculties of command respecting a military apparatus concern both the chain of authority within and the system of guidance and control exterior to and above it. The interlaced functions of command are broadly four: first, determination of doctrine underlying and motivating the force, its character as a social entity, and traits to be cultivated through control of members' careers; second—and closely related—the magisterial function of judging and punishing derelictions; third, choice of weapon systems and

[13] The French Foreign Legion as an example might have seemed more persuasive before the French government's decision in 1961 to disband its paratrooper battalions because of their recalcitrance and potential for mutiny. In any event, the Foreign Legion is a *French* Foreign Legion. The members are subject to French indoctrination and authority, serve on missions ordained by the French government, and use French as their operational language. Company officers are largely French and senior officers entirely so. Some Frenchmen serve in ranks. The rest are drawn mainly from European cultures somewhat assimilated to the French. Alien members usually serve in expectation of receiving French nationality upon completion of service. All are judged and rewarded or punished according to standards authorized by the French government. Discipline, however, emphasizes rigorous punishment for strictly military infractions but is indulgent with respect to social offenses, as would be usual in a service based on a mercenary principle—that is, without a high degree of identity between the outfit and the frame of authority. Withal, desertions have been a perennial problem, as gang tendencies also have been. The Legion's suitability is limited to duties in marginal areas with high incidence of combat rather than to routine duties in metropolitan areas (see Adrian Liddell Hart, *Strange Company* [London: Weidenfeld & Nicolson, 1953], *passim*).

inculcation of proficiency in them, conceived in relation to putative missions; fourth, competence to decide upon and to effect
deployments in actual operations. The first two aspects—characteristically taken for granted or summarily dealt with in projects
for universal forces—are foundations of accomplishment with
respect to the other two.

A fundamental aspect concerns the moral basis of the faculty
of command. To a superficial view, obedience flows from establishment of a command framework: create authority, and compliance will follow in consequence. This approach involves a
simplification amounting to distortion. Command authority is in
essence a grant from those subject to it. Command conceived of
as a product of obedience comes closer to basic truth than a statement putting the relationship vice versa.[14]

A second key aspect concerns the cultural base of a military
organization's responses.[15] This base is linked integrally to the
concept of reliability. Reliability standing alone conveys little.
The term requires a referent: reliability with respect to what? To
be reliable, a force must have unity of character—a unity reflecting a common doctrine, reflecting agreement about values. The
range of possible moral and cultural bases for creating an effective force are wide, but no universal base—no generally accepted

[14] Chester Barnard, *The Functions of the Executive* (Cambridge, Mass.:
Harvard, 1938), pp. 163–64. Also James G. Harbord, *The American Army
in France* (Boston: Little, Brown, 1936), p. 259. Military annals are replete
with instances of units rendered actively mutinous or passively unresponsive,
whereupon power of command was left intact.

[15] "Military institutions are intimately bound up with the state of culture
which the nation has obtained," in the words of Rudiger von der Goltz
(quoted by Hoffman Nickerson, *The Armed Horde* [New York: Putnam,
1939], p. 3). Literature constituting what might be called a sociology of
military organization is not abundant. Stern (*The Citizen Army*), Nickerson
(*Armed Horde*) and Alfred Vagts (*A History of Militarism* [New York: Macmillan, 1959]) are useful, however. Two relevant points emerge from a
perusal of such works: the basic and complex social character of military
organization in contrast to the relatively simple technical aspect; the fallacy
of thinking of military culture as a culture *per se* rather than as an aspect
of culture normally related to a national base. Niccolo Machiavelli's insights
into the national basis of military morale, though brief, are incisive (see his
Discourses [New York: Random House, 1940], i. 42).

ethic of authority, responsibility, and the like—exists to be invoked as a basis for a world peace force. Such an ethic would have to be agreed upon and given reality as a motivating body of ideas as a precondition to creating a structure of command and control. Because of its importance, this simple point deserves elaboration.

An Underlying Ethic for a Global Force

It is accurate but inadequate to conceive of a force as a body of men organized and equipped to bring destructive energy to bear against designated adversaries upon the proper command. A force is not a collection of depersonalized entities. A force, moreover, should be thought of as spending the larger part of its existence under peaceable conditions, rather than in hostile operations. The problem of relation to environment mostly concerns pacific environment. The members represent some pattern of identities and associations. In the usual case, a member has affective ties with some place inhabited by his own kind—a place in whose security against enemies he is personally involved.

Peaceable associations, sense of identity, and affective connections are basic to the assumptions, responses, and motivations underlying the character and effectiveness of a force. These characteristics vary in detail and strength from one member to another. In the degree of their existence and likeness, however, as between one member and another, they afford some basis for essential community. They do not account for all constituent traits of a force. Many other intertwined factors enter into determining a force's character, meaning the sum of what it can be relied upon to do or not to do: such matters as indoctrination, development of common habits and general proficiency by training, cumulative common experience as a group, systems of preferment and promotion, qualities of administered justice, standards of leadership, and the moral basis of authority. The sum total of the determinants of a force's character is great and complex, and the sum differs from one culture to another, so that respective armed forces, however much alike from a technical standpoint, are widely variant as social entities. Such moral aspects are basic, and their paramountcy over material factors is recognized in a well-known Napoleonic maxim.

Persons from alien cultures may indeed be assimilated into a force associated with some particular culture. This circumstance does not gainsay the main point: a force cannot be cogently considered apart from a cultural base and an underlying ethic. Outsiders must be assimilated. A force must reflect a character—not a patchwork. Forces may have roots in variant schemes of identity and value. A force must have, and be limited to, one basis: otherwise, it constitutes not a force, but a congeries of forces, not susceptible of being equated against putative missions.

The considerable variations possible may be illustrated by a force, on the one hand, with preponderant attitudes and associations scarcely distinguishable from those characterizing the civil community to which the force relates and, in contrast, a force disassociated from its surroundings, centered on its own existence, and characterized by inward affective connections, so that the outfit becomes a moral equivalent of a homeland, and barracks life becomes the engrossing focus of loyalties. The Swiss army or a force based on the ethic delineated by Frederick Martin Stern in *The Citizen Army* would typify the first. Any force of the Janissary of Praetorian-Guard type could typify the latter.

What the *Outline* contemplates is a force. It would be synthesized from pre-existing forces associated with particular cultures—an assemblage of fragments taken over from disbanded national components. Three, and only three, elements of its binding ethic are made apparent: first, an affirmation of the unconditional heinousness of unauthorized violence; second, as a corollary, the rightness of authorized violence; and third, the repose of relevant authority (meaning the faculty determinative of the difference between violence authorized and violence unauthorized) in some prescribed consensus, as yet undefined, of local representatives in an international collectivity.

For a moment, at whatever cost in effort to suspend disbelief, it is appropriate to hypothesize achievement of a force on the

basis of the ethic stipulated and to ponder its possible effectiveness, whether active or deterrent. The two aspects would be
linked. The deterrent effects would be a product of estimates of
the force's probable efficacy on being called into action.

A decision is made by a requisite majority in the establishment
vested with control of the global peace force. It deems some act,
whether in connection with an international quarrel or a contest
for power within a national domain, to be a malefaction deserving
or requiring interposition of the peace force, designates the malefactors, and summons the force to bring to bear its irresistible
capabilities. The decision is conveyed to the apex of authority
within the confines of the force establishment proper—presumably
some global equivalent of a ministry of defense. Appropriate
orders thence are relayed to the military command apparatus.
The immediate results conceivable fall into two general categories: an effective strike against the designated malefactors, or a
default. The implications of these two broad possibilities deserve
further consideration.

An effective response might reflect either an identification, on
the part of a determining number within the force, with the
requisite majority's view on the merits of the matter at issue
or an unreflecting acceptance of the directive as conclusive *ipso
facto*. The first would not necessarily constitute a precedent for
subsequent compliance under different circumstances. The
second, unreflecting compliance, would *apparently*—with the
emphasis on that qualifier—tend to sustain the frame of authority
unequivocally.

The possible forms of failure to comply, which would signal
the collapse of the ethic and the derogation of the authority,
would be various, for the ways of mutiny are multiple: dissent
and cleavage within the command structure, resulting in a withholding of orders or even a commitment of force to the opposite
side; or divided identities within the force as a whole, rendering
it inert in the particular instance or even sundering it, dividing
its irresistibility into two or more parts, and bringing on an internal struggle for ascendancy. A potential for such developments
would remain in any force with national identities and a lingering

sense for the merits or issues in the command structure or the cadres,[16] and calculations of that potential and of ways of affecting it would become a central consideration in world affairs.

It would be presumptuous to dismiss the possibility, as distinguished from the probability, of achieving a force to suit the prescription and to sustain authority by bringing its overwhelming capabilities to bear unquestioningly. Some may uphold the possibility on a premise of recruiting members with a zeal for universal peace.[17] This is an improbable hope. A force's capability must depend on a fighting *élan*—not a zeal against fighting. Theoretically, however, such a force might be realized in either or both of two ways: by recruitment of individuals free of antecedent loyalties, moved by an urge to identify with paramount power or desirous of opportunity to fight on the overwhelming side without fear of formidable retribution, or by a rigorous method of indoctrination to expunge its members' antecedent loyalties and identities, to inculcate purely reflex responses to mandate, and so to transform personalities as to render members willing to operate even against their erstwhile homelands because a vote has determined them to do so in the name of enforcing peace.

In reason and prudence, a word must be added. One should rule out the assumption of achieving a complete departure from the lessons and limits of experience through international concord on the ethic of a global force. A force of such overwhelming corporate spirit, imbued with absolute obedience, disassociated from the considerations which move others, divorced from cultural ties, and committed to so peculiar an ethic would in all probability be characterized by a high Janissary or Praetorian potential—a potential for developing its own momentum, a potential for passing almost momentarily from subordination to

----

[16] Paul Kecskmeti, "Nuclear Absolutism," *Commentary*, July, 1963, pp. 43, 47.

[17] See for example Dicks, *loc. cit.*, p. 252. The author envisions a force imbued with and motivated by zeal for peace. He suggests the Churkas and the French Foreign Legion as possible prototypes. The inappositeness of these two traditional groups, with high reputation as fighting men, needs no laboring.

presumption of authority or from absolute obedience to absolute mutiny.[18]

Doubts and Queries

In the mind's eye, one can visualize the component parts of the new ordering of force predicated in the United States project: first, the basic force itself; above, yet part of it, a command and staff structure; higher still in the chain of formal authority, and equivalent of a world defense ministry; and in supreme or political charge, a collectivity of representatives of erstwhile independent governments.

The peace force itself would be a body of fighting men chosen in accordance with some criteria, supposed to be moulded to a common set of habits and responses, equipped and trained not for some abstractly conceived mission of peace but to interpose and to wage havoc in particular theaters of operations under specific assumed operational conditions. Necessarily, it would be garrisoned somewhere, maybe in a diversity of locations. It would have some social relationship within itself and with surrounding populations. The members might conceivably be cut off from women and familial ties. They might be permitted fuller

[18] This danger is dealt with, and a solution offered, by one highly reputed writer in this field: "The danger of Caesar worship may be avoided if the command of the force is entrusted, not to a single person, but to a committee of five or seven persons, all of whom preferably ought to be nationals of small nations. At the same time, to ensure the impartiality of decisions, the majority of the command group should come from the noncommitted nations rather than the two major blocs" (Sohn, in Larson [ed.], *A Warless World*, p. 5). No demonstration is given of the relevance of such concepts as "major blocs" and "noncommitted nations" under conditions of complete national disarmament. No links between "impartiality" and "noncommitted nations" are shown. No proof is offered for the assumption of the likelihood of small nations being resourceful in affording talents and experience for the intricate and subtle problems of command under the contemplated conditions. No experiential data on the efficacy of command by committee are offered. Nothing is adduced to support an assumption in favor of the appropriateness of plural command as a means of averting the perils. The passage quoted is an interesting example of how to project the future in disregard of experience.

lives in enclaves set apart from the surrounding societies, or they might even enjoy that combination of aloofness and prerogative associated with a conqueror's status. The way of life might be that of blending into surrounding cultures as full sharers. The basis chosen would, of course, have a bearing on the degree of feasible admixture into a conglomerate homogeneity or of assortment into diverse components attempted in the force, and that factor in turn would have much to do with how the force could be used.

The higher command and staff structure—itself presumably drawn from diverse cultural sources and struggling with language barriers as well as internal divergencies of outlook—would be concerned with trying to realize a cogent, unified, operationally reliable instrument out of culturally varied men. The men must be either admixed into a uniformity of diversities or separated into a diversity of uniformities. With small inherent unity within itself, the structure would be trying to cope with unexampled complexities of human relations. What notional missions should be prepared for, inasmuch as military doctrine and training cannot be formulated against abstractions?[19] Staff work and command would be unremittingly involved in that most prickly of questions.

The ministerial agency, itself internally diverse, would be trying to perform prodigies of superintendency in integrating the force over a world scope. It would be seeking and trying to apply formulas for qualification, selection, promotion, brigading, compensation, retirement, and conditions for a common life covering throngs of persons of divergent backgrounds, different senses of reality, highly varied value systems, and discrepant expectations and taboos. It would face baffling problems in the formulation and administration of justice resulting from the interspersion of cultures in an intensively organized body. It would

[19] Schelling, loc. cit., p. 233, puts the matter succinctly: unless conceived as a purely ceremonial or symbolic entity, such a force would have to have a strategy. A set of purposes and assumed missions would have to be built into the organization and reflected in its doctrine. Determining that strategy would be a central concern in world politics, because in turn that strategy would have a determinative influence on world politics.

be charged with measuring operational requirements and procuring accordingly, against unforeseeable missions.

The supreme authority, the political collectivity itself, would be engrossed in parallel attempts in trying to translate the rhetoric of unity and world order into measurable realities. Basically, the collectivity must determine the distribution of authority. The participants would be in an ambiguous position. The entities for which they would speak would be putative targets of, as well as participants in, the amalgam of force. This duality would affect a wide range of questions requiring decision. One such question would be that of selecting a site for the force's headquarters. Others would arise in connection with locating the force's main bases and main normal concentrations of personnel and determining its main supply sources. Obviously, except under incalculably distraught conditions, the force would never be ordered to proceed against its own establishment or sources. Hence a host area, or a significant contributor, might presumably be exempt from ever becoming an operational target. On the other hand, the continuing presence of large numbers of global troops would probably be an important political conditioning factor in any land. The issues would be deep and enduring.

Further, questions would arise as to who should command from one stage to another, what should be the extent of his or their prerogative to determine subordinates in the chain of authority, and who should have the determining voice in displacing commanders. The questions, obviously, would bear upon what the force might be relied upon to do or not to do. The participating entities would have to be vitally alert because they would be vitally concerned.

A basic matter would be that of settling who should lay down the binding doctrine for the force and how the inculcation of the doctrine should be supervised. These would not be theoretical questions. Academies, staff and command schools, and the like would have to be instituted in view of the abolition of national establishments of such character. Who would be in charge? What precepts and methods should be imposed in them? The pattern of fidelity and reliability for a globally irresistible force might well turn on such questions, and every significant unit of government would feel vitally concerned.

How and by whom would specific questions of equipment and specific objects of training exercises be determined? In a related way, how, and at whose say-so, should operational intelligence be gathered? The implications do not need to be labored. Forces must be prepared to operate in one kind of mission or another, in one sort of terrain or another, and amid one populace or another, against specific rather than abstract operational targets. The force runs maneuvers under simulated Alpine conditions. It concentrates on desert training. The staff studies Baltic or Red Sea oceanography. Some officers are assigned to study Arabic. Data on land approaches to Kashmir are gathered. One can readily imagine the sort of reverberating issues bound to arise as plans, exercises, and the gathering of operational information are directed toward particular countries. One may predicate the vesting of control of nuclear weapons in the projected apparatus and ponder the question—and its implications—of what particular capitals or industrial complexes should be targeted.

Such questions, by no means exhaustive, are illustrative of what would be involved in creating links to ensure control and response with respect to such a force. The aspects are myriad, and all delicate. The authority of a central collectivity over such a peace force may sound engagingly simple when confined to considerations of authorizing a pre-established and ready force to blast away at some hypothetical miscreant. In practice, the elements of control would be integral to the character of the force itself and would have to be built into the force from its origin and continuously superintended.

If the whole idea were to work at all, the collectivity, however organized, with the force under its charge as an instrument of presumed reliability, would have to exercise effective power in suppression of attempts to undermine the arrangement. The irresistible force would need to be brought to bear at once and rigorously against any effort to offset its irresistibility. Any move by a formerly independent state to resume military autonomy would need to be regarded and dealt with as an act of rebellion and secession. In consenting to become a participant in, and putative beneficiary of, a world monopoly of military force, a state would, *ipso facto*, consent to becoming a target in event of a later attempt to renounce the contract. Under other conditions— and without an effective will to maintain paramountcy in the central arrangement—the force would fail of irresistibility, and states could not afford to commit their security to its care unconditionally. Yet the paramountcy premised for the force must rest on such commitments made in an engrossing pattern. With respect to the whole undertaking, the peace force's irresistibility is thus premised both as a condition precedent and as a consequence. In any event, and in practical terms, it is at least subject to doubt that the constituent elements of the stipulated quality are accessible.

The collective authority, with its irresistible coercive instrument, would become arbiter of questions of legitimacy touching the regime in every land. To its jurisdiction would come questions of enlarging quotas of force permitted to particular governments for internal security. It would have to develop a basis for approving and rejecting such petitions. It would presumably inquire into the necessities in view of the methods and purposes of an applicant government and in relation to the purposes and interests confronting it. It would be in a position to grant effectiveness, to license oppression, or to deny a beset regime the requirements for maintaining itself against internal challenge.

In an extremity involving a regime's inability to counter a domestic challenge with its permitted quota of internal security forces, it would fall to the world collectivity to lend or not to lend a hand with a fraction of its irresistible components—a political question of sweeping import. A factor in the life and stability of regimes would be their standing, as measured by political favor, with whatever consensus might prevail in the apparatus of control over the central force and the apparent probability, again calculated in political terms, of their being able to obtain its assistance in an exigency. In an instance of rival claims to a local seat of authority, the advantage falling to a claimant enjoying favor with the determining voices in the central apparatus might well prove conclusive. In like fashion, the suffrage of the central apparatus would be dominant in issues of secession arising within any constituent area.

These considerations have a basic importance to every scheme for integrating and centralizing the organization of force over a great expanse. Characteristically—and, one should add, essentially—such projects in the past have faced the attendant problems squarely. They have started from postulates of the legitimacy of every regime engrossed and of the propriety of its span of jurisdiction. In predicating a central authority in possession and control over paramount forces, they have complementarily undertaken to guarantee each participating regime in perpetuity.

Thus it was, for example, with the Duke of Sully's Grand Design in the sixteenth century and with the Abbé de St. Pierre's *Projet* in the eighteenth. Thus it was, and remains, with the Constitution of the United States. A provision, in Section 10 of Article I, that "No State shall, without the consent of Congress, . . . keep troops, or ships of war" goes hand in hand with provisions, in Sections 3 and 4 of Article IV, that "no new State shall be formed or erected within the Jurisdiction of any other State; nor any State be formed by the Junction of two or more States, or Parts of States, without the Consent of the Legislature of the States concerned as well as of the Congress" and that the "United States shall guarantee to every State in this Union a Republican form of Government, and shall protect each of them . . . against domestic violence." The integrity of every span of domain and the continuity of legitimacy for every participating regime are clearly stipulated. Every state is secured against disruption of its domain. Every state is promised a duly elected and representative regime and guaranteed constitutional continuity.

The *Outline* omits equivalent provisions for guaranteed peaceful continuity. To the contrary, it bespeaks peaceful change. Yet assurance of what can be counted on to last—not what can be counted on to give way—forms the foundation of order. It is difficult to see how any significant regime could afford to sign away command over factors of force without some such set of guarantees as those cited from the Constitution of the United

States. Yet the idea of agreeing *ab initio* on a universal frame for legitimacy, undertaking to guarantee licit continuity of authority in every land and predicating the fixity of all territorial dispositions, only underlines the remoteness from actuality of preconditions for a world monopoly of force.

To assume such preconditions as fulfilled is to construe the underlying problems of world order and security as solved. To attribute to governments individually and collectively such plenitude of power—such omnificent capacities—as to enable them to achieve these conditions as an exercise in policy involves disregarding the actual limitations bearing upon their actions. As an element in the United States disarmament plan, the project for a world peace force may promote an aura of abstract good intentions for United States policy. Its usefulness with respect to the credibility of United States policy is another matter.

7.

CONTROL AND ACCOUNTABILITY OF A UNITED NATIONS PEACE FORCE

Livingston T. Merchant

THE PURPOSE of this paper is to examine the question of how political control might be exercised over the United Nations peace force contemplated in the *Outline*. The examination will include an attempt to assess what form of political control over the peace force would be compatible with the national security interests of the United States.

The first section of this study will consider this question within the confines of the *Outline* and the United Nations Charter, as now written and interpreted.

The second section will consider what changes in the United Nations Charter would be required to ensure that an effective peace force would operate under effective political control, in terms of United States interests. This section will discuss briefly the present political environment of the world and the likelihood of imminent constitutional change in that environment.

Finally, this study will suggest, within the realm of what is deemed possible, the sort of peace force that could be expected to play a constructive role in world affairs and the nature of its controlling political authority.

The *Outline* is concise in its treatment of a United Nations peace force. The following first reference to a peace force ap-

pears under the heading "Objectives." "To ensure that during
and after implementation of general and complete disarmament,
states also would support and provide agreed manpower for a
United Nations Peace Force to be equipped with agreed types
of armaments to ensure that the United Nations can effectively
deter or suppress any threat or use of arms."[1] It is provided that:

The Parties to the Treaty would undertake to develop arrange-
ments during Stage I for the establishment in Stage II of a
United Nations Peace Force. To this end, the Parties to the
Treaty would agree on the following measures within the
United Nations:

A. Examination of the experience of the United Nations
leading to a further strengthening of United Nations forces for
keeping the Peace;

B. Examination of the feasibility of concluding promptly the
agreements envisaged in Article 43 of the United Nations
Charter;

C. Conclusion of an agreement for the establishment of a
United Nations Peace Force in Stage II, including definitions
of its purpose, mission, composition and strength, disposition,
command and control, training, logistical support, financing,
equipment and armaments.[2]

In Stage II the parties to the treaty would undertake to
strengthen further the arrangements for keeping the peace
through the establishment of a United Nations peace force. It is
further provided that the peace force (under terms negotiated in
Stage I) would actually come into being within the first year of
Stage II and be progessively strengthened during the balance
of the period defined as Stage II.

In Stage III the parties would make available agreed manpower for the peace force and would progressively strengthen it
"until it had sufficient armed forces and armaments so that no
state could challenge it."

From the foregoing it seems clear that the intention is first to
negotiate and then to create an irresistible military force in an

[1] *Outline*, A. Objectives, 4.
[2] *Ibid.*, Stage I, H, 5.

otherwise completely disarmed world. This force is designed to be able, by the end of Stage III, to deal, by deterrence or suppression, with the military challenge that might come from the internal security forces of any nation using or threatening the use of force. For practical purposes it is assumed here that its strength as calculated would also be sufficient to deal with a challenge from the aggregate internal security forces of any likely combination of nations. It might be noted in passing that one can expect difficulty in arriving at an agreed size for the force in the light of the various combinations of future possible aggressors. It should further be noted that this force would be multinational. States would provide agreed manpower, and states would support it. Finally, it is clear from its name that the peace force would be a *United Nations* peace force and hence would operate under the United Nations Charter as it now reads and is interpreted or as it may in the future be amended, in law or in practice.

This, then, is the concept. It is bold and simple. It envisages only one army, navy, and air force in the entire world. This military establishment would constitute the most powerful military force in being in the world. By definition it could not be successfully challenged by the internal security forces maintained by any nation-state or any likely combination of nation-states. For practical purposes, it would provide the individual or the body who controlled its employment with a monopoly of coercive power in the world. This is a formula for political control of the globe.

To the United States—and indeed to any nation, whether it be weak or powerful—the crucial question within the confines of this paper is who would exercise the political control over it? Who would "instruct" the military officer commanding this force to move against a nation judged by the instructing authority to have breached the peace or to be engaged in an act of aggression? Such an effective "instruction" can be described as "positive" political control over the force. This is to intervene as a new and, by definition, irresistible coercive element in some particular situation.

Of importance equal to that of "positive" control is what can be defined as "negative" control. This is to assure effectively, looking at it from an American viewpoint, that *no* "instruction" is issued to the force to intervene in some particular situation contrary to the interests of the United States.

The Charter of the United Nations is quite clear as to the political authority that would issue "instructions" to any peace-keeping forces subscribed to the United Nations. It is equally clear on the composition of that political authority and the rules under which it arrives at decisions.

Article I of the Charter, in stating the purposes of the United Nations, gives, as its first purpose, "To maintain international peace and security, and to that end: to take effective collective measures for the prevention and removal of threats to the peace, and for the suppression of acts of aggression or other breaches of the peace . . ." This section defines the function to be performed by the peace force described in the *Outline*.

Article 24 of the Charter clearly establishes the authority which will exercise political control in the discharge of the function. This Article reads *in toto:*

1. In order to ensure prompt and effective action by the United Nations, its Members confer on the Security Council primary responsibility for the maintenance of international peace and security, and agree that in carrying out its duties under this responsibility the Security Council acts on their behalf.

2. In discharging these duties the Security Council shall act in accordance with the Purposes and Principles of the United Nations. The specific powers granted to the Security Council for the discharge of these duties are laid down in Chapters VI, VII, VIII, and XII.

3. The Security Council shall submit annual and, when necessary, special reports to the General Assembly for its consideration.

A number of subsequent articles under Chapter VII deal with action with respect to threats to the peace, breaches of the peace, and acts of aggression. They cover, *inter alia,* questions of how forces are to be made available to the United Nations for the stated purposes, criteria for their use, and related matters. For the purpose of this discussion, we need only be concerned with identifying the political authority established under the Charter for the control of the peace force, the composition of the body constituting that authority, and the essential voting formula whereby it arrives at decisions.

We have noted that under the Charter the "political" authority for this purpose is the Security Council. Article 23 describes its composition. It has eleven members, of which five—China, France, the Soviet Union, the United Kingdom, and the United States— are permanent members. The other six are elected for two-year terms by the General Assembly from among its membership.

Article 27 prescribes the voting rules for the Security Council. Each member casts a single vote, and on procedural questions an affirmative vote by any seven members settles the matter. On all other matters—and beyond doubt a decision to send the peace force into action would be an "other matter"—a different voting formula obtains. On such matters an affirmative vote of at least seven is still required, but among the majority must be found all five of the permanent members. There is one exception. This is that in voting on matters relating to the *pacific* settlement of disputes, any member of the Security Council—including a permanent member—is deprived of its vote if it is a party to the dispute in question.

One should carefully note that each and every permanent member retains its veto and hence its right to prevent the use of force—in pursuit of the prescribed purposes of the Charter— against any country, even though it may be the country judged to be in violation of those purposes.

To sum up, the peace force envisaged in the *Outline* under present circumstances would be "politically" controlled by the Security Council of the United Nations. The Security Council could be frustrated in reaching an effective decision to act— however overwhelming the majority might be in favor of a particular "peace-keeping" action—by the veto of any one of the five nations who compose the permanent members of the Council.

What conclusions pertinent to the use of the peace force can be drawn from the foregoing provisions of the Charter? First and foremost, the peace force would be legally powerless to act against any of the five permanent members of the Security Council contrary to the wishes of that member, even though every other member of the Security Council—and the entire balance of the United Nations membership, for that matter— favored such use of the peace force.

It is inconceivable that any nation would invite or voluntarily agree to the use of the militarily irresistible peace force against itself. On the assumption that national interests will persist in a disarmed world and that collisions between nations' interests can therefore occur, it would seem equally unlikely that any nation now possessing the legal right to prevent the use of superior military force against it in the pursuit or protection of what are deemed to be its vital interests would willingly renounce that legal right. Accordingly, the conclusion is inescapable that the peace force could never act legitimately through Security Council action under the Charter as it reads today against any of the five permanent members of the Security Council even if one, or several of them in combination, incontestably breached the peace or committed an act of aggression in a totally disarmed world.

A second conclusion can be drawn. It is in the realm of the probable and not as certain as the first conclusion. This is that a nation possessing the veto would exercise it in any situation— such as one involving an ally—where it considered that its own vital interests were involved, even though it was not itself charged by others with a breach of the peace. A hypothetical case might be the situation of the United States in the event of an armed intervention in Cuba designed to expel the Castro regime undertaken by Venezuela and the Central American states. It would seem predictable that under such circumstances the United States would exercise its veto to prevent the employment of the peace force against Venezuela and its partners. Similarly, one could predict that the Soviet Union would veto the intervention of the peace force if East German forces attempted to occupy West Berlin.

At this point it is worth pausing to examine the past experience of the United Nations with peace-keeping forces. The dreary years of failure to reach the agreements contemplated under Article 43 of the Charter are sufficiently well known to require no recitation here. Rather, it is more constructive for the purposes of this paper to select, for the practical examination of difficulties and achievements, certain episodes in which armed forces were deployed by the United Nations for peace-keeping purposes. The episodes selected are Korea, Suez, and the Congo.

Korea is the one instance in the nineteen-year history of the United Nations in which the Security Council did take effective "peace-keeping" or "police" action to resist an aggression in the commission of which a permanent member of the Security Council clearly aided and abetted the aggressor. It is still occasionally cited as an illustration of the ability of the United Nations, through the Security Council, to move promptly and effectively to resist force with force.

The fact is, of course, that the successful United Nations action which followed the invasion of the Republic of Korea by the North Korean armies on June 25, 1950, was the result of a combination of unrelated factors which are unlikely to be duplicated in the future. First of all, the Soviets were boycotting the Security Council at the time of the invasion, and for some little time thereafter, for reasons totally unrelated to the event. They did not attend the first emergency meeting of the Security Council, held on a Sunday, the day after the invasion. Being physically absent, the Soviet representative was unable to cast the negative vote which would have vetoed the crucial Security Council resolution which called on all members of the United Nations to come to the assistance of the victim of aggression, the Republic of Korea.

Second, there was no real difficulty at the time in identifying the aggressor. There was in the Republic of Korea at the time a United Nations Commission on Korea, composed of representatives of Australia, China, El Salvador, India, the Philippines, and Syria. The commission had been charged with the responsibility of inspecting the Thirty-Eighth Parallel, which divided North

Korea from the Republic of Korea. Though blocked by the regime from entrance into North Korea—which was widely recognized as a satellite of the Soviet Union—this commission in the course of its routine inspections had published a report only a few days before the attack which certified that the troops of the Republic of Korea were strung out along the southern side of the parallel in routine defensive positions, with no evidence of any capability on their part to launch an invasion of North Korea. The world Communist propaganda apparatus loudly asserted at the time that the Army of the Republic of Korea had invaded North Korea, an assertion which it has continued to this day. There was incontestable proof to the contrary in the commission's report.

Third—and in many ways most important—the South Koreans fought back with great courage. Understandably demoralized by the suddenness of the surprise attack, they retreated but did not surrender. They slowed the advance, and their desperate bravery aroused the sympathy and respect of the free world.

Fourth, there was military help close at hand across the Tsushima Strait in Japan in the form of the United States Army of Occupation. Poorly trained and under-manned as they were, these troops, with United States air and naval support, were thrown into Korea as fast as they could be moved after the authorizing resolution of the Security Council.

Fifth, in the person of General MacArthur, the Supreme Commander of the Allied Powers in Japan, there was ready at hand a renowned military leader who commanded the respect of the world when the Security Council asked the United States Government to assume the United Nations Command in Korea.

Last, North Korea was the only satellite with which the U.S.S.R. was not linked by a mutual security treaty. This little-noticed fact is not without significance. In the final outcome the aggression was defeated and thrown back to the line from which it was launched. This result could be accepted, however reluctantly and bitterly, by the Soviet Union without calling into serious question the reliability of its pledge to come to the assistance of those satellites to which it was actually bound by treaty obligations.

The Korean case, accordingly, is *sui generis*. It provides no guide or hope for effective future action by the Security Council in meeting an aggression by the Soviet Union or by any other country whose action is deemed by the U.S.S.R. to be in its own national interests.[3]

Let us now turn to Suez in 1956. The history of the United Nations Emergency Force is marked by the fact that it was created during the liquidation of the Suez incident of 1956, after the fighting had ended. The incident serves to illustrate certain essential conditions for the successful operation of a United Nations Force. The relative ease of the creation of the UNEF and the tranquility of its operation rested on the essential twin base of its acceptance by all the parties to the original dispute, except initially by Israel but including France and Great Britain, and the overwhelming support it received in the General Assembly, which established it. All consenting nations judged that their own national interests under the circumstances were being best served by an end to hostilities in the area of the Suez Canal.

[3] The entrance of Communist Chinese troops into the Korean War is not dealt with in the foregoing analysis because this intervention is irrelevant to the point being made. The point under discussion concerns the ability, or the inability, of the Security Council as it is now set up to act with effectiveness and dispatch under conditions of a demonstrably clear act of aggression. The seat of China on the Security Council was not occupied, then or now, by the Communist mainland regime. Hence it had no role to play in the United Nations' consideration of the problem of Korea. Incidentally, although the generally accepted view at the time was that the Chinese Communists misread United Nations (or United States) intentions when General MacArthur advanced to the Yalu after the successful Inchon landings, there is today a basis in the light of the deep differences now revealed between Peking and Moscow, to chance another interpretation. This is that the Chinese decision to put their "volunteers" into North Korea was based on open contempt for what they regarded as a Soviet policy of excessive timidity and on the desire to replace the then-dominant influence of Moscow over the North Korean regime with their own. Be that as it may, Peking in 1950 had no veto to use in the Security Council. It can further be argued—though more tenuously—that exclusion of Peking from the United Nations freed that regime from any of the restraints on behavior which, it is sometimes asserted, the fact of membership *ipso facto* imposes on its members, as well as the more direct pressures of "world opinion" which the United Nations can to some degree mobilize and direct.

One other element in the genesis of the United Nations Emergency Force is crucially important, as Dr. Julius Stone lucidly points out. This is the fact that its functions and responsibilities, as set forth in the relevant resolution of the General Assembly, were sufficiently narrow and circumscribed as to make clear that it had none of the true attributes of a United Nations military organ for peace enforcement.[4]

Before considering the Congo as the third experience selected from military or quasi-military peace-keeping operations attempted by the United Nations, we should note that in the Congo from 1960 until now the United Nations has relied heavily on the Uniting for Peace Resolution passed by the General Assembly in 1950. The history of this resolution is instructive. As a result of Soviet efforts to frustrate the conduct of the United Nations' action in Korea during the summer and early fall of 1950, there developed in the United Nations—under the leadership of the United States—an effort to maximize the use of the peace-keeping powers of the General Assembly. This effort took the form of the Uniting for Peace Resolution, which the General Assembly passed on November 3, 1950. In some modest degree in the years since passage this resolution has proved successful. The formula relies heavily on the recommendatory powers of the General Assembly and on the first sentence of Article 51 of the Charter, which reads: "Nothing in the present Charter shall impair the inherent right of individual or collective self-defense if an armed attack occurs against a member of the United Nations, until the Security Council has taken the measures necessary to maintain international peace and security."

If one disregards the possible constitutional question of usurpation by the General Assembly authority and assumes that a

[4] Dr. Stone makes the point that its modesty of function (it was virtually an observer force and only quasi-military in character) clothed the United Nations Emergency Force with an acceptable degree of legitimacy under the Charter which under a more robust assignment would have been denied it (see Julius Stone, *Aggression and World Order* [Berkeley: University of California, 1958], p. 954).

United Nations peace force were sent into action in a particular situation by General Assembly vote against the will of a permanent member of the Security Council, there still exist many ways in which the accomplishment of its mission could be frustrated.

The United Nations action in the Congo from 1960 to date is indicative of some of these. Troop units originally contributed by friendly associates of the dissident permanent member can be suddenly withdrawn at a critical moment (as Ghana did in the Congo operation) or utilized for actions subversive to the purposes of the United Nations action (as did forces of the United Arab Republic in Orientale Province at a later stage of the Congo operation).

Then, the United Nations Secretary-General can be personally harassed and threatened if he shows the personal courage to strain or stretch the Charter's description of his powers. Dag Hammarskjold suffered this experience in the early stages of the Congo operation. Withdrawal of support of the Secretary-General for the reelection can be announced. He can be sabotaged in the discharge of his manifold duties by hostile propaganda and by actions of nationals of the offended permanent member who are serving on his staff.

Finally, there remains the club of refusal to contribute to the financing of the entire operation. The refusal of such contribution to the Congo operation on the part of the Soviet Union (with an assist from France) has forced the United Nations into heavy borrowing, notwithstanding an advisory opinion of the International Court of Justice confirming the obligation on the part of all United Nations members to contribute to the cost of the Congo operation. All this has been done in the face of an overwhelming majority in the General Assembly favoring the operation. Use of this financial club has injured the Congo operation and threatens to bring it to a premature end.

The history of the Congo operation, partially successful though it has been, is instructive, for it demonstrates the variety of means available to a determined permanent member of the Security Council to defend its interests as it judges them. If this is a case of a clash of Communist and Western interests occurring in the remote heart of a continent regarded by neither side as truly strategic and distant by thousands of miles from the closest border of either the Soviet Union or the United States, one realizes how much more vigorously and promptly all the available measures of sabotage would be tossed into the contest in the United Nations from the very outset if, for example, a majority of the General Assembly voted that a United Nations peace force be sent into Canada or Mexico or into Poland or Rumania. As a consequence, one is forced to conclude that an attempt to rely on the Uniting for Peace Resolution would not transform the General Assembly into an effective and reliable political authority to order the peace force into military action in a situation where one or more permanent members of the Security Council decided that such action would threaten its or their vital interests.

It is well to recapitulate at this point, having drawn on the experience of the United Nations in its efforts to intervene with armed force in the three differing situations described earlier. Countering the aggressor in Korea with United Nations forces worked because the crucial resolution in the Security Council was able to be passed by the absence of the Soviet representative. A quasi-military United Nations force was created successfully and operated in the Suez area *after* a cease-fire had gone into effect because an overwhelming majority of the General Assembly, as well as Egypt, the host government, was agreeable to its establishment and operations. Only Israel was initially opposed, and its consent was not crucial to the functioning of the force.

In a totally different situation, in the Congo, the problem was the internal breakdown of law and order. Here, in the face of widespread, though by no means unanimous, African sentiment favoring the United Nations operation and substantial financial and logistic support by the United States, the Soviets were able, with a considerable degree of success, to dally, obstruct, and financially starve the whole operation when it went against them even though they were not prepared to strangle it in the cradle or to cut its throat crudely.

We now have dealt with existing conditions, with the United Nations Charter as it reads today and with our experience under it, and with the current world environment and the mutual suspicions beclouding relations between the Sino-Soviet bloc and the United States. We confront explosive situations not quieted, let alone solved, such as West Berlin and the division of Germany, the offshore islands in the Formosan Strait, the truce in Korea, the wars in Southeast Asia, and Castro's Cuba as a Soviet base in the heart of the Western Hemisphere.

How would the interests of the United States be served reliably by a United Nations force with international relationships as they now are? What role in support of United States interests could be realistically expected of a United Nations peace force?

Let us consider these questions on the assumption that general and complete disarmament has been achieved and that a United Nations peace force has been created, trained, and fully equipped, also with its own transports. It would seem incontestable that from the point of view of "positive" control by the United States (by which is meant reliable, prompt, and forceful action to suppress or deter an aggression against what were considered United States interests) nothing could be expected of the United Nations under the present adversary relationships if a remedy were sought in the Security Council, where the Soviet veto is unbreakable. If reliance were placed, instead, on the General Assembly under the Uniting for Peace Resolution, the chance of effective action would be at best highly dubious. The paralyzing effect on the Afro-Asians—and many other members—of being forced to stand up and be counted in a direct confrontation between the United States and the Soviet Union, coupled with the opportunities that the latter would have to threaten, filibuster, and withhold financial support, would reduce almost to zero any assurance of effective action by the United Nations General Assembly.[5]

[5] One must take into account the expansion of membership in the United Nations, the changes in its composition, and its recent voting pattern when one relates the actions of the United Nations General Assembly in 1950, at the time of the Korean affair, to what could be expected in the way of performance by the General Assembly in another similar incident today.

One is forced to conclude that a United Nations peace force would offer small comfort to the United States, under existing circumstances, if it were in the interest of the United States to have such a force utilized to deter a threatened aggression or to fight one in which our adversary, the Soviet Union, was directly or indirectly implicated.

So much for positive control. In regard to negative control—that is, ensuring that the peace force would not be used against what the United States judged to be its interests—the situation is different. Here the United States would have open to it the same capabilities available to the Soviets in the case *contra*. The United States has the veto in the Security Council too. In the General Assembly the United States could, if it wished, obstruct and financially cripple the use of the force.

In short, the peace force could not be brought into action legitimately by the Security Council contrary to the will of the United States, nor is it conceivable that it could operate effectively, if at all, under the General Assembly or the Secretary-General in a situation where the United States was determined to frustrate its use. All this is equally true for the Soviets and, indeed, for any permanent member of the Security Council.

Accordingly, it can be concluded that under the present Charter, even if its provisions were stretched to their maximum, the United Nations peace force envisaged in the *Outline* could never be effectively employed in a situation where one of the permanent members of the Security Council considered that the intended use would operate against its own interests. Logically, one must conclude that an effectively controlled peace force would require the elimination of the veto of the permanent members of the Security Council. One could further conclude that the financing and composition of the peace force would have to be such as to safeguard it against being crippled by actions of one or more objecting members of the United Nations.

The first of these changes in the Charter would be clearly unacceptable to the United States. We come then to consider what theoretically conceivable changes in the Charter would enable the establishment of a political authority over the peace force acceptable to the United States under present circumstances.

In the judgment of the writer, there would have to be two changes, at the least. The first is simple—to make the veto, now granted to all five permanent members of the Security Council, an exclusive right of the United States. This change would not be necessary if it were a matter of granting negative control over the peace force to the United States. The existing veto rights of the Charter ensure that the peace force could never be sent into action contrary to the expressed determination and vote of the United States government.

The existing veto formula, however, does not assure positive control of the peace force to the United States because its use as a means of protecting vital American interests could be blocked by a single contrary vote from any one of the four other permanent members. Under the Charter change suggested above, it would still be necessary for the United States to secure six other votes in the Security Council, in addition to its own, in order that an instruction be given to the peace force to move in on any particular situation. As a calculated risk, the United States could probably live with this requirement, although bitter contests could be expected every year in the election of members to the nonpermanent seats on the Security Council.

In the world of today, however, the proposed change is impossible. In the absence of an overwhelming preponderance of power on the part of the United States that would enable it to impose this change in the Charter on others, there is no chance that so onesided a Charter revision would be acceptable to more than a handful of other United Nations members. The peace force being *ex hypothesi* an irresistible military force, the change would cede world hegemony to the United States. The Soviet Union would certainly not be alone in its resistance to such a surrender.

The other change in the Charter necessary to meet this writer's view of an acceptable political control over the peace force would be equally obnoxious to others. It would be a redefinition of the

qualifications of the Secretary-General or of the method of filling
the office to ensure that the occupant always would be responsive
to the interests of the United States. Only by such a change
could the operation of the peace force be assured of freedom
from bureaucratic sabotage. But such a capture of the office of
the Secretary-General by the United States is likewise unthink-
able.

It is accordingly impossible to believe that the minimum
changes in the Charter that the United States would have to require for the protection of its interests under existing circumstances are capable of achievement.

It is important to stress the phrase "under existing circumstances," which is intended to describe the world as it is today,
where the presence of bitter unsolved conflicts, suspended hostilities, and guerrilla actions approaching full-scale war are all too
numerous. It is impossible for this writer to believe that the fact
of adherence by all nations, including Communist China, to a
treaty for general and complete disarmament, and even substantial progress towards that ultimate goal, would of and by
itself so change the political climate of the world that all quarrels
and disputes—however ancient—would miraculously dissolve.[6]

    [6] Certainly the United States negotiators at Geneva are victims of no such
innocence. Ambassador Dean in his intervention of May 24, 1962, reflected
a sure grasp of reality when he said:
        I am sure that no one here is naive enough to believe that, just because
    armies and armaments have been eliminated, all forms of external inter-
    ference directed against the sovereignty and independence of one State
    by another will cease. It is true that the means of mass destruction and
    devastating wars will be eliminated by general and complete disarma-
    ment. However, one State can still send into the territory of another
    subsversive agents, persons who can instigate strikes, terrorists who can
    use home-made bombs, persons who can agitate groups of people into
    angry mobs, or who can advocate work stoppages or otherwise interfere
    in the domestic life of the other country. If States engage in such prac-
    tices during the process of disarmament, there is considerable doubt that
    we can succeed in reaching the goal for which we are all striving, that
    is, general and complete disarmament. I will go even further: If States
    indulge in such practices after general and complete disarmament is
    reached, it is entirely possible that the condition of general and complete

While to a limited extent quarrels might subside, it runs counter to human experience to expect that the reduction or even the prospect of the ultimate elimination of national armaments will remove, for example, the determination of West Germany to unite with East Germany or of East Germany to control West Berlin or of the Afghans to agitate for Pushtunistan or of Peking to seek to incorporate Taiwan into Communist China, to name only a few of the present deeply divisive and dangerous political issues. This list leaves aside the ideological Communist claim to the domination of the world.

The terms on which settlements of any or all of these situations may be reached affect importantly, though with varying weight, the interests of the United States. The role of leadership of a good part of the world which has devolved on the United States in the Cold War requires the maintenance of its power position. For this reason, it is necessarily concerned with any and every shift of allegiance towards it or away from it.

Assuming, then, that conflicting and unresolved international issues will remain even in a rapidly disarming world, can one seriously contend that any nation capable of defending its own vital interests by its own military power, alone or in association with reliable allies, will surrender that control over its own destiny? Stage III of the *Outline* contemplates such a surrender as national armed forces with their weapons are steadily reduced to the final point where the peace force emerges as militarily irresistible. Accordingly, one must conclude that it would be fruitless—barring a radical change in the world environment—to embark in Stage I on negotiations designed to lead to the creation in Stage III of a militarily irresistable peace force.

---

disarmament will not endure, that the scope and frequency of such violence as I have described will increase and that the United Nations force, despite our very best planning, will be unable to cope with the situation.

I do not mean to paint a picture of unlikely events just for the sake of indulging in drama. I believe it is incumbent upon us, as responsible representatives of governments, to recognize these possibilities, and I believe that it is also incumbent upon us . . . to take the most effective steps that we can devise to prevent them from becoming realities.

(ENDC/P.V. 41, p. 13.)

The United States cannot hazard subcontracting its ultimate ability to defend its vital interests with force unless the subcontractor (which by definition is the peace force in the matter under examination) will at all times be reliably responsive to decisions by the United States government as to where its interests lie in a particular situation.

There can be a further argument—although this paper is not the place for it—that the existing circumstances of an antithetical bipolarization of power in the world (essentially based on the possession of great nuclear striking power) will not endure forever; instead, the great-power harmony hoped for when the United Nations Charter was signed could be restored, thereby enabling the Security Council to maintain the peace with a peace force under its command and with little risk of any veto over its employment. Power factors and power relationships can indeed be changed by war, revolution, scientific breakthroughs, and, even more likely, by gradual evolution or erosion. Certainly one can hopefully cite today the evidence that the Sino-Soviet camp is no harmonious monolith. One can similarly see gaping fissures within the western world, reflecting on our side the forces of what George Kennan calls polycentrism. One could possibly be more comforted by this evidence if the confrontation between the Soviet Union and China with their satellites, on the one hand, and the United States and its allies, on the other, were solely ideological or religious. But it goes beyond that. It has equally deep roots in what many nations, including the Soviet Union and China, regard as a maldistribution of real estate, of resources and of other economic advantages. The pressures for change, painful for prospective losers to contemplate, will accordingly remain, even if a magic wand waved away the fears of each side that the other implacably seeks to impose its own system of political, social, and economic institutions and values upon the other. To this writer, at least, the sort of great-power harmony that would make the veto in the Security Council meaningless would be conceivable (in the absence of a total conquest of one side by the other) only over so long a time span as to render it suitable for speculation only by theoreticians. It belongs to a future so remote as to make it of little concern to statesmen charged with the welfare and security of the nations they govern. They face present dangers and are forced by their responsibilities to deal with reasonably foreseeable alternatives and contingencies.

If it is impossible to believe, as is the case with this writer, that any significant military power in the world today would be willing to trade the capability for self-help inherent in its military establishment for an omnipotent United Nations peace force, envisaged in the *Outline* as coming into existence in Stage III, one need not leap to the conclusion that it is useless or futile to seek to develop *any* peace force under the conditions envisaged in Stages I and II. There has been ample proof during the lifetime of the United Nations that situations may arise in which some sort of United Nations peace force can play a valuable role in preventing the outbreak of violence or deterring its renewal. As the earlier discussion sought to demonstrate, any peace force established on a more permanent basis than the improvisations of the past would go into action or abstain from action legitimately by decision of the Security Council with its existing veto provisions. Accordingly, it could not appear completely reliable in the eyes of any member of the United Nations that was calculating its possible future employment in support of its vital national interests. The advantages in creating it, however, are twofold.

In the first place, it would be a force in being. Hence, at a time of crisis, if the decision were reached to engage it, the peace force could move without the loss of important time which in past episodes has necessarily been required to negotiate for contingents and then to assemble and transport them to the scene of trouble. Second, an established peace force would give the United Nations valuable experience in the continuing administration of such a force, from which practical lessons could be learned that would become applicable in case of a later creation of the kind of peace force proposed for Stage III of the *Outline*. Hopefully, it might also contribute in some measure to an improvement in the political environment. The advantages seem well worth the effort of creating it.

We need first of all, however, to remind ourselves of the limitations under which it would function. In a reflection of the argument made earlier, the peace force necessarily would operate in compliance with the existing United Nations Charter provisions granting political authority over it to the Security Council. Consequently, it could not be used against any of the five permanent members or in a fashion that one or more of the five deemed contrary to its or their interests. This could be assumed to be the case even though the objecting permanent member or members were not intended to be the direct target of peace force intervention.[7] It can also be assumed to rule out a peace force action against any country formally allied with the Soviet Union or the United States. Its use, therefore, could not be contemplated in Europe, where the lines are drawn with North Atlantic Treaty Organization and Warsaw Pact forces confronting each other. It also seems improbable in the foreseeable future that it could operate in the Western Hemisphere, either against a member of the Organization of American States or, on the other hand, to expel a Soviet military presence in Cuba.

It is conceivable, if one assumes that Communist China adheres to a disarmament treaty but does not occupy China's seat on the Security Council, that the peace force could be used in Asia in the event of aggression by Peking. In practical terms, what this means is that the arena of potential operation of the peace force would be Africa, the Middle East (excluding Turkey and Pakistan because both are formally allied with the United States), and

---

[7] Given the depth of the division between the Communist countries and the United States with its allies, the big-power veto principle is the only formula on which agreement is conceivable. It is of interest to note that in discussions of the political control formula for the multilateral force, the principle of unanimity (i.e., each major participant possessing the right of veto) seems to be the only formula on which even tentative agreement could be reached, and this dialogue was between countries bound by common ties and all of them members of the North Atlantic Treaty Organization.

probably Asia, including the East Indies, and the Pacific Islands. The exclusions are large, but, generally speaking, they are the part of the world where political maturity runs relatively high and where positions between the United States and the Soviet Union are clearly drawn and (with the exception of West Berlin and a divided Germany) relatively well stabilized and accepted. It is elsewhere that one finds the most active dangers and disorders, as witness the Congo, Angola, Mozambique, and half a dozen other spots of present or potential danger. There is also the chronic Arab-Israeli tension, and in other places in the Middle East trouble could erupt. The problems in Southeast Asia are all too familiar. Other disputes in Asia, such as that between Malaysia and Indonesia or India and China, exist or could easily develop.

Beyond question, the immediate availability of a trained and mobile United Nations peace force, not dependent on being organized *ad hoc* after trouble arises, would provide a stabilizing deterrent and, if need be, a force capable of intervening promptly and effectively. Such a peace force falls short of what the *Outline* contemplates as the ultimate goal. Apart from its usefulness as a force in being, however, it could well provide the base on which could gradually be built, as trust displaced existing international distrust and "constitutional" changes in the world took place, the more ambitious and all-powerful peace force that a totally disarmed world would require.

One must then ask oneself what should be the general shape and underlying concept of a permanent United Nations peace force for at least the earlier stages of disarmament. The choice would seem broadly to be between two concepts. The first would be a force that would be composed of military units of existing national military establishments belonging to selected United Nations members. Such a peace force seems to be contemplated by the Charter through arrangements to be concluded under Article 43. A second and opposed concept would be a United Nations peace force in being, recruited and financed wholly by the United Nations and possessing a logistics system of its own, together with adequate transport and at least one base and training center. It would be homogenized and not made up of national units.

The first of these concepts has the virtues of simplicity, tradition, and lower cost to the United Nations. The second, however, can be argued to be more reliable when needed and capable of going into action with greater swiftness. It would, moreover, provide the essential experience for the sort of peace force that would be needed if genuine progress were made toward general and complete disarmament.

Either type of force would respond to some of the lessons of experience. Every past United Nations effort at peacekeeping has involved a crash creation under pressure of crisis. All have suffered from the absence of a United Nations logistics and transport system and adequate financial support. They have also reflected an undue dependence for manpower on the European neutrals (Sweden and Ireland) or on the smaller members of NATO and the Warsaw Pact (Canada, Norway, Denmark, Poland, and Czechoslovakia). They have all depended heavily on the United States for transport facilities. The military command structure, with the single exception of the action in Korea, has been ramshackle, improvised, and at times hamstrung by compromise arising from the particular combination of the countries participating.

On balance, it appears to the writer that it would be worth the greater effort and the greater expense to the United Nations to attempt to negotiate a more ambitious and novel type of peace force than one constructed out of diverse contributions of national military units. In considering what such a peace force might look like, there might be value in taking into account the areas in which it would be most likely to operate.

With quite clear geographical areas of feasible activity in mind, and given the intensity of racial feeling in Africa, Asia, and even the Middle East, it might well be desirable to have the United Nations peace force divided into three divisions, each one trained and based in the area in which it would operate. These areas would be Asia, the Middle East (including what was French North Africa), and Africa south of the Sahara. Each of the three bases would be adequately stocked with equipment, spares, ammunition, etc. Each of the three divisional units would possess its own transport, both to lift it to an area of operations and to make it mobile in the field. The top command would presumably be at the United Nations headquarters in New York. In case of need, the area divisions would of course be capable of mutual reinforcement. The manpower—both officers and men—would be recruited as individuals rather than as organized units under Article 43 agreements negotiated with the governments of the contributing countries.

Two other aspects of this force will be considered here, its financing and its composition. Assurance must be provided that the peace force would not be starved in periods of nonemployment or subjected to crippling actions in the middle of an operation, such as withdrawal of financial support by one or more important contributors.[8] Interesting suggestions have been made to the effect that the force should be financially self-supporting. However, to devise an equitable tax would be difficult, and collecting any special levy might turn the peace foce into the role of revenuers in mountain moonshine territory. A better solution would be to include the appropriation for the establishment and annual maintenance of the peace force in the general budget of the United Nations. An added device might be used to render its financial future more secure. This would be to budget an amount each year in excess of estimated annual costs by a figure of 25 per cent or thereabouts. The excess would be held by the Secretary-General of the United Nations in a special reserve fund to accumulate for a possible future year or years in which an unpopular peace force action led to default on payments of United Nations assessments by one or more United Nations members.

The problem of recruitment and composition also deserves attention. There may well be matters of value and relevance to the

[8] According to one estimate, the annual cost of a standing peace force of four hundred thousand men would run about nine billion dollars (Grenville Clark and Louis B. Sohn, *World Peace through World Law* [2d ed.; Cambridge, Mass.: Harvard, 1960], p. 320).

peace force that could be learned from the intensive study accorded the project for a multilateral nuclear force for the North Atlantic Treaty Organization by the United States government beginning in 1959. This study, in all its political and technical aspects, was the foundation for the United States concept for such a nuclear force as it was explained in detail to interested members of the alliance in 1962–1963.

An initial political requirement laid down in the United States study was that the force should be so designed as to ensure that no single unit of it could be rendered ineffective by mutiny, or be sabotaged, or be withdrawn by one of the participants for purely national purposes. This led to the conclusion that mixed manning should be central to the entire concept. Each ship would for this purpose be manned by a mixture of officers and enlisted men of the participating countries, with no more than 40 per cent of any single nationality serving on any single ship. Moreover, in function the crew would be fully homogenized, so that the engine crew, the missile maintenance and firing squad, and every other division in the ship would be mixed, thus none of them composed of national units.

This essentially political conclusion led to detailed studies by the United States Navy of the technical feasibility of such a staffing pattern and the resultant effect on combat efficiency. The conclusion was reached that, given high caliber personnel recruitment, a considerable span of time for training (including initial concentration on a common language), and the continuing support of the contributing governments, a first-class fighting force could be produced.[9]

---

[9] Admiral Claude Ricketts, United States Vice Chief of Naval Operations, has written on this point:

Recognizing that responsibility for the operation of such a force would rest upon Navy personnel, we of the U.S. Navy have made a very thorough analysis of this concept from every pertinent point of view. We have come to the definite conclusion that such a force is feasible, that it would be effective, and that its survival probability is such that its nuclear retaliatory capability could not be eliminated, or substantially reduced, by present or foreseen forces and tactics of an enemy.

(*Time*, July 5, 1963, p. 5.)

Common sense would argue that, given this authoritative certificate of the feasibility of mixed manning for such a sophisticated military force as a fleet of Polaris missile warships, this concept should be capable of adoption in the peace force. It has a direct bearing on the political control of such a force in that it would minimize the risk of its being crippled by withdrawal of one or more national units or paralyzed by a threat to do so.

Moreover, in the plan developed by the United States Navy for the multilateral force, the training period would run between two and three years, during which a sense of collective loyalty to the North Atlantic Treaty Organization, rather than exclusive emphasis on purely national patriotism, would be inculcated. It is not unreasonable to suppose that a United Nations peace force, in genuine service to a great ideal, would attract young men of intelligence and high ideals with a consequent strengthening of the United Nations force in its sense of purpose and reliability.

Another relevant conclusion emerging from the United States technical studies of the essential elements of a multilateral force was that it should have its own shore establishment and its own logistical and administrative organization so that the multilateral force would not be dependent on national facilities and organizations to ensure that the force was properly supplied, maintained, and serviced in the whole complex range of functions performed for national navies by national ministries of marine or admiralties or navy departments.

The difficulties of recruiting, training, and supporting a mixed-manned peace force are formidable. Given, however, the authoritative character of the studies testifying to the technical feasibility of producing an effective combat force of such composition, the argument is powerful for insisting that the United Nations peace force should be organized on this basis. To do so would strengthen the reliability of its responsiveness to the political authority governing it.

It can be argued, but with less assurance, that the principle of mixed manning should apply regionally in each of the three areas of the peace force command. In other words, Asian officers and men would compose the Asia division, with no single nationality dominant in any unit down to the platoon. Similarly, black Africans would make up the Africa south of the Sahara division and Arabs the Middle East division. The problem in mixed manning arising from different religions, customs, cultures, diet, etc., would thereby be alleviated and the racial angle eliminated, since a white force would never be sent into territory inhabited by black peoples and vice versa. In opposition to this proposition it must be said, however, that the position of the Republic of South Africa and of Israel, for example, in their respective areas under such a manning system must not be overlooked. The diversity of political coloration of regions and nations in all three areas might compel the conclusion that regional divisions are impractical for the peace force. This conclusion would not, however, in the writer's opinion, affect the validity and desirability of the principle of mixed manning.

It should also be noted that this program would eliminate from participation in the peace force the chief adversaries in the Cold War, the Soviet Union and the United States. It would also exclude most European nations who still are identified in the eyes of the underdeveloped peoples as colonial powers.

In addition, it might be useful for permanent or standing advisory committees to be set up for each of the three regions of possible United Nations peace force action and composed in each case of representatives from United Nations member nations in the area. The Congo experience with such an advisory committee has, on the whole, been useful. These committees presumably would be appointed by the Secretary-General with the approval of the General Assembly, and the appropriate committee would advise him during a peace force operation in any one of the three areas. The essential political control, however, would rest with the Security Council.

The size, cost, method of recruitment, training procedures, and many other technical aspects of the homogenized peace force suggested here and preferred by the writer would require detailed and careful study. None of these complicated questions seems unsurmountable, although serious questions can be raised.

In any event, this modest beginning in United Nations permanent peace-keeping machinery for a disarming world would have the virtue of operating with legitimacy under the existing United Nations Charter and on a basis that would mute rather than exacerbate the sharpest conflicts between the opposed interests of the Soviet Union and the United States. Making a hopeful assumption, the process of disarming in stages, with all parties acting in good faith, would in fact affect the climate in which existing sources of tension and conflict of interests could be eased. The now narrow area of generally accepted international law might expand. For example, the failure of the Conferences on the Law of the Sea was in part due to the need for safeguarding the security interests of naval powers. With the ultimate elimination of national navies under general and complete disarmament, this factor would diminish in importance and proportionately increase the chances for international agreement on the extent of territorial waters.

Little by little in the years to come the world might approach a consensus on fundamental principles and values which ultimately would enable the establishment and functioning of an "irresistible" peace force. However, the dawn of that day is far distant.

APPENDIX

Summary of the *Outline* and Complete
Text of Its Peace-keeping Provisions

Summary of the Outline

PRINCIPLES AND PROCESS OF DISARMAMENT

Disarmament would be implemented progressively and in a balanced manner, so that at no stage could any state or group of states obtain military advantage. Compliance with obligations would be effectively verified. As national armaments were reduced, the United Nations would be progressively strengthened.

Disarmament would be accomplished in three stages: the first to be carried out in three years; the second, also in three years; and the third, as promptly as possible within an agreed period of time. Stage I would be initiated by the United States, the Soviet Union, and other agreed states. All militarily significant states would participate in Stage II, and all states possessing armaments and armed forces, in Stage III.

Transition from one stage of disarmament to the next would take place upon a determination that all undertakings in the preceding stage had been carried out and that all preparations for the next stage had been made. [The full text of the *Outline* makes it clear that the consent of at least the U.S. and the U.S.S.R. would be required.]

DISARMAMENT MEASURES

A. *Armaments.* During Stage I, inventories of major categories of both nuclear delivery vehicles and conventional armaments would be reduced by 30 per cent. Fixed launching pads would be reduced with associated missiles. Half of the remaining inventories would be eliminated during Stage II, and final reductions would be made in Stage III. Upon the completion of Stage III, states would have at their disposal only agreed types of non-nuclear armaments for forces required to maintain internal order and protect the personal security of citizens.

Production of armaments during Stage I would be limited to agreed allowances and would be compensated for by the destruction of additional armaments, to the end that reductions would not be impaired. In Stage II, production of armaments would be halted except for parts for maintenance of retained armaments. Any further production of national armaments would be ended in Stage II except for production of agreed types of nonnuclear armaments for internal forces.

Military research, development, and testing would be subject to increasing limitations during the disarmament process. During Stage III, appropriate action would be taken to ensure that new scientific discoveries and technological inventions of military significance were not used for military purposes.

B. *Armed Forces.* Force levels of the United States and Soviet Union would be reduced to 2.1 million men at the end of Stage I. Half of the remaining forces of these two states would be disbanded during Stage II, and final reductions would be made in Stage III. Other states would also progressively reduce their force levels. By the end of Stage III, states would have at their disposal only those agreed forces and related organizational arrangements required to maintain internal order and protect the personal security of citizens.

C. *Nuclear Weapons.* Production of fissionable materials for use in nuclear weapons would be halted in Stage I, and limitations would be imposed on the production of fissionable materials for other purposes. The availability of fissionable materials for use in nuclear weapons would be reduced during Stage I and subsequent stages by safeguarded transfers to nonnuclear weapons purposes.

If nuclear weapons tests had not already been halted under effective international control, arrangements to this end would be undertaken in Stage I. States which had manufactured nuclear weapons would agree in Stage I not to transfer control over nuclear weapons to states which had not manufactured them or to assist such states in their manufacture. States which had not manufactured nuclear weapons would refrain from seeking them. Transfers of fissionable materials between states would be limited to peaceful purposes and would be safeguarded.

Beginning in Stage II, nonnuclear components and assemblies of nuclear weapons would be destroyed, and limitations would be imposed on further production or refabrication of nuclear weapons. At the end of Stage II, remaining nuclear weapons would be registered internationally to assist in verifying the fact that by the end of Stage III states would not have such weapons at their disposal.

D. *Outer Space.* The placing of weapons of mass destruction in orbit would be prohibited in Stage I, and limitations would be imposed on the production, stockpiling, and testing of boosters for space vehicles. States would support increased co-operation in peaceful uses of outer space.

E. *Military Bases.* Reduction of military bases, wherever they might be located, would be initiated in Stage II, and final reductions would be made in Stage III.

F. *Military Expenditures.* Military expenditures would be reported throughout the disarmament process.

VERIFICATION

The verification of disarmament would be the responsibility of an International Disarmament Organization, which would be established within the framework of the United Nations. Reductions of armaments and armed forces would be verified at agreed locations; and limitations on production, testing, and other specified activities, at declared locations. Assurance that agreed levels of armaments and armed forces were not exceeded and that activities subject to limitation or prohibition were not being conducted clandestinely would be provided through arrangements which would relate the extent of inspection at any time to the amount of disarmament being undertaken and to the risk to the disarming states of possible violations.

Such assurance might, for example, be accomplished through arrangements under which states would divide themselves into a number of zones through which inspection would be progressively extended. By the end of Stage III, when disarmament had been completed, all parts of the territory of states would have been inspected.

REDUCTION OF THE RISK OF WAR

To promote confidence and reduce the risk of war during the disarmament process, states would, beginning in Stage I, give advance notification of major military movements and maneuvers, establish observation posts to report on concentrations and movements of military forces, and ensure rapid and reliable communications among heads of governments and with the Secretary-General of the United Nations.

An International Commission on Reduction of the Risk of War would examine possible extensions and improvements of such measures, as well as additional measures to reduce the risk of war through accident, miscalculation, failure of communications, or surprise attack.

Peace-keeping Provisions of the Outline[1]

STAGE I

1. Obligations Concerning the Threat or Use of Force
The Parties to the Treaty would undertake obligations to refrain, in their international relations, from the threat or use of force of any type—including nuclear, conventional, chemical or biological means of warfare—contrary to the purposes and principles of the United Nations Charter.

2. Rules of International Conduct
a. The Parties to the Treaty would agree to support a study by a subsidiary body of the International Disarmament Organization of the codification and progressive development of rules of international conduct related to disarmament.

b. The Parties to the Treaty would refrain from indirect aggression and subversion. The subsidiary body provided for in subparagraph a. would also study methods of assuring states against indirect aggression or subversion.

[1] Complete text taken from U.S., Arms Control and Disarmament Agency, *Blueprint for the Peace Race, Outline of Basic Provisions of a Treaty on General and Complete Disarmament in a Peaceful World,* Publication 4, General Series 3, Released May 1962, pp. 1–3, 19–21, 27–28, 33.

3. Peaceful Settlement of Disputes

a. The Parties to the Treaty would utilize all appropriate processes for the peaceful settlement of all disputes which might arise between them and any other state, whether or not a Party to the Treaty, including negotiation, inquiry, mediation, conciliation, arbitration, judicial settlement, resort to regional agencies or arrangements, submission to the Security Council or the General Assembly of the United Nations, or other peaceful means of their choice.

b. The Parties to the Treaty would agree that disputes concerning the interpretation or application of the Treaty which were not settled by negotiation or by the International Disarmament Organization would be subject to referral by any party to the dispute to the International Court of Justice, unless the parties concerned agreed on another mode of settlement.

c. The Parties to the Treaty would agree to support a study under the General Assembly of the United Nations of measures which should be undertaken to make existing arrangements for the peaceful settlement of international disputes, whether legal or political in nature, more effective; and to institute new procedures and arrangements where needed.

4. Maintenance of International Peace and Security

The Parties to the Treaty would agree to support measures strengthening the structure, authority, and operation of the United Nations so as to improve its capability to maintain international peace and security.

5. United Nations Peace Force

The Parties to the Treaty would undertake to develop arrangements during Stage I for the establishment in Stage II of a United Nations Peace Force. To this end, the Parties to the Treaty would agree on the following measures within the United Nations:

a. Examination of the experience of the United Nations leading to a further strengthening of United Nations forces for keeping the peace;

b. Examination of the feasibility of concluding promptly the agreements envisaged in Article 43 of the United Nations Charter;

c. Conclusion of an agreement for the establishment of a United Nations Peace Force in Stage II, including definitions of its purpose, mission, composition and strength, disposition, command and control, training, logistical support, financing, equipment and armaments.

6. United Nations Peace Observation Corps

The Parties to the Treaty would agree to support the establishment within the United Nations of a Peace Observation Corps, staffed with a standing cadre of observers who could be despatched promptly to investigate any situation which might constitute a threat to or a breach of the peace. Elements of the Peace Observation Corps could also be stationed as appropriate in selected areas throughout the world.

STAGE II

1. Peaceful Settlement of Disputes

a. In light of the study of peaceful settlement of disputes conducted during Stage I, the Parties to the Treaty would agree to such additional steps and arrangements as were necessary to assure the just and peaceful settlement of international disputes, whether legal or political in nature.

b. The Parties to the Treaty would undertake to accept without reservation, pursuant to Article 36, paragraph 1 of the Statute of the International Court of Justice, the compulsory jurisdiction of that Court to decide international legal disputes.

2. Rules of International Conduct

a. The Parties to the Treaty would continue their support of the study by the subsidiary body of the International Disarmament Organization initiated in Stage I to study the codification and progressive development of rules of international conduct related to disarmament. The Parties to the Treaty would agree to the establishment of procedures whereby rules recommended by the subsidiary body and approved by the Control Council would be circulated to all Parties to the Treaty and would become effective three months thereafter unless a majority of the Parties to the Treaty signified their disapproval, and whereby the Parties to the Treaty would be bound by rules which had become effective in this way unless, within a period of one year from the effective date, they formally notified the International Disarmament Organization that they did not consider themselves so bound. Using such procedures, the Parties to the Treaty would adopt such rules of international conduct related to disarmament as might be necessary to begin Stage III.

b. In the light of the study of indirect aggression and subversion conducted in Stage I, the Parties to the Treaty would agree to arrangements necessary to assure states against indirect aggression and subversion.

3. United Nations Peace Force

The United Nations Peace Force to be established as the result of the agreement reached during Stage I would come into being within the first year of Stage II and would be progressively strengthened during Stage II.

4. United Nations Peace Observation Corps

The Parties to the Treaty would conclude arrangements for the expansion of the activities of the United Nations Peace Observation Corps.

5. National Legislation

Those Parties to the Treaty which had not already done so would, in accordance with their constitutional processes, enact national legislation in support of the Treaty imposing legal obligations on individuals and organizations under their jurisdiction and providing appropriate penalties for noncompliance.

STAGE III

1. Peaceful Change and Settlement of Disputes

The Parties to the Treaty would undertake such additional steps and arrangements as were necessary to provide a basis for peaceful change in a disarmed world and to continue the just and peaceful settlement of all international disputes, whether legal or political in nature.

2. Rules of International Conduct

The Parties to the Treaty would continue the codification and progressive development of rules of international conduct related to disarmament in the manner provided in Stage II and by any other agreed procedure.

3. United Nations Peace Force

The Parties to the Treaty would progressively strengthen the United Nations Peace Force established in Stage II until it had sufficient armed forces and armaments so that no state could challenge it.

INDEX

A

Africa, 31, 170, 204, 212, 214, 218

Aggression: ambiguity of definitions, 72, 123, 157, 158n–59n; countered by alliances, 47; Korean War and, 199–201; proof of, 154, 155, 199–201; restrictions on, 72–74, 115; self-preservation and, 151; mentioned, 33, 42, 43, 47, 103, 115, 196, 198, 205. *See also* Indirect aggression

Algeria, 95–96

Alliances: aggression countered by, 47; cohesion of, 81; collective defense and, 24; effects of disarmament on, 129; ideological aspect of, 44; military balance and, 44, 46; military basis of, 28, 61–62, 80–81, 84; rigidity of U.S. policies, 87; stability and, 43–45; U.S. influence in, 28; mentioned, 6, 60. *See also* North Atlantic Treaty Organization; Organization of American States; Warsaw Pact

Arms race: Communist expansion and, 22, 48; dangers of, 8n, 94–95; existing armaments as cause of, 6, 7; expense of, v; peace force control and, 15; rearmament and, 52–53, 126n; mentioned, 7, 62

Asia: racial tension in, 214; U.S. involvement in, 61, 68; vulnerability of, to Communist expansion, 47–48; mentioned, 31, 212, 213, 217. *See also* Far East; Southeast Asia

B

Balanced disarmament. *See* Proportionate disarmament

Balance of power: alliances and, 43–45; defined, 25; dependent on threat of force, 44; deterrence and, 25; effects of disarmament on, 36, 39–40, 43–46, 101–2; international law and, 146; legal freezing of, 40; rearmament and, 50, 52–53; security dependent on, 37–38; U.S. effort to preserve, 24–25, 30; mentioned, vii, 22, 51

Baruch plan, v

Berlin: blockade of, 30; containment in, 23; economic vulnerability of, 27; isolation of, 10; mentioned, 25, 47, 198, 205, 209, 213

Biological weapons, 66

C

Caroline case, 148n, 149n

Chemical weapons, 66

China. *See* Communist China

Collective defense, 20, 24–25, 132–37 *passim*

Colonialism, 30, 31, 55–56

Communist China: containment of, 23–25; economic coercion by, 27, 29; expansion of, 16–17, 26, 27, 29, 47–48; ideological warfare by, 27–28; India and, 24, 213; indirect aggression by, 27, 36; internal security forces of, 48; Korean War and, 201n; national liberation wars and, 48; peace force operations against, 212; Soviet Union and, 210; subversion by, 27; Taiwan sought by, 209; U.S. and, 205; mentioned, 17, 61, 82, 83, 197, 208

Congo, 29, 95, 105, 202-4, 213, 218

Containment, 20, 23–25, 36, 47

Cuba: Soviet missiles in, 145–6, 149n, 150n; mentioned, 23, 27, 56, 198, 205, 212

Cyprus, 95, 105

Czechoslovakia, 17, 23, 214

THE UNITED STATES IN A DISARMED WORLD

by Arnold Wolfers and others

designer: Edward King

typesetter: Baltimore Type and Composition Corporation

typefaces: Caledonia (text) and News Gothic (display)

printer: The Murray Printing Company

paper: Lindenmeyr Schlosser Paperback M.F. Offset

binder: William Marley Company